**Deschutes
Public Library**

D0429902

Shorter

Previous Books by Alex Soojung-Kim Pang:
Rest
The Distraction Addiction

Work Better, Smarter, and Less—

Here's How

Shorter

Alex Soojung-Kim Pang

PUBLICAFFAIRS
New York

Copyright © 2020 by Alex Soojung-Kim Pang
Cover design by Pete Garceau
Cover images © iStock/Getty Images
Cover copyright © 2020 Hachette Book Group, Inc.

Hachette Book Group supports the right to free expression and the value of copyright. The purpose of copyright is to encourage writers and artists to produce the creative works that enrich our culture.

The scanning, uploading, and distribution of this book without permission is a theft of the author's intellectual property. If you would like permission to use material from the book (other than for review purposes), please contact permissions@hbgusa.com. Thank you for your support of the author's rights.

PublicAffairs
Hachette Book Group
1290 Avenue of the Americas, New York, NY 10104
www.publicaffairsbooks.com
@Public_Affairs

Printed in the United States of America

First Edition: March 2020

Published by PublicAffairs, an imprint of Perseus Books, LLC, a subsidiary of Hachette Book Group, Inc. The PublicAffairs name and logo is a trademark of the Hachette Book Group.

The publisher is not responsible for websites (or their content) that are not owned by the publisher.

Print book interior design by Amy Quinn.

Library of Congress Cataloging-in-Publication Data
Names: Pang, Alex Soojung-Kim, author.
Title: Shorter: work better, smarter, and less—here's how / Alex Soojung-Kim Pang.
Description: First Edition. | New York: PublicAffairs, 2020. | Includes bibliographical references and index.
Identifiers: LCCN 2019048304 | ISBN 9781541730717 (hardcover) | ISBN 9781541730700 (ebook)
Subjects: LCSH: Work. | Time management. | Communication in management. | Creative ability in business.
Classification: LCC HD4904 .P26 2020 | DDC 650.1—dc23
LC record available at https://lccn.loc.gov/2019048304
ISBNs: 978-1-5417-3071-7 (hardcover); 978-1-5417-5712-7 (international paperback); 978-1-5417-3070-0 (ebook)

LSC-C

10 9 8 7 6 5 4 3 2 1

For Elizabeth and Daniel

Contents

If masters would always listen to the dictates of reason and humanity, they have frequently occasion rather to moderate, than to animate the application of many of their workmen. It will be found, I believe, in every sort of trade, that the man who works so moderately, as to be able to work constantly, not only preserves his health the longest, but, in the course of the year, executes the greatest quantity of work.

Adam Smith, *The Wealth of Nations* (1776)

The whole development of wealth rests on the creation of disposable time.

Karl Marx, *Grundrisse* (1858)

Introduction

MAIN STREET, HUNTINGTON BEACH, CALIFORNIA

When he first heard about the five-hour workday, David Rhoads thought, *I want to give this to my employees.*

David is CEO of Blue Street Capital, a Huntington Beach, California–based company that arranges financing for enterprise IT systems. He's also an avid surfer: Huntington Beach is one of Southern California's iconic surf towns, and Rhoads is "in the water as much as I can," he tells me. So when he saw an article about how Tower Paddle Boards—an online, direct-to-consumer company that sells stand-up paddleboards—had moved to a five-hour workday, he was intrigued.

Stephan Aarstol founded Tower in 2010. An appearance on the TV show *Shark Tank* won him an investment from Mark Cuban, and the company had grown steadily since then. As an e-commerce company, Tower was constantly experimenting with new technologies and business processes, and Stephan was convinced that they could use the same technologies to change how his employees worked, not just how they sold paddleboards. If they focused on their most important work, cut out distractions, and used technology to automate routine tasks and make their hard jobs easier, he thought, they could dramatically improve their performance—and give him more time for surfing.

So in June 2015, Stephan offered his employees a deal: if you figure out how to do the same work in less time, you can keep the same salary and leave at 1:00 pm. He also implemented a 5 percent profit sharing plan, further increasing people's hourly pay. Finally, he shifted focus away from revenue growth to building company culture.

What happened? The day they announced the change on their website, Tower broke its previous daily sales record and booked $50,000 in sales for the first time. They did it again a couple days later, and three more times in the next two weeks. By the end of the month, they had sold $1.4 million worth of paddleboards, breaking their previous monthly sales record by $600,000.

By the time David Rhoads read about the five-hour day, Tower Paddle Boards had been on the new schedule for nearly a year. It hadn't been easy, but it had been a great success: the company was one of the fastest growing in San Diego, customers saw the five-hour day as an expression of a "work hard, play hard" beach lifestyle, and revenues had gone from $5 million to $7.2 million.

You couldn't find two products more different than bespoke financial deals that fuel high-tech investments and surf equipment inspired by Polynesian sailors, but David started thinking about whether a shorter workweek could be implemented at Blue Street Capital too. He had run Blue Street since 2003, and after a couple "brutal" quarters, he was looking for ways for the company to improve and start taking on challenges again, rather than just responding to them. He had dedicated workers, but "if we took out our breaks, took out our lunch, and took out all the [unproductive] nonsense that we do over the course of the day," he thought they could compress the workday to five hours. They'd need to figure out how to keep customers happy during a shorter workday—companies depend on Blue Street Capital to help them finance mission-critical upgrades or expansions, and since every deal is different his employees spend a lot of time on the phone to clients—but he was sure they could figure it out. "We knew it would be a huge productivity tool for the business," David says, "but we also knew we were going to get part of our lives back."

Business development manager Alex Gafford remembers David announcing the five-hour day at an all-hands meeting. "I was kind of burned out that day," Alex tells me. "It was after lunch, I'm tired, and I'm going to be in the office till at least five o'clock doing emails and calls and stuff.

"David says, 'All right, at the end of this meeting everybody can go home for the day,'" Alex remembers. "We look at each other like, What? It was . . . unexpected. Then David says, 'Hold on, let me explain what we're going to do. We're going to try a ninety-day experiment.'"

David explained the idea, talked about Tower Paddle Boards, and explained why he wanted to try a five-hour day. "I want you to have the lifestyle that I have," Alex recalls him saying, "and I believe that you'll be as successful as I am or more successful as a result." David answered a few questions. No, salaries wouldn't be cut. No, the company wasn't about to go under. Yes, the new schedule would become permanent after ninety days if productivity remained the same and if customers didn't complain. As one of the company's leading sales managers, Alex knew that the summer was a slow period at Blue Street, so it was a good time to start a trial.

During the trial, "there were not really any other instructions," Alex recalls. "We had to figure it out on our own." David had advice he had picked up from productivity experts—avoid multitasking, focus most of your effort on your most valuable work, take quick, purposeful breaks to stretch the muscles and get the blood flowing—but people were largely left to their own devices.

A single quarter wasn't enough time to see a big change in revenue—in contrast to Tower Paddle Boards, Blue Street Capital has a long sales cycle—but after three months David could measure the impact of five-hour days on their leading key performance indicator (KPI), the number of calls per salesperson. More calls means more business: working the phones, staying in touch with clients, and pitching to new customers is essential if people are going to meet their sales targets and the company is going to grow. What did he find? When they cut the length of the workweek by three-eighths, calls per person . . . actually doubled.

How did they do it? Alex says that it wasn't any single thing that helped them be more efficient; that steep increase in productivity was made from a bunch of little steps, not one giant one. A couple people had actually quit, because after years of working long hours, they couldn't give up the idea that sixty-hour weeks were the price of success and didn't like having to be so careful with their working time. "It was a culture shift for the whole business," David says.

David made the new schedule permanent after three months in late 2016, and Blue Street has operated on an 8:00 am to 1:00 pm schedule ever since. After three years,

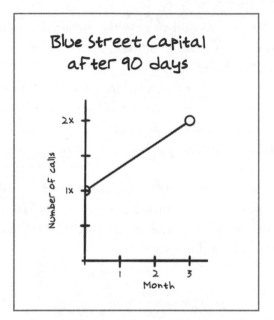

Blue Street Capital after 90 days

Number of calls (y-axis): 1x, 2x
Month (x-axis): 1, 2, 3

At the end of its ninety-day trial, Blue Street Capital had shortened its workday by three hours a
day, but the number of calls each salesperson made
had doubled.

revenues have gone up every year—30 percent the first year,
30 percent the second—and the company has grown from
nine to seventeen employees.

Few things sound more Southern California than "Let's
shorten the workday to have more time to surf!" But shortening the workday to boost productivity and improve the
company? That's pretty counterintuitive. When you get a
late-night email from a boss or a last-minute request from a
client, you don't think, *I know how to deal with this—I'll take
Friday off.* You don't prove your dedication and passion by
leaving work early. We live in a world in which business operates 24/7, the global economy never stops, and competition

is relentless. And even if you can become productive enough to finish early, customers and bosses still expect you to be available at all hours.

And yet in the last few years, hundreds of companies in a variety of industries around the world have followed the same path as Tower Paddle Boards and Blue Street Capital: they've shortened their workweeks without cutting salaries, lowering productivity, sacrificing quality, or driving away clients. They're solving immediate problems in their businesses, often with surprising or dramatic results. They're also building a movement that could improve how we all work and could create a brighter future for work.

WHAT'S WRONG WITH WORK

And we really need to improve work. A century ago, philosopher Bertrand Russell and economist John Maynard Keynes argued that by 2000—eight decades in their future and two decades in our past—we could all be working as little as three or four hours a day. In Russell and Keynes's lifetime, technology, labor union demands, rising educational standards, and greater prosperity had reduced the length of the average workday from fourteen to eight hours a day. They thought that as technology continued to advance through the twentieth century, productivity could continue to rise, economies could continue to grow, and working hours could fall further.

But Russell also warned that while "modern methods of production have given us the possibility of ease and security for all," if productivity gains and profits were hoarded by factory owners, executives, and investors, those same

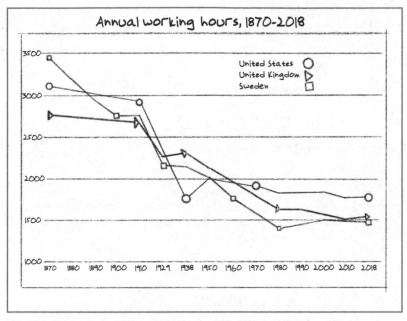

Working hours from 1870 to 2018 in the US, UK, and Sweden. Working hours fell substantially between 1870 and 1930, and that decrease led Russell and Keynes to believe that they could fall much further by 2000, to as low as one thousand hours per year. Instead, especially since the 1970s, working hours have held relatively steady or fallen only modestly.

advances could be used to create a world that offered "overwork for some and starvation for others." That's not a bad description of work today. In the United States, working hours have slowly fallen since World War II, despite enormous productivity gains and economic growth. The growth of mass-consumption-oriented economies in the West made ever-increasing wages and hours more desirable than a shorter workweek for most workers. When economic growth slowed in the 1970s and labor unions lost power, companies offshored factories, outsourced jobs, replaced stable work with part-time gigs, and demanded longer hours from employees. The development of sophisticated models for predicting

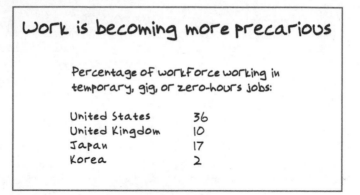

Work is becoming more precarious

Percentage of workforce working in
temporary, gig, or zero-hours jobs:

United States	36
United Kingdom	10
Japan	17
Korea	2

The percentage of workers employed in temporary work, gig-economy jobs, or zero-hours contracts has grown dramatically in the US, with other advanced economies following.

labor demand and the growth of online freelance market-places have accelerated the expansion of the gig economy in advanced nations and the growing precariousness of work.

Executives learned they could boost profits by shredding workforces, tapping global manufacturing and transportation networks, or using "disruptive innovation" to drive established companies out of business. The rise of Silicon Valley in the 1980s brought with it a new model of work and success that glamorized long hours, made workaholics into heroes, and turned overwork into a badge of honor. As a result, we now live in a fast-moving, unstable world in which overwork is a source of riches for some and a necessity for survival for the rest.

But this way of working is costly for individuals, for companies, and for economies. The human cost of over-work and burnout—in lost earning potential, happiness, and creativity—is huge. Overworked people suffer from higher rates of chronic disease and depression. Stanford business professor Jeffrey Pfeffer argued recently that the health costs

Overwork is a global problem

Percentage of workers who average
more than 50 hours/week:

Turkey	32.6
Korea	25.2
Japan	17.9
United Kingdom	12.2
United States	11.1
OECD average	11.0
Sweden	1.1
Switzerland	0.4

Overwork is common in many developed countries.

of badly designed workplaces make work as significant a health hazard as smoking.

Overwork is also counterproductive for companies. Overworked or burned-out employees are actually less productive than well-rested workers. They're also less engaged at work, more likely to leave, and even more likely to cut ethical corners or steal from the company. People who drop out of promising careers are expensive to replace—especially in professions like law and medicine in which long hours, high standards, and intense pressure are common. And employee burnout costs the global economy an estimated $300 billion a year in sick days and lost productivity.

Even in countries where formal workplace discrimination ended decades ago, long hours make it difficult for women to manage the demands of bosses, professions, and family, and to maintain their careers after they become parents. Despite decades of corporate policies for improved maternity leave, flexible work schedules, and exhortations for women to lean in or manage their time better, solutions to the problem of

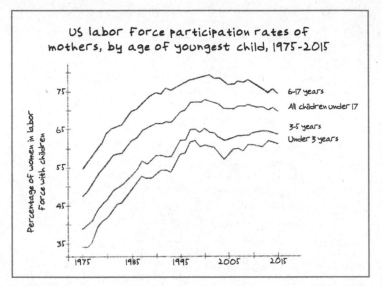

Labor force participation of mothers, by age of youngest child, 1975–2015. Participation rates rose steadily through the 1990s, but in the last twenty years have barely improved—and sometimes have dropped.

work-life balance remain elusive. In the United States, mothers flocked to the labor force in growing numbers between the 1970s and late 1990s. For the last twenty years, though, those participation rates have stalled, suggesting that family-friendly policies have not had as large an impact as their designers, and many users, would have liked.

To different degrees, in the United States, United Kingdom, and Japan, women's full-time participation rates in the workforce decline when they have young children and take years to recover; even after they return to work full-time, they often earn less than men (including fathers with dependent children) and have lower lifetime earnings. Managing part-time or flexible work while raising children even has a measurable impact on women's health: a recent study

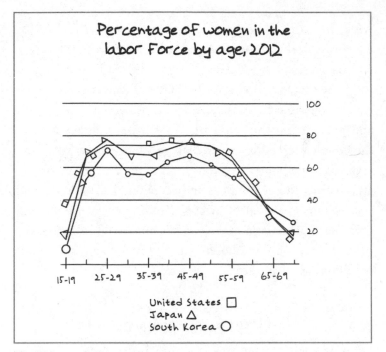

Percentage of women in the labor force by age, 2012

United States □
Japan △
South Korea ○

The "M curve" of women's employment. In many countries, women's participation in the labor force climbs steadily until they start families; at that point, participation rates drop and remain low for some time. The size of the curve varies from country to country: as the chart above shows, in the United States it's flatter than in South Korea.

of stress-related biomarkers (which provide a more objective measure of stress than surveys) found that women with children who worked part-time or in flexible schedules actually had higher stress levels than women working full-time.

Our worship of overwork also creates problems of recruitment, retention, work-life balance, career and financial stability, and burnout. Piecemeal solutions might help one of those problems but leave the rest untouched. Indeed, the limited success of programs for workplace wellness and flexible work, added to the economic and technological forces that drive overwork, the number of voices that sing its praises, and its sheer overwhelming pervasiveness all contribute to the sense that long hours are natural and inevitable.

At the same time, the growing gap between the richest and poorest and the sense that modern economies are designed to enrich elites rather than generate prosperity for everyone are fueling a dangerous level of populism, discontent, and distrust in our political and economic institutions. And the imminent arrival of artificial intelligence, robots, and other new technologies threatens to further widen economic gaps, destroy jobs, and hollow out industries and the futures of billions of people around the world.

DON'T PATCH, REBUILD

So for many people, and many industries, work isn't working. Today's economy is capable of amazing but unsustainable things, demands time and loyalty from workers while withholding security, and shows blithe disregard for sharing the benefits of rising productivity or using new technologies to improve everyone's lives. Workers are caught between a present that feels unbalanced and unsustainable and a future full of uncertainty, disruption, and inequality. Small-scale solutions to these problems are no longer enough. We need bigger, more holistic approaches that help fix today's problems and give us the means to build a better future.

At the risk of sounding like one of those internet ads that promise "one weird trick" for losing weight or getting rich, the shorter workweek offers a solution to all these problems—the culture of overwork, gender inequity, and unequal division of economic gains, and the massive indirect costs of burnout and shortened careers. After a year visiting and studying companies, I've seen that the four-day week, six-hour or five-hour day, or other shorter workweeks—you'll meet a variety of them in this book—help make them more focused and productive. It boosts recruitment and lowers turnover. It helps service workers be more engaged, creative workers more imaginative, chefs and servers more energetic, and salespeople more focused. It distributes productivity gains, using the one commodity even the richest of us can't buy—time. It helps level the hidden obstacles that drive women out of the workforce, that burn out hard-charging professionals, and that undermine valuable employees. It helps people give equal attention to work and family life and to derive satisfaction from being good workers and great parents.

I became convinced of the need for this sort of systemic change when I was promoting my last book, *Rest: Why You Get More Done When You Work Less*. In that book, I argued that many of history's most creative and prolific people—Nobel Prize–winning scientists, and authors, painters, and composers—worked far fewer hours than you would imagine necessary for producing world-class work. Rather than grind away, these figures worked in intense bursts of four to five hours each day and alternated time at their desks with long walks, exercise, or other activities. This looks at first like a poor use of time, but recent research in neuroscience and the psychology of creativity shows that our brains actually keep working on problems when we turn our attention elsewhere, and that scheduling rest periods after intensive work gives us time to recharge our batteries while allowing our creative subconscious to continue searching for solutions to problems that have eluded our conscious effort. Rest, it turns out, is not work's competitor; it is work's partner.

While I was promoting the book on radio call-in shows and podcasts, with book readings and talks, people rarely challenged the idea that we should all rest more. Rather, I would almost always get a variant of the question "If I'm working a nine-to-five job, how do I convince my boss that rest is valuable?" Or "What are some tips and tricks for working mothers about how to get more rest?"

Of course, I had answers. The science clearly shows that overwork is counterproductive, I said. It stresses both companies and workers, hurts productivity, and contributes to burnout. Smart managers will recognize the value of letting workers go home on time, have email-free evenings, and use their vacation days. It's good for people to reclaim control over their own time; it's not easy, but that only makes it more rewarding.

But to tell the truth, I never really felt satisfied by those answers. Most of us work in environments where we don't have a lot of control over our daily schedules. Some of us are members of professions where overwork is the norm. For managers and entrepreneurs accustomed to offering perks to keep people on the job, rest sounds like a drag on productivity. I still think it's important for people to see that they have more control over their time than they realize. But we have to acknowledge that our control is limited by social expectations, the demands of bosses and organizations, and the economy. Personal solutions to problems of work-life balance can only take us so far. To put it another way, what I should have said to those radio-show callers was, "Working mothers don't need tips and tricks. They need a workplace and career model that doesn't expect them to work as if they don't have kids, raise children as if they don't work, demand that they do both at exactly the same time, and say it's their own fault if they can't do that to some poorly articulated, impossible standard. They've gotten all the personal advice they need. What they need now is structural change."

So I was intrigued when I heard about some companies that were putting the lessons of *Rest* into practice, moving to four-day weeks or six-hour workdays, reducing their working time by 20 or 25 percent without cutting salaries, productivity, or profitability. I found software companies in Tokyo and New York, advertising agencies in London and Glasgow, financial services firms in Norwich and San Diego, organic cosmetics makers in Melbourne and Los Angeles, and even Michelin-starred restaurants in Copenhagen and Palo Alto. They're all led by entrepreneurs who are full of ambition, but who also think they can fix what's broken in their industries. They share worries about risks to productivity, missed deadlines, disappointed customers and clients, and skeptical investors and employees. But they also find similar ways of dealing with the challenges of doing the same amount of work in less time. And everyone sees similar benefits: higher productivity and profits, happy clients, improvements in recruitment and retention. The shorter workweek becomes an important part of many companies' brand; in a world where everyone is young, scrappy, and hungry, finishing by Thursday shows you're more efficient than the competition.

As a futurist, I've been trained to look for "weak signals," strange events that can be the leading edge of big social and economic changes. To me, these companies look a lot like weak signals. They are young and small, distributed across a variety of industries, and spread all over the world. Even though they didn't know about each other, they're all moving down the same path. They're part of a larger movement that just isn't aware of itself yet.

ABOUT THIS BOOK

This book is meant to introduce you to that movement and to show you how you can join it yourself.

In these pages you'll meet the leaders who have taken their companies on a journey to four-day weeks. You'll see how they do it: how they plan and design trial periods, how they redesign the workday to become more focused and effective, how they change their cultures and processes to get the same work done in four days rather than five, and how they convince clients and customers to go on the ride with them. You'll learn how they conduct efficient meetings, use technology thoughtfully, and support an innovation mindset that helps them shorten the workday. You'll discover the benefits that four-day weeks bring to companies, employees, and clients alike, how they make companies more productive, people more creative, careers more sustainable, and clients happier and more satisfied. You'll learn why many companies succeed in moving to a shorter workweek, and why a few fail. Finally, you'll see how by treating work and time as things that we can redesign using the same tools that cutting-edge companies use to create world-class products and services, we can make our work better, our workplaces happier and more prosperous, and the future of work brighter.

Reducing business hours runs against every instinct we have about work and success and requires defying professional norms and ignoring social expectations. Yet it can work. Shortening the workweek can help make companies run better, encourage leaders and workers to develop new skills, enhance focus and collaboration, make work more sustainable, and improve work-life balance. It can even help the environment, reduce traffic and congestion, and make people healthier.

In today's always-on, globally connected, 24/7 world, it's easy to think that overwork is inevitable and inescapable. The companies you're about to meet prove that it's not. They show that you can reinvent the way your business works today, right now.

Let's get started.

1

Frame

SOWOL-RO, SEOUL, SOUTH KOREA

"Maybe it's because I have a design background, or maybe it's my personal tendency, but I really like to find patterns and flip them, or tweak them, and think about why things are the way they are," Bong-Jin Kim, the CEO of mobile app developer Woowa Brothers, tells me. We're sitting in a Japanese restaurant in Seoul, a parade of exquisitely made *kaiseki* dishes floating past us as we talk. After spending several winter nights grazing my way across Seoul's vibrant street-food scene and following a strict diet of skewers of food grilled on open-air braziers, the private tatami room at the Millennium Hilton is a pleasant change; the quiet also makes it easier for me to hear the pair of interpreters who are with us.

Korea is an unlikely laboratory for experiments in shortening the workweek. In 1953, after decades of Japanese colonial rule, World War II, and the devastation of the Korean

War, South Korea was one of the poorest countries in the world. Nearly seventy years later, its economy had grown an astounding **31,000 fold**, and it was one of fifteen countries in the world with an annual GDP of more than $1 trillion. Hard-driving high-tech companies like Hyundai, Samsung, and LG helped transform this small, resource-poor, and rugged country into a global economic and cultural powerhouse. But it's come at a cost: Koreans now work more hours per year than almost any other country in the world (only Mexicans work more). Suicide rates have tripled since 1990. The Korean language now has its own word for "working yourself to death"—*gwarosa*.

Yet despite (or maybe because of) this history, a number of companies in Korea are experimenting with ways to shorten working hours. In 2018, in an effort to ease pressures caused by long hours, the Korean government passed legislation capping working hours at forty-eight per week. Companies struggling to find and retain workers are giving them the option of working four ten-hour days. A few are going further and adopting four-day or thirty-five-hour weeks. Probably the best known of them is Woowa Brothers.

Bong-Jin is one of the country's most famous tech entrepreneurs, a star of what Koreans call O2O (online-to-offline commerce) and one of the more colorful figures in the normally buttoned-up world of Korean business. After what one biography diplomatically called an "eventful adolescence," Bong-Jin studied interior design at the Seoul Institute of the Arts, then earned an MA in typography at Kookmin University's Graduate School of Design. After a short-lived venture making furniture, he worked as a web designer and art director for Nike Korea and credit card company Hyundai Card, before cofounding Woowa Brothers in 2010. Baedal Minjok,

Woowa Brothers' restaurant delivery app, was the first Korean smartphone app to be downloaded more than 10 million times and is now the Korean market's version of DoorDash or Deliveroo. The fledgling company attracted funding from Korean venture capitalists, and then foreign investors. By 2015, Woowa Brothers had grown from a scrappy startup to a five-hundred-person company that made *Fortune* Korea's list of fifty best places to work and landed Bong-Jin on lists of top CEOs in Korea.

But then Bong-Jin did something unexpected: he decided to shorten the workweek for his employees. Koreans work some of the longest hours in the world, and Woowa Brothers had been no exception. He implemented a 37.5-hour workweek in 2015, then in March 2017 cut hours further, to 35 hours a week, without cutting anyone's pay. "We didn't introduce this so we could slack off," he told *Bloomberg* reporter Sam Kim in 2019. "My goal was to create a workplace where we could concentrate better. We should never stop thinking about how we can change the way we work so we change the way we live."

I ask Bong-Jin to tell the story of how he decided to shorten the workweek at Woowa Brothers. The company spent its early years like any lucky startup, growing fast, burning cash and midnight oil. But eventually, "I realized that putting more hours into work did not lead to higher productivity," he recalls. "For a company like this, an IT company and a creative company, longer working hours are not very useful." Logically, if "the link between time and productivity was blurry," he continues, the company should try not to maximize working hours but instead aim "to promote more efficient work, to remind workers of what kind of people we are and what kind of work we are doing."

Further, "I was curious why we take a forty-hour week for granted," Bong-Jin says. He found that the first labor laws establishing a forty-hour workweek were passed in Europe in the late 1800s, after decades of labor action and political negotiation. But he wondered, "Why forty, not forty-five or thirty-five?" The idea of "eight hours for work, eight hours for rest, eight hours for what we will" had been a rallying cry for unions since the nineteenth century, but why couldn't the workweek be different today? What was preventing it from being different at Woowa Brothers? he wondered.

Did his investors put up any resistance? I ask. No, Bong-Jin says, because "I just did it. I posted about the decision on Facebook, and that was the first announcement the investors got." As a charismatic founder and CEO, he could get away with that. Fortunately, he adds, "they clicked 'Like.'"

They should like the decision. Woowa Brothers has enjoyed 70 to 90 percent annual revenue growth since

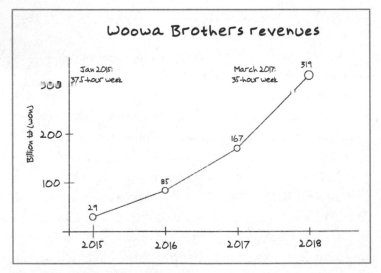

Woowa Brothers revenues, 2015–2018.

shortening its workweek in 2015. By July 2019, its user base has grown from 3 to 11 million, and monthly orders have risen from 5 million to 35 million.

By 2019 the company was valued at $2.6 billion, vaulting it into the elite global club of tech "unicorns," startups worth more than $1 billion. They moved into new offices overlooking Seoul's Olympic Park and now employ over a thousand people. Even as they've tripled in size in the last five years, from 400 to 1,300 employees, they've become more selective in their hiring and are now able to compete with giants like Samsung and LG. Starting the week on Monday afternoon hasn't made the company any less innovative: it's collaborating with tech giants to develop delivery drones and robots, artificial intelligence, and conversational interfaces and has a new service to help traditional small businesses sell online. Their whimsical apps remain fun and easy to use, a model of Korean companies' love of good design.

A number of other O2O startups have adopted shorter workweeks with similar success. So the decision to shorten working hours is paying off for these companies. Still, I feel like there's more to understand about Bong-Jin's thinking. What allowed him to spot this opportunity?

DESIGN THINKING

"Most companies look at what other companies are doing and then follow that path," he says. But "if everyone else is doing it this way, maybe we should do it differently." He credits his training in design for teaching him to think this way. Design taught him to dig deep, ask questions that challenge conventional thinking, and look closely at things that we usually take for granted. Indeed, Bong-Jin has never shed his identity as a designer. "People call me the CEO," he told a journalist once, "but I'm still a designer and I still design these days."

Bong-Jin's design training didn't provide him with fuzzy inspiration for rethinking the workday, and it wasn't just about rearranging schedules or shifting the normal workday. "People usually think design is using the right part of your brain, or is more emotional, but in fact design is very logical," he says. Intuition and feeling are important, but they build on a foundation laid by the left brain. So while they were planning to shorten the workweek, "my directors and I spent a lot of time thinking about what kind of company we are, what kind of work we do as a company, how to transform the market, and things like that," Bong-Jin tells me. But they weren't just engaged in philosophical speculation. They were asking the kinds of basic questions that you pose when you start reimagining a product or redesigning a service.

Bong-Jin wasn't the only CEO to talk about shortening the workweek this way. In many of the companies I visited, leaders spoke about "prototyping" shorter workweeks. Employees collaborated to invent new ways of working together. Companies were constantly trying new things, evaluating their experience, and using lessons learned to improve their practices.

Whether they explicitly did so or not, all these companies were taking the same approach to figure out how to shorten the workday, I realized. They were treating it as an exercise in design thinking.

The discipline of design thinking evolved in Silicon Valley in the 1970s and 1980s, when industrial designers working on the first generation of personal computers were trying to turn cutting-edge but often hard-to-use technologies like personal computers, the computer mouse, and laser printers into products that everyone could use. For engineers accustomed to mastering difficult technologies, complexity represented power, not a problem, but most users didn't want to join a priesthood in order to keep better inventory or write term papers.

A few designers realized that making computer technology accessible would require understanding what users wanted to do, studying how they worked, and developing products that fit their needs. They needed a method that was technically grounded but also observant and insightful, and could draw on a variety of disciplines, from engineering and psychology to materials science and anthropology. But design thinking also needed a set of practices that would deliver to ambitious clients in a fast-moving environment. (Steve Jobs was one of design thinking's earliest supporters and most demanding clients.) Over time, design thinking evolved into a

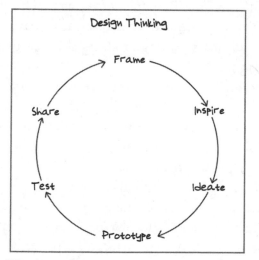

The design thinking process.

formal set of processes. In a version developed by IDEOU, the design thinking studio IDEO's online school, it's broken down into six steps.

- **Frame.** This involves reflecting on the problem you really need to solve and the ways you can go about solving it. For companies, this is an important phase because it can broaden their thinking and ultimately generate better products. You might go into this phase asking, "How can we update this product that used to be a big moneymaker?" but realize that you face a deeper opportunity—say, using the product as a platform to provide an ongoing (and much more profitable!) service.
- **Inspire.** This phase is about better understanding users' needs. Depending on the company, you might analyze quantitative data or surveys, listen to focus groups talk about their experiences with your product, or send researchers out to offices or surgical theaters to watch how people work with your product. This phase can often reveal unmet needs or creative ways that users are adapting existing products that can inform your design.
- **Ideate.** In this phase, you use what you've observed to start generating ideas for products or designs. This is often associated with brainstorming sessions, walls filled with Post-its, lists of specifications, or rough-hewn prototypes or sketches.
- **Prototype.** Time to build! Prototyping is a critical practice for design thinking because it's an intellectual discipline and exercise, not just a physical craft. Prototyping can help identify technical problems with your design, gaps in your thinking, or cool ideas that just

turn out to be impractical. The act of building something can also reveal new opportunities to improve a product before it gets into a user's hands. But the prototyping stage is also essential because in order to test your ideas, you need to create something that people can actually use and respond to—and you need to observe those interactions. People are complicated, the world is often a messy and unpredictable place, and most jobs are more complex than we realize; the best way to appreciate and make sense of that complexity—to understand which pieces of that complexity you really need to pay attention to and which ones you don't—is to prototype.

- **Test.** In this stage, you put the prototype before users. You see what they make of it, what they like, and what they struggle with. This is where abstract ideas start to grind against reality, and it's a phase that can be illuminating, bracing, or inspiring. Your favorite cool feature may turn out to fall flat. A feature that was included on a whim might prove to be incredibly useful. Or a rough prototype might draw out ideas or user behavior that you hadn't seen before.

- **Share.** In the last stage, you share your work: the product itself, of course, but also the story behind it. That might sound like an afterthought, but the stories can help frame how users think about and use products, and storytelling itself is a powerful medium for attracting customers. (Think about how much packaging now has stories about what inspired the product or the company's origins.) And for other designers or colleagues, stories can help illuminate issues they're working on and point the way to better solutions.

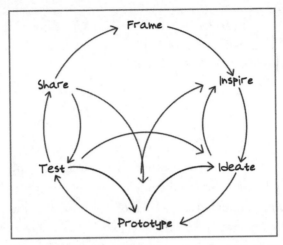

The design thinking process in action. In most cases there's lots of feedback between the different stages, as conceptual work, prototyping, and user testing all influence each other.

I've described these as separate steps, but in reality designers move back and forth between these stages. Testing generates feedback from users that inspires a new prototype, which then generates more feedback from users, which might drive a change in the design brief and another round of prototyping. So what looks at first like a cycle is more like a medieval model of the solar system, filled with epicycles.

And as with any professional practice, different studios and designers will have their own takes on the process. But they all agree on the importance of empathy, focusing on users, exploring ideas through prototyping, learning from experience, and incorporating feedback. No matter how you organize it, the design thinking process is always "open-ended, open-minded, and iterative," as Tim Brown put it in his book *Change by Design*.

Design thinking has driven the creation of some of the world's most familiar products. Apple's computer mouse was designed by a young team that went on to form IDEO, now the world's foremost design thinking studio. IDEO has played a role in designing products ranging from the PalmPilot, to the Swiffer, to the coaster bike. Today, design thinking reaches beyond the physical. "In Korea, we have the term 'design management,' or 'design *gyeong-yeong*' in Konglish," Jin Ryu, Woowa Brothers' vice president of public relations, explains. "It means adopting design thinking to management." "You can design a thing, but you can also design how people behave," Bong-Jin says. "Designers can use management as a tool to shape the behavior of people." (If you guessed that Korean companies take design pretty seriously, you'd be right.) Futurists use design thinking to help clients see emerging problems and opportunities in new ways. Banks, airlines, and governments use it to more effectively provide services. My son's high school organizes its curriculum around design thinking. A palliative care doctor uses it to help patients think about end-of-life issues.

And, as the companies that have shortened their working hours show, you can use design thinking to redesign time.

It might not be obvious that you can apply the same techniques that designers use to create products to thinking about meetings and schedules and workflows. Time, like money or love, is something we all want to accumulate and conserve—and usually we want more of it—but it feels largely outside our control (especially these days). Companies that move to four-day weeks or six-hour days don't just cut a couple things from their schedules, or add a new HR program, or urge employees to "work smarter, not harder." They take a more holistic view of the problem.

The idea that you can use design thinking to redesign the workday—to uncover hidden assumptions about how we work, replace them with principles of our own choosing, think more clearly about what matters in how we work, build experiments and prototypes that help us make our workdays more productive and happier, and iterate and improve our working styles—is one you'll encounter a lot in these pages. As we tour companies that are redesigning the workweek, hear from the leaders who are driving change, and follow the workers who are putting it into action, design thinking can help us see the underlying logic in particular choices and extract the principles that specific cases illustrate. The aim of analyzing these case studies and stories isn't to figure out who to copy. It's not to "look at what other companies are doing and then follow that path," as Bong-Jin puts it. It's to stimulate thinking about "what kind of company we are" and "what kind of work we do."

Since I encounter design thinking so often in the companies I'm studying, I'm using the six-stage model to organize this book, though I take a little literary license. We've already started to "Frame" the big question and to explore the idea that what we often regard as separate issues—work-life balance, burnout, career development, inequality, the future of the high-tech workplace—can be approached and managed more holistically. "Inspire" talks about what moves leaders to embark on the risky adventure of shortening the workweek, and about the companies and industries in which the movement is taking off. "Ideate" explains how companies get started: how people react to the idea of shortening the workweek, what companies do to prepare for trials, and how they deal with uncertainties and potential problems. "Prototype" is all about the practical steps companies take when redesigning the workday: how they change daily routines, meetings, and cultural norms; how they exploit technology; and how people learn to manage and collaborate in new ways. "Test" presents the results: how shorter working hours affect recruitment and retention, productivity, and profitability; the impact it has on work-life balance and creativity; and how clients and customers react. Finally, "Share" explains how shorter workweeks could change the future of work, how they could help us deal with rising levels of stress and burnout, how they create new ways of solving problems posed by automation and AI, and how they could even contribute to fighting inequality and climate change.

Using design thinking as a framework also keeps us focused on the question of "How can I do this?" I don't just want to present an abstract or moral case for a shorter workweek; others, like historian Rutger Bregman and the New Economics Foundation in London, are already making that argument. Instead, I want to show how companies are actually doing it and show you how you could redesign the workday at your own company. If you're a manager or company owner, this book will lay out the steps you can follow to implement a four-day workweek or six-hour day: how to design a trial period; how to sell it to clients and investors; how to get your employees on board; how to redesign meetings, technology, and the workday itself to become more focused, effective, and productive; and how to measure the results. If you're an employee at a company that's trying it out, this book will help you navigate the transition by pointing out the pitfalls, highlighting the opportunities, and documenting the benefits of moving to a shorter week. If you want to convince your manager that a shorter workweek would be good for your team or department, this book will help you make your case. And even if you're self-employed, this book can help you find ways to work more efficiently and sustainably.

AT THIS STAGE . . .

The experiences of Blue Street Capital, Tower Paddle Boards, and Woowa Brothers might have you thinking that a shorter workweek is worth exploring. They highlight two things in particular:

- Companies and leaders today face a variety of challenges, which they usually address through a patchwork of bespoke efforts and policies: outreach programs for recruiting new talent, parental leave for better work-life balance, mindfulness and exercise classes for stress, flexible work options to increase retention and productivity. Many leaders recognize that these workers' issues aren't just isolated, personal problems, but are interconnected and systemic, and that approaching and dealing with them more holistically would provide better, more stable solutions.

- Design thinking offers a useful way of making sense of these problems, thinking about their underlying causes, and constructing novel solutions to them without being overwhelmed by their complexity. It provides a way of gaining new insights by looking across a company and taking a broad view of its issues, a discipline for challenging convention and exploring alternatives, and a process for generating insights that lead to action. And for leaders who need space to think strategically, are at risk of burnout from decision fatigue, and are weary of dealing with the same problems over and over again, a design thinking approach offers a more efficient way to manage complexity and boost both personal and organizational sustainability.

Everyone wants more time, but for most organizations, giving back time to workers is a zero-sum game: either workers have to take a pay cut or the company has to spend more. By taking a design thinking approach to the problem and redesigning the workday, it's possible to reduce working hours without losing customers or money.

Ready to get inspired?

2

Inspire

In the inspiration phase of the design thinking process, you cast a wide net around a problem in an effort to refine the question while still staying in touch with a wide range of ideas and disciplines. If you were thinking about designing a hospital admitting room, you would talk to doctors, nurses, and patients and their families about the space, the admitting process, and the worries and anxieties people have when coming into a hospital. You might also spend some time in airport security checkpoints, department stores, and churches to see how different spaces balance security, route people efficiently, and communicate empathy and reassurance.

In this chapter, our inspiration will come from the companies that have already moved to four-day workweeks, six-hour days, or other forms of shorter working hours.

ST. LEONARD'S STREET, EDINBURGH, SCOTLAND

"From a very young age, I would say from sixteen, I was already working fifty hours a week," Stuart Ralston tells me. It's late morning at Aizle, the restaurant that Stuart owns with his wife, Krystal Goff. We're at an immaculate table across from the bar, and while it's quiet, staff are drifting in. Aizle has been one of the best-known restaurants in the city since it opened in 2014 and has only gotten better since it moved to a four-day week in 2018. I want to understand what drove Stuart to that decision, and how Aizle has stayed afloat opening one day fewer.

Like many chefs, Stuart started out washing dishes as a teenager. He rose through the ranks at restaurants in Scotland and England before Gordon Ramsay hired him to work in his New York restaurant. Stuart learned a lot, but the hours were crazy: he'd be on "from seven in the morning to one or two in the morning, six days a week, covering people's holiday, and as soon as someone went on holiday, you're working ten days straight." His parents and older brother are chefs, and while working in New York was exhausting, it was work to be proud of. Few people ever get the chance to work in a Michelin-starred restaurant, and even fewer can stand the heat. Surviving makes you part of an elite.

After working for Gordon Ramsay for two years, Stuart became executive chef at the CORE: Club in New York, then head chef and chef de partie at resorts in England and Barbados. But he had always wanted to be his own boss, and eventually he and Krystal returned to Edinburgh, found a location on St. Leonard's Street in the Newington area near the university, and opened Aizle. They refinished the floors, wallpapered, and installed the shelves and appliances themselves. "The first seven weeks here I didn't take a day off," he recalls. "It was crazy how many days in a row I spent working from eight in the morning till twelve o'clock at night. And I didn't realize what is entailed in being the head chef of a place and at the same time being a business owner."

With Stuart's focus on seasonal ingredients, a prix fixe menu, and a flair for unusual combinations of ingredients and cuisines, Aizle won some good early reviews with critics and quickly became a favorite with patrons too; out of more than 1,800 Edinburgh restaurants reviewed on the travel website TripAdvisor, it's consistently been ranked number one or two. Krystal stopped working the bar when she had their first child, but Stuart stayed on. "The whole business is built around me cooking my cuisine," he explains, and "we were trying to do lots of stuff, we were trying to push for lots of accolades and awards and manage the business." Any small business owner would rather deal with the problem of too much business than too little, but Stuart was spending up to sixteen hours a day at the restaurant. "Then I get home, I've got a young baby who's awake all night." For two years the three of them survived on a few hours' broken sleep per day. "I think that's when we really started noticing that the hours I was working were not helping in the family situation," he says drily.

After three years of eighty- or ninety-hour workweeks, "I was overweight, stressed, tired, drinking too much. I was super-tired all the time, I was losing my temper quickly with people, losing staff by the minute." At home, meanwhile, "I didn't feel like I was bonding enough with my son. The first two years of his life, I pretty much missed it." However, as a father and business owner, "you have responsibilities to both your family and the ten people that work here who depend on you to pay their rent." As is often the case, the success of the business came at a high personal cost. "Even though the restaurant was doing really well and we had a lot of business, it wasn't going anywhere positive. It just felt like I was caught in this really dark spiral."

In the restaurant industry, the pressure to succeed is enormous. Chefs feel it every night, with every dish; when doing the books at the end of the week; when trying to create new dishes and hone their craft. The industry prides itself on welcoming misfits and people with quirky or sketchy backgrounds, but it also struggles with high turnover, intense stress, and long hours with low pay. Drug and alcohol abuse are common problems, and many chefs battle depression. Success brings its own perils. The glare of the spotlight, the feeling like you can't afford to turn down an opportunity, the worry that you'll lose it all—these create new anxieties. As Kat Kinsman, food writer and founder of the mental health project Chefs with Issues notes, even chefs who've built profitable, critically acclaimed restaurants can feel tremendous pressure to maintain their reputations.

By late 2017, it was clear to Stuart that he faced a choice. He could change the way he ran Aizle and risk failure, or keep going the way he had been and fail for sure. "At that point, I didn't feel like I had anything to lose, because I was losing too much of myself and my family time," he tells me. "So in January 2018 we decided that's it, something needs to change." Aizle couldn't add another chef to the staff; it was too small, and too much a reflection of Stuart's distinctive vision. "The only way to do it," he realized, "was to shut. If there's no business, there's no reason to be here. It forces us to have that day off."

Stuart made two big decisions. First, he decided to close Aizle three days a week, and to remain open Wednesday through Saturday. "Sunday was always fully booked," he tells me, "but I wanted that day because in the future, my son will be going to school, and Sundays he'll still be off." To cover the potential lost revenue, they renovated the dining room, adding six more seats, allowing them to serve an average of twelve more people per night, or forty-eight more per week—almost enough to make up for closing on Sunday. Stuart bought a larger stove, allowing him to work more efficiently. And if they need to, they can go back to a five-day week during the Edinburgh Fringe festival in August, when more than two million visitors descend on the city, and in December during the busy holiday season.

Second, Stuart decreed that the restaurant would shut for six weeks a year to give everyone a vacation at the same time, so nobody has to work overtime covering for people who are on vacation. Stuart once worked three weeks of twenty-hour days covering for other chefs. "I don't think it's healthy," he says with grim understatement, "and [now] at thirty-five, I don't think I've got the energy." It also guarantees that he'll have time with his family. As he told a journalist in 2018, "I grew up in a world where family time was sacrificed for the business. I've decided I don't want to do that any more."

So how is it working out? After almost a year, "the staff are happier," Stuart tells me, "and they work harder in four days than in five. So the place is cleaner, more organized, we're getting stuff done." General manager Jade Johnston agrees. "I have more energy, and I feel happier. When I come to work, I'm only thinking about work. I can work at a faster pace and work better—I won't miss anything, I will care about all the guests consistently, and care about the business."

And the food? "With a four-day week, I've had time to do more research and development into products," Stuart says. "I'm definitely spending more time designing the dishes, spending more time with the staff doing the dishes. So I'd say in the last ten months, the standard of what we're doing, across the board, has been much better than it ever has been. You see the feedback from customers. We're fully booked— there's not an opening on a Saturday for two months." In fact, business was strong enough to allow Stuart to expand: in mid-2019 he opened a second restaurant in Edinburgh, a more casual eatery named Noto.

Before he started Aizle, Stuart had worked as a chef de cuisine at a Caribbean resort, and the skills he acquired there proved decisive in making a four-day week a success. Unlike many chefs, "I was used to managing orders and people and numbers," so when he was considering a four-day week, he could examine the restaurant's balance sheet and cash flow, "look at the numbers and say, yeah, this could work." But that didn't just mean having something in the bank in case business fell off. "We've been here four and a half years, we're popular, and we've already made money and reinvested it." You might think that a new business would have an easier time starting a four-day week, but Aizle's history suggests that a more mature business, with a proven infrastructure and staff and roots, can better handle the challenges of redesigning the workday.

Aizle is one of a number of restaurants that have shortened their workweek in recent years. It's a notable trend because world-class chefs exemplify the best and worst of creative life. They're constantly looking for new ideas, ingredients, and inspiration, then turning creative breakthroughs into viable products that can be prepared by chefs on the line, night after night. The work is open-ended: the quest for new dishes and ingredients and ways of cooking never stops. It's almost a textbook example of creativity at a high level.

It's also as high-pressure and intense an occupational world as you can find. Cooking demands perfection, minute after minute, day after day. It's physically and mentally exhausting; you're working in a high-stress atmosphere. The industry gives a lot of power to chefs who are visionaries, and some of them are deeply imaginative, inquisitive, curious, and perfectionist; others just turn difficult, demanding, and even abusive. It's also a field that has more than its share of burnout, substance abuse, and other problems.

Now some of the best-known and most critically acclaimed restaurants in the world are reducing the number of nights they open. In Palo Alto, California, Baumé went to a four-day week not long after winning its second Michelin star; to the south, Los Angeles kaiseki restaurant n/naka (another Michelin two-star winner) also operates on a four-day week. In Melbourne, Australia, Attica adopted a forty-eight-hour weekly cap for staff in 2017. Two of the most famous centers of "new Nordic" cuisine have also experimented with shorter hours. When it reopened in 2017, Noma in Copenhagen decided to serve four nights a week; as they explained, "Noma's strength lies in its staff; we've come to this decision in an effort to give them a better quality of life, both at work, and outside it." In Oslo, Norway, Maaemo has gone even further: it shifted its staff to four-day weeks in 2016, and in 2017 let everyone work a three-day week. Giving chefs and staff more time off reduces stress, helps them stay innovative, and raises the odds that they'll stay in the kitchen.

Stuart and Aizle's story is also more broadly illustrative of how leaders come to shorten workweeks at their companies. A lot of their motivation is personal: they want better lives for themselves, they want the means to deal with the problems of stress and work-life balance that we all confront. There are also a host of practical considerations: no matter what business they're in, they face challenges with recruitment, problems with turnover, a need to compete against bigger and better-funded companies, the demand to be constantly innovative and fresh. They also want to push back against negative trends in their industry, to ease the pressures that drive dedicated people away, and to show how to create businesses that will support more sustainable careers and lives. Finally, whether they've spent their careers in the United States or Europe or Asia, they have the professional experience and knowledge necessary to fix their own companies and chart a new course for their industries.

THE COMPANIES

You've probably heard about a few companies that have experimented with shorter workdays or workweeks. In newspapers and the business press, you're likely to have read about San Diego–based Tower Paddle Boards or Philadelphia software company Wildbit, financial trust Perpetual Guardian in New Zealand, or Radioactive PR in the United Kingdom. In fact, the movement to shorten working hours is broad, diverse, and global. I've researched, visited, and conducted interviews with leaders and employees at more than a hundred companies that have reduced their working hours, many of which have received little or no attention in the English-speaking press. To get a better sense of the movement to shorten working hours, and to understand how widespread it is, let's look at these companies as a group, what industries they're in, and where in the world they are.

Most of the companies share three qualities that allow them to be early innovators. First, they're mainly small- to medium-size businesses, where significant cultural and managerial changes are easier to implement. Second, almost all are still led by their founders, whose formal position and moral authority give them the power to make big changes. Third, many companies already trade on reputations for being creative, innovative places and can sell experiments in shorter hours as yet another expression of those qualities. This explains why these companies have been early adopters, but overall, the diversity of companies, industries, and geography suggests a movement that's just getting started.

The appendix lists the companies I discuss in this book, the countries where they're located, the industries they're in, and the kind of schedule they've adopted. Note that I'm not focusing on companies that offer employees reduced working hours for reduced wages (as Amazon has done with some of its employees), and with only a couple interesting exceptions, I'm also not including companies (like 7-Eleven in Japan) that have moved from five days to four but have extended the workday to ten hours in order to keep the same working hours. These companies are helping normalize the idea of a four-day workweek, but they generally don't have to change their internal processes or company cultures.

I also talk only briefly about government agencies or public school districts that have moved to four-day weeks, though it is worth noting that there is a movement in government and education to experiment with alternatives to the traditional five-day week. In Utah, the state government adopted a four-day week/ten-hour day between 2008 to 2011, and the government of the city of El Paso likewise had a four-day week/ten-hour day between 2009 and 2018; other city governments have likewise trialed four-day weeks. Between 1996 and 1998, the Finnish government sponsored a program that allowed municipal governments to reduce working hours for employees. In Iceland, the city of Reykjavik began trialing a shorter workweek in 2015; by 2018, it had expanded to include more than two thousand workers, or a quarter of the city's workforce. In 2019, three other Icelandic municipalities implemented their own trials with reduced working hours.

In the United States, public schools have also been experimenting with four-day weeks. In 2019, twenty-five states had districts whose schools operated on four-day weeks, and in Colorado, more than half of districts now operate on four-day weeks. Many districts shorten the school week when budgets are tight, but some rural districts are switching to four-day weeks in an effort to reduce the time children spend on long bus rides and to improve teacher recruitment and retention.

Instead, in this project I'm focusing on companies that have done three things at the same time: shortened their total working hours, kept salaries the same, and maintained the same levels of productivity, profitability, and customer service.

This is not an exhaustive list, because new companies around the world are trying four-day workweeks all the time. Tash Walker, the founder of "human behavior agency" The Mix, tells me that several dozen companies contacted her for advice about moving to a four-day week after The Mix published a report in early 2019 describing their transition. Likewise, Andrew Barnes at Perpetual Guardian, a New Zealand firm that received global attention when it shifted to a four-day week in 2018, says that he has heard from companies all over the world that are interested in launching their own trials.

The first thing to note is that while Western European and Scandinavian countries are well known for having the shortest working hours thanks to a combination of legislation, union contracts, and support for flexible and part-time work, the movement to four-day weeks and six-hour days is actually very international. Thirty-five of the companies I studied are in the United Kingdom, and twenty-four are in Europe. Twenty-four are in the United States and Canada, and nine are in Australia and New Zealand. The companies aren't just in the West: fourteen are in Korea and five are in Japan, both countries notorious for long hours.

Likewise, the companies range across a wide variety of industries. Twenty-four companies are restaurants, from world-famous establishments like Noma to casual chains like Shake Shack. Twenty-five are software firms or e-commerce companies. Twenty-seven are creative agencies of various kinds: digital agencies; marketing, advertising, and PR firms; video production companies; design studios. Nine are in consulting, insurance, or financial services. Eight are in manufacturing or maintenance, ranging from a Japanese maker of rice mills to an auto repair center. Six make health and beauty products. Three are nursing homes, and three are call centers.

Restaurants, creative agencies, and software firms are heavily represented because all three are dealing with systemic problems with mental health, stress, and burnout.

The restaurant industry is one that's long struggled with low pay, long hours, and difficult working conditions—and all too often, abusive behavior and sexism in the workplace. In a 2015 survey, 17 percent of full-time restaurant workers admitted to having substance abuse issues. Another survey three years later found that job stress had led to unhealthy behaviors among 43 percent of restaurant workers and affected the family lives of 50 percent of workers.

Things are a little better in advertising, if only because the fires dealt with are only metaphorical. In a 2019 survey in the United States, 33 percent of advertising industry professionals worried about their mental health; among people working more than fifty hours a week or making less than $50,000 a year (in other words, most young professionals), the rates were above 40 percent. The same year, an Australian survey of workers in marketing and advertising found that 56 percent exhibited symptoms of depression. A 2018 study in the United Kingdom found that 64 percent of workers thought about leaving their jobs, 60 percent thought their work had a negative impact on their mental health, 36 percent described their mental health as "poor," and 26 percent said they had a long term problem like chronic stress or depression. Little wonder that the industry as a whole has a 30 percent turnover rate or that half the people who quit their jobs leave the field entirely.

The tech industry has its share of problems too. In a 2018 survey of 12,500 workers in the software industry, 39 percent described themselves as depressed, and 57 percent said they felt burned out. A lot of this was thanks to toxic workplaces: 48 percent said that their workplaces contributed to their poor mental health, and 91 percent said that burnout was a problem at their companies. A 2019 Stack Overflow survey found that 30 percent of software developers deal with mental health challenges like ADHD, emotional disorders, and anxiety, or are not neurotypical.

While almost two-thirds of the companies in this book are from these three industries, the remaining third are quite varied. They include manufacturers of rice-milling machines and bespoke pressed-metal parts, organic cosmetics companies, nursing homes, an auto repair shop, insurance and financial companies, hotels, online and print publishers, and call centers. Two—Japanese e-commerce company Zozo and Korean O2O company Woowa Brothers—have over a thousand employees; most are much smaller, with under a hundred employees. Some shorten working hours by closing an extra day; others have maintained or even extended their opening hours while shortening workers' shifts. They operate at a range of time scales: some have months-long projects, others serve customers every night, and a few have to be open 24/7. Some companies review their financials and key performance indicators quarterly, while others have real-time visibility into how their workers performed that day.

In other words, this is not a movement consisting only of fat, happy companies in slow industries. Moving to a shorter workweek requires that firms rethink everything about how they operate, who they hire, how they incentivize workers, how they divide labor and authority, how they measure performance, and how they distribute the benefits of new technology and higher productivity. Shortening working hours isn't about working less. It's about working better—better economically, but also ethically. Nor are these companies in industries that already offer great work-life balance and gender balance; to the contrary, these fields have well-earned reputations for hard-charging cultures, leaders who treat overwork as a badge of success, and problems with gender disparity, recruitment, turnover, and burnout.

For companies in these industries, shortening working hours isn't a sign of laziness. It's an act of resistance.

KINDS OF TIME REDUCTION

The resistance takes several forms. The most popular is a four-day workweek: about two-thirds of the companies I studied are on some variation of a four-day week. Of these, many work a thirty-two-hour week over four days; a few others trialed or adopted, then abandoned, the four-day week. A few combine a four-day week with remote, flexible work. Japanese software company Cybozu offers the four-day week as part of its "100 styles for 100 people" policy of flexible work.

Other companies have built schedules inspired by Google's 20 percent model, where workers spend four days on company work and have a free day for personal projects. At applications developer thoughtbot and New York software company Cockroach Labs, for example, employees work on company products or client work for four days; on the fifth day, workers have what thoughtbot calls "investment time," when they can take classes, learn new programming languages, cultivate other skills, or do other things that broaden their intellectual horizons. At London design consultancy ELSE, Fridays alternate between totally free "yay days" and self-improvement "play days." A number of restaurants have moved to four-day weeks; they still have long days, and chefs and staff may still work fifty-hour workweeks. But that's a big drop from the seventy- or eighty-hour weeks their colleagues face at conventional restaurants.

Some companies maintain a five-day workweek but shorten the workday. In Korea, the thirty-five-hour week pioneered by Woowa Brothers is popular. Other companies work thirty-hour weeks, with workers on six-hour shifts. Finally, a small number are working five-hour days, either full-time or during the summers.

For other companies, simply holding the workweek to forty hours represents a big step forward. The London office of global advertising agency Wieden+Kennedy started a policy in 2016 to cap working time at forty hours per week. For an agency famous for its fast-working, pressure-cooker environment (it was even nicknamed "Weekend and Kennedy"), returning to a regular workday was a significant move. Clyde Group, a Washington, DC–based strategic communications agency, implemented a forty-hour-a-week cap after losing half its staff to burnout in a year. New York–based Skift discourages employees from working longer than forty hours. Denver's Never Settle IT actually penalizes people for overwork: if they clock more than eighty hours in a two-week period, they lose vacation hours.

There are a number of companies, municipalities, and even states that have offered workers the option of working four ten-hour days. These programs date back to the 1960s and early 1970s, when factories in the United States experimented with four-day/ten-hour-day workweeks in an effort to reduce energy costs and inefficiencies. In the 2000s and 2010s, large companies like General Motors and Amazon, state offices in Utah, city offices in El Paso, Texas, and rural school districts in the United States all experimented with four-day weeks. Today some Japanese companies—including quite large ones like Uniqlo, 7-Eleven, and KFC—offer employees the option of working ten-hour days, four days a week. Some American companies, including Amazon and New York advertising agency Grey, have also offered employees the option of working four-day weeks at reduced pay. But they're not fundamentally redesigning the workweek; these companies are just reshuffling the forty-hour workweek.

THE LEADERS

Let's look closer at the leaders of these companies and what makes them take the leap. Experiments with shorter working hours begin at the top, so it's important to understand leaders' backgrounds and motivations and why they came to believe that shorter hours will make their companies better.

In interviews, almost all the founders describe how their earlier careers featured long hours, poor work-life balance, and brushes with personal or professional burnout. "We all describe ourselves as recovering workaholics," Marei Wollersberger, cofounder and managing director of London design firm Normally, says. They have previous experience working in high-tech companies (including Facebook, Google, and other hard-charging organizations), restaurants, consulting companies, and advertising agencies; many are also serial entrepreneurs. Their decision to move to shorter hours is informed by their own experiences with highly competitive cultures, long hours, and sometimes burnout.

Every one who moved their company to a four-day workweek contrasts their own background and experience with the kind of environment and schedule they now want to create at their companies. Spencer Kimball, Peter Mattis, and Ben Darnell, the cofounders of cloud-based SQL database startup Cockroach Labs, are all Xooglers (as Google alums are called in Silicon Valley); Kimball and Mattis were a co-founder and a senior engineer at payments company Square. Before they founded Never Settle IT, cofounders Kenn Kelly, Shaul Hagen, and Andrew Lundquist worked eighty-hour weeks in "hyper-growth tech startups" and were "highly immersed in Silicon Valley culture." John Peebles, CEO of SaaS training software company Administrate in Edinburgh, Scotland, "literally worked every waking minute" building his first startup. When he left his second company, "I'd made a lot of money and learned a lot, but I didn't really remember the preceding seven or eight years. It was just black. That seemed like a problem."

Software industry veterans aren't the only ones who have these backgrounds. Annie Tevelin founded organic skin-care company SkinOwl in 2013 after working fourteen-hour days as a makeup artist in Hollywood. Anna Ross founded natural nail polish company Kester Black after leaving an eighty-hour-a-week job in fashion. "I cried all the time, ate badly and was so stressed," she told the BBC in 2016, "and I decided I never wanted anyone to experience that kind of bad work environment." After ten years in advertising and "a lot of late nights, a lot of overnighters in some cases," Michael Honey realized when he founded digital interactive agency Icelab that he "wanted to work a relaxed forty hours, rather than a frenetic fifty hours."

Interestingly, they don't come from places like the University of Pennsylvania (where I studied) or Stanford University (where I taught)—the kinds of institutions that congratulate themselves on educating the world's disruptive innovators and business visionaries. In Korea, where many corporate executives are drawn from elite universities like Seoul National and

KAIST (Korea Advanced Institute of Science and Technology), Bong-Jin Kim studied graphic design. Yusaku Maezawa, Zozo's colorful founder and CEO, dropped out of Waseda University. In the United States, United Kingdom, Australia, and New Zealand, aside from a couple Berkeley-trained software engineers, none of the founders who've moved their companies to four-day workweeks are from Oxbridge or the Ivy League; rather, they're from respectable but not elite institutions like the Universities of Arizona, Southampton, and Tasmania, Temple University in Philadelphia, the Glasgow School of Art, and Otago Polytechnic.

WHAT MOTIVATES LEADERS TO TRY A FOUR-DAY WEEK

At some point in their careers, these leaders reach a tipping point: they continue to love their work, but become disillusioned with conventional ways of working.

Ryan Carson had worked for a design firm in London before founding online education provider Treehouse, and sleep deprivation left him "regularly delirious with exhaustion" and "frustrated with his output," according to one reporter. Working long hours is "an adrenaline rush" when you're younger, Kenn Kelly tells me, "but it's just not sustainable. You see that with attrition and burnout." No one denies that for young workers, periods of hard work can build confidence and professional identity, strengthen group ties, and accelerate learning, but chronic overwork carries health hazards, increases risk of burnout, and eventually makes it harder to do good work. Spencer Kimball discovered while working fourteen-hour days at his first startup that "there's a point after about ten hours when you're just useless. You're just not thinking creatively, and you're not even solving problems you should be able to solve."

They also come to realize that in creative and knowledge-intensive industries, work is never done, no matter how many hours you put in. Overwork isn't a sustainable source of competitive advantage. Marek Kříž, cofounder of Czech company Devx, says, "We hate the narrative that when you are doing a startup, you have to grow fast, work unbelievable hours, and just squeeze every drop of your energy out." For company founders, who never run out of prospects to call and pitches to make, new ideas to pursue, or new products to develop, it can be challenging to accept that "done" is an unattainable state, but once they do, they're free to rethink how their companies should work.

• •

Cockroach Labs CEO Spencer Kimball on Long Hours

Part of what drove me with this company to try to steer clear as much as possible of long hours is that even in my first startup, right out of school, I remember I'd often work like eighteen-hour days. It felt virtuous, you know, I felt like, "Wow, I'm really burning the midnight oil, we're getting some crazy work done here, and this is so productive." But there were more than a couple of times where, fourteen hours in, I'd still spend the next four hours just kind of staring at the screen. And believe me, that was much more routine work than what we're doing now. Here we're building a complicated product, and it seems to be getting more complicated with time. And you know, that kind of a product is best approached by people who aren't on a course for burnout.

When you're burning the midnight oil, even when you're young, if you go past twelve hours, you're just kidding yourself. So twelve hours would be my limit, even if you're doing routine stuff. But with the kind of stuff that we are doing at Cockroach Labs? With the complexity of some of the problems and the different moving pieces in the system, if you are overworked and stressed out and haven't gotten much sleep, there's just no way you can be effective.

• •

Sometimes heath issues drive experiments with shorter hours. In Iceland, Margeir Steinar Ingólfsson and Þórarinn Friðjónsson decided in 2016 to try a six-hour workday at their twenty-year-old, twenty-four-person digital marketing consultancy, Hugsmidjan. Ingólfsson became interested in shortening the workday after a spiritual awakening and chronic health issues; Friðjónsson reevaluated his priorities after being seriously injured in a skiing accident. They also wanted to create a workplace that was more family-friendly and avoid the presenteeism (the phenomenon of employees working while sick) that Ingólfsson felt was becoming more common in Icelandic business.

Presenteeism and overwork are particularly toxic in creative industries, because they crowd out opportunities for the constant learning and exposure to new ideas that feeds creativity. Pushing back against it requires learning to respect the value of varied experiences and apparently "unproductive" time. "Clients come to us because of who we are, the perspective we bring, and the application of our experience to their problem," Warren Hutchinson says. He's the CEO of ELSE, a design consultancy. This requires hiring smart people, giving them interesting work, but also giving them time to have other experiences. "If all you do is the work that comes to you, you become your experience, and your learning becomes defined by that." Clients want experience, but they also want inspiration and novelty, and you can't get that by staying late at the office.

Many leaders discover that they can be far more efficient with their time when they become parents. Having her first child made Marei Wollersberger rethink her ideas about overwork. Returning to work after maternity leave, "I was a lot more productive than I had ever been before," she says, because she had to focus more, work faster, and make decisions more quickly. "It was a big myth that I needed to sit there until ten o'clock to make it work." The CEOs of Australian financial services firm Collins SBA and German IT firm Rheingans Digital Enabler both transitioned their companies to five-hour days after moving to part-time schedules to care for family and discovering that they were able to get as much done working part-time as full-time. Having children made Ryan Carson more aware of the brief period we have to do important things like be a parent. "With kids, you realize you have this eighteen-year window, and it's done," he says. "I don't have that long to spend with people I love."

It's not enough to be disillusioned with conventional ways of working, though; you need to believe that different, more sustainable ways of working are possible.

Some are inspired by stories of other companies' experiments. When Warren Hutchinson heard about Normally's four-day week, he thought, "Well, why wouldn't we do this?" at ELSE. Hutchinson and Normally cofounder Chris Downs had both worked at the same big firms in London before starting their own agencies. Like Downs, Hutchinson was now a parent, an industry veteran who worried about the effects of late nights and burnout on his agency and the profession as a whole, and could immediately see the advantages of a four-day workweek.

Others are moved by science. Weiden+Kennedy London executive creative director Iain Tait was moved to experiment with shorter days by Scott Barry Kaufman and Carolyn Gregoire's book *Wired to Create* and essays about the cognitive importance of silence. Daniel Kahneman's *Thinking, Fast and Slow* convinced IIH Nordic cofounder Henrik Stenmann that shorter hours would help improve productivity. "If people are going to change habits, if we are going to be creative," he realized, "we need to have more rest."

Several leaders I interviewed talked about the eight-hour day or five-day week as an artifact of the Industrial Era, not something meant for the twenty-first-century workplace. History shaped the workday, they realize, and changes in technology and the workplace can make it obsolete. A few have lived through such changes themselves. When John Peebles moved with his parents to China in 1985, companies operated on a six-day week. Young John loved it: it meant he could go to the amusement park on Saturdays and there were no lines. Long working hours had been the norm for decades as China worked to increase its standard of living, but as government officials and policy makers spent more time abroad in the 1980s and early 1990s, they began to consider how China could move to a five-day workweek. In 1995, the country officially moved to a five-day workweek without slowing its breakneck growth. The lines at the amusement park got longer, but Peebles had more students in the English language classes he taught as a teenager—reflecting a dramatic rise in spending on consumer goods, tourism, and education that officials attributed to people having more leisure time. It was an experience that Peebles recalled when he moved Administrate to a four-day week twenty years later.

But this isn't a story of solitary, heroic individuals bending reality to their will. In lots of companies, the key drivers are a small group, often a founding director and operations manager. In many cases one person is male, the other female, which may give the process a little more perspective: a few studies have indicated that working women (particularly working mothers) tend to be more pragmatic about how they spend their time and have first-hand experience juggling the competing roles of professional and parent in a world that manages to demand and penalize women for pursuing both.

While they're often motivated to move to shorter hours to attract new talent, many companies that successfully move to a four-day week are led by executive teams that already know how to work together. IIH Nordic cofounders Henrik Stenmann and Steen Rasmussen had previously worked together at digital marketing agency Deducta Search. The cofounders of Pursuit Marketing were all veterans of the Glasgow call-center world and worked together, and competed against each other, for years. Such teams are better able to deal with the challenges they'll face when redesigning the workday, learning to work more intensively, and being more mindful about priorities and tasks.

RECRUITMENT AND RETENTION

External pressures also push companies to experiment with four-day weeks. For many, recruitment and retention is the big driver for adopting a four-day workweek. For Edinburgh software company Administrate, a four-day workweek was a good way "to make ourselves a bit different, and offer something that would attract the attention of candidates at a time when the market in Edinburgh was quite hot," operations manager Jen Anderson recalls. The city's tech scene has grown rapidly in recent years, and homegrown startups like Administrate now have to compete with international tech giants like Adobe and Amazon for talent. There's an "industry-wide epidemic" of people leaving full-time jobs to become freelancers, says Ffyona Dawber, founder and CEO of medical communications company Synergy Vision, and she hopes that a four-day workweek can help keep more people in the workforce. Restaurants that have moved to four-day workweeks do so partly to stem the 70 percent annual turnover rates that plague the industry. Programs to shorten nurses' shifts in hospitals and nursing homes are driven partly by a desire to retain skilled staff.

In Japan, competition for new workers and the need to keep older people in the workforce is pushing a number of companies to experiment with shorter working hours. "I want to compete with Google and Microsoft in the global market," Cybozu CEO Yoshihisa Aono says, "yet we can't recruit all the smart engineers from Stanford like Google and compete with them technically." But he can change the game by creating "an amazing company where employees work only three days a week and working mothers all work from home." In 2016, Yahoo Japan announced a plan to phase in a four-day workweek over several years, first by allowing staff to use holidays to get a four-day week, then formally shortening the workweek. In 2017, package delivery company Sagawa, convenience store chain FamilyMart, retailer Uniqlo, and nursing home manager Uchiyama Holdings all introduced four-day weeks in which employees either work ten-hour days or take a pay cut and work eight-hour days.

Most of these companies say these policies were driven by a need to improve recruitment of younger workers, boost retention of older workers with aging parents, or increase the number of women in management. The Japanese labor ministry estimates that 6.9 percent of companies with more than thirty employees offer some form of a four-day workweek, up from 3.1 percent a decade ago.

Likewise, companies in Korea began experimenting with shorter working hours mainly out of concerns about recruitment and retention. Enesti, a cosmetics maker in the city of Chungju, started experimenting in 2010 with a four-day workweek after working mothers demanded a change in their working hours. The new schedule was such a success Enesti eventually made it standard for all workers. The company, in turn, has inspired other firms in Korea's booming cosmetics industry to try their own shorter workweeks—in part to avoid losing workers to Enesti.

SUSTAINABLE COMPANIES AND CAREERS

In a startup world that values fast burn rates, rocket-ship growth, and always has one eye on the exit, founders who shorten their workweeks want to creating lasting companies. "My motivator is to have a good life, a comfortable life, a business that I'm in control of, that's not growing too much," Annie Tevelin says. "I'd rather grow this company to something that feels very special ten years from now than something that's worth ten million dollars two years from now." IIH Nordic aims to create an environment in which "people feel safe when they're working for us," Henrik Stenmann says, even as they're pushed to develop new skills and more effective ways of working. Shorter hours are a tool for building companies that are not meant to be acquired by bigger, better-funded corporations, but instead are stable and long-lived.

While they risk being outworked in the short term by more conventional companies, founders are betting that more-focused, limited hours will help their companies be more productive and more innovative in the long term. For Chad Pytel, CEO of product design and development consultancy thoughtbot, designing ways of working sustainably in the software industry reflects both experience and a desire for greater stability. "We've been at this for fifteen years, we don't plan on going anywhere. We're planning on doing it for another fifteen," he tells me. And sustainability doesn't have to come at the expense of great work. "The results speak for themselves," Chad says. "You put our portfolio and our work and our track record and our team against any team, and we're just as productive, if not more." The popular view of software is that it's written quickly and discarded, but that's not really the case. Code can last years, even decades. Microsoft Word's early classic versions, like Word 5.1 for the Macintosh, came out seven years after the first release, and legacy code can survive in video games even as game platforms become faster and more powerful. Given this, it's actually important for software companies to survive long enough for their products to grow and mature.

Put another way, these leaders treat the company as an end in itself, not merely a vehicle for getting rich and famous. In interviews, they talk about their desire to build something that would be distinctive and would outlive them, and company culture is a means to that end. When you launch a company with the assumption that you have only a few years to cash in before you implode or become obsolete, you're likely to have a culture that satisfies the preconceptions of venture capitalists, has the right look, and demands superhuman hours. In contrast, founders who shift to shorter workdays and workweeks are playing a long game, and trying to build a company that will last and will be the last one they start. The language of sustainability also extends to careers. Chefs have been talking about the sustainability of food for years, and they're starting to apply those ideas in conversations about improving the lives of people who work in restaurants. "It's kind of crazy that we as cooks focus so much on sustainability, but we kind of forget" about "creating a sustainable environment for ourselves," Maaemo chef Esben Holmboe Bang said in 2017. For him, a shorter workweek was an experiment to "see if we can make this business sustainable" and "make a more sustainable life for our cooks, our waiters, our busboys, our dishwashers." But nearly everyone who experiments with shorter hours wants to build sustainable companies that support sustainable careers.

● ●

Company Profile

Pursuit Marketing: Using Four-Day Weeks to Boost Recruitment

Glasgow, Scotland–based Pursuit Marketing is "not a bums-on-seats call center, where it's just a numbers game and it's just a commodity transaction," operations director Lorraine Gray wants me to know. It's one of the first things she tells me when I meet her and CEO Patrick Byrne in Pursuit's offices in the newly hip neighborhood of Finnieston. Founded in 2011 by Gray, Byrne, and managing director Robert Copeland, Pursuit was built on a model of contracting with major technology companies to sell their products to other large businesses, not cable TV providers trying to upsell retirees on package internet-and-phone contracts. This requires training, and then retaining, highly skilled telemarketers. "You could be speaking with the CFO of a FTSE 250 business about their financial plans for the coming year, so you have to have a deep commercial and credible conversation with him," Lorraine says, and that means "a lot of training at the beginning to get our team up to speed."

It also requires having employees who understand the economics of the business better than the average telemarketer. Employees at the average company think that "you put in long hours and you've done a good job," Lorraine explains to me, "but actually, if you just speak to answering machines for twelve hours a day, that means nothing. For us, success is about meaningful engagement and positive outcomes, and if it takes someone thirty dials to get five positive outcomes, or one hundred fifty dials to get two, I'd rather have fewer calls and more positive outcomes. It's more about quality of work than time. That's what the training's all about. With us it's about knowing your product, knowing your brand, knowing your market space, and positioning yourself correctly to do that so you get more meaningful engagement. That's the key."

Glasgow is Europe's call-center capital and has a "culture of job hopping," as people jump to new companies in pursuit of higher salaries and bonuses. Lorraine realized "if we were going to invest in that training, we didn't want them leaving six months later." By early 2010, they had grown to fifty people and added a variety of perks to keep them: gym classes, free breakfast, a wellness coach and personal trainer, even a company-wide vacation to Tenerife during the depths of the Scottish winter. But the slow economic recovery in the United Kingdom, and the uncertainty generated by Brexit and the Scottish referendum, were starting to squeeze the company.

If they responded by cutting costs, Pursuit would risk turning into just another call center racing to the bottom. That would lower employee loyalty and create an opening for competitors to start poaching their highest performers. That was becoming a huge concern. "Some larger IT vendors had moved into Glasgow, and because they were new to the city they were offering big salaries to attract talent," Lorraine says. "And we knew our team would be first on their lists, because our staff are not just trained on Microsoft products, but on Oracle, Sage, everybody else. In terms of competitive landscape, they're the best-trained about the market space, and we knew they'd be in high demand. So we had to do something to make radical changes. We had to protect our sales and grow and achieve what we wanted to. And we had to make sure the team remained happy and wouldn't be tempted to move off."

Rather than respond to the pressures by cutting costs or squeezing salaries, they went in the opposite direction. In September 2016, they announced that they were moving to a four-day workweek while maintaining everyone's salaries at the same level. The leadership calculated that a shorter workweek would "really change the business and transform it," not just be "a token gesture," Patrick Byrne says. He also wanted a move that the outside world would see as bold and confident. To him, austerity measures—like those the UK government had introduced in the wake of the recession—looked sensible in the short run, but were mad in the long run. "The more you invest," he tells me, "whether it's your business or your economy or your country, the more value there is; the more you value people, the more productive they are; the more productive you are, the more tax receipts you generate. On a very small scale, that was what we were thinking when we said, 'We've got to do something to kick-start this business. Cutting it is killing it; investing in it is building it.' So that's what we did."

Two things in particular convinced them that they could make the transition successfully. First, a study revealed that 90 percent of employees reached their weekly sales targets by Thursday afternoon, and those who missed them by Thursday weren't very likely to get caught up on Friday. Second, they looked at the revenues generated by working mothers who had already moved to three- or four-day weeks and found that "they actually achieved the same or more than people working a conventional thirty-eight-hour week," Lorraine says.

Because their salaries are higher than the industry average, Pursuit was already "aspirational" and "an employer brand of choice," Lorraine says, but they still saw an immediate jump in recruitment after announcing the four-day week. "Unsolicited job applications were up five hundred percent after the launch, and every week we get loads of applications through our website." The company's annual retention rate skyrocketed to 98 percent, which meant less disruption to the business and big savings in fees paid to headhunters. A slew of industry awards—from the Scottish Business Awards in 2016, Family Friendly Working Scotland in 2017, Working Families in 2018, and a shelfful of others—followed.

Despite paying higher salaries for a four-day week, the company has remained profitable. "We're more efficient, we deliver more to our clients, and we're earning more money," Lorraine says. People have more time to go to the doctor, exercise, or simply recover from the week; sick days have dropped to "practically zero, which is unheard of in the call center world."

Clients posed no objections. Many of them have their own flexible or remote work systems and understand the need to experiment with working hours to maximize productivity while accommodating employees' needs outside work. They also had little reason to complain: Patrick estimates that Pursuit's efforts contributed $2.1 billion to their clients' sales pipelines in 2018 and generated sales in thirty-four countries.

The four-day week hasn't slowed Pursuit's own growth. By late 2019, the company had expanded operations in Europe, opening a fifty-person office in Malaga, Spain, and was looking at adding a North American office. They joined with Glasgow-based Fierce Digital and London consultancy Software Advisory Service to form a new data-driven sales and marketing enterprise, the 4icg Group. Those companies have also adopted a four-day workweek and have seen similar improvements:

Software Advisory Service's productivity jumped 30 percent while working hours dropped 22 percent.

I ask Lorraine what advice they'd give to companies interested in trialing a four-day week themselves. "You've got to have your measures," she says. "Our mantra is, 'If it can't be measured, it can't be improved.' So, how do you currently measure your performance, how do you know what success looks like just now across five days, and what would your expectation be across four days and how you would achieve that—that would be the first thing I'd look at."

You might not imagine that a numbers-driven, sales-oriented company would have a four-day workweek in its DNA, but the very fact that Pursuit Marketing combines clear metrics, a focus on meaningful engagement over sheer volume, and a culture of continuous improvement means that while "everyone's very performance driven and focused," Lorraine says, "they know they can leave on a Thursday and know they've had a successful week."

• •

INEFFICIENCY

Lots of founders rail against the inefficiencies of the traditional workplace and are motivated to experiment with shorter workweeks by a desire to optimize their (and their employees') workday. "Every single time I've worked in an office, there have been one or two hours that are just not super-productive," Annie Tevelin observed. "Most people could get done what was expected of them, and more, in five or six hours." For founders, overwork isn't just bad because it consumes people's lives; it's also offensive because it's unnecessary and avoidable.

For developers, that inefficiency is most visible in the obstacles and distractions that modern work throws at people trying to focus. "I can't tell you how many people I interview who are like, 'I do my best work at night,'" Natalie Nagele, cofounder of Philadelphia software firm Wildbit, tells me. "You get your best work at night because you're not given the space to do good work during the day, right? In software development, to do your best work, you really need to get into the zone and really focus and have uninterrupted time to do that work. Any kind of distraction takes hours out of your day, and it's extremely frustrating and demoralizing." For software companies, the appeal of the four-day workweek is that it encourages teams to concentrate, to eliminate distractions and let people focus and get into flow.

Sometimes experiments in personal productivity—which are especially popular among software developers—light the spark of organizational change. Jan Schulz-Hofen, the founder of Berlin-based software company Planio, "started an experiment early in 2017 not to work on Fridays, not look at my laptop, not look at my emails too much," he tells me. Planio makes cloud-based productivity and collaboration software, so they think a lot about how work happens, and how to improve it. Schulz-Hofen "quickly realized that it was really helping me regain my focus and recharge my batteries, and be much more efficient at work Monday through Thursday. So I suggested that the entire company start an experiment of cutting down one day each week."

WORK-LIFE BALANCE

Some leaders also want to make work less exploitative and more balanced. For some, this means pushing back against cultural norms that put work over rest, prioritize busyness over leisure, and encourage us to define ourselves by our economic productivity. "We have all these tools that make us more productive, but we don't turn that extra time into more free time that we can enjoy," says Jan Schulz-Hofen. Instead, in today's working world, "we fill that time with even more tasks. I wanted to find another way to do things."

Figuring out how to use technology more thoughtfully is an important part of that search. Rich Leigh, founder of Gloucester, England–based Radioactive PR, argues that "technology was supposed to have made work-life balance improve, but it's made it, if anything, arguably worse. You'll find that it's eleven o'clock at night and you're emailing somebody back. That's a sad reality for us. The four-day week helps jump-start a change." We're all familiar with this paradox. Mobile devices that were supposed to allow us to work anywhere and give us greater flexibility instead create the expectation that we'll work everywhere. In 2017, a Gallup survey found that 47 percent of American workers checked work email occasionally or frequently after hours; another survey found 46 percent checked their email before getting out of bed. This has contributed to a world in which, as Virginia Tech professor William Becker put it, "'flexible work boundaries' often turn into 'work without boundaries.'" By encouraging companies to use technologies to both become more productive and create more free time, leaders of companies moving to four-day weeks aim to change that pattern, and to uproot the unconscious habits that create it.

AT THIS STAGE . . .

You've seen that a wide variety of companies have successfully moved to shorter workweeks. In the following chapters, we'll explore in detail how they do it, and what costs and benefits they report. At this point, I hope you'll see that it's worth exploring a four-day week if you're dealing with one or more of these issues:

- **Burnout.** For founders and leaders, a four-day week offers time to rest and recharge; it also encourages greater organizational discipline and gives everyone a reason to develop practices that can reduce the stresses that cause burnout.
- **Recruitment and retention.** Companies have adopted shorter hours in response to industry-wide problems with retention, to compete for talent against bigger rivals, or to attract more experienced workers.
- **Work-life balance.** After decades of experiments, it's clear that there are hard limits to what even well-intentioned company programs can do to improve work-life balance. Most companies expect people (especially women) to simultaneously work as if they don't have families, raise children as if they don't work, blame them if they don't do both to perfection, and punish them for making use of programs meant to give them more time with children. A shorter workweek offers a simpler, more radical way to improve work-life balance.
- **Organizational sustainability.** Many leaders begin thinking about shorter hours because of their own need to avoid burnout; others want to build companies in which high performers are less likely to burn out and leave, and that can build deep stores of collective knowledge and the patience to work on products that need years to mature.
- **Creativity.** Having time off away from your desk, being exposed to new ideas or experiences, or simply

letting ideas incubate in the subconscious can be important for stimulating and sustaining creativity. Companies can either treat creativity like a raw material, extracting it from employees and casting them aside when they're exhausted, or they can treat it like a sustainable resource, developing strategies that allow creative people to refresh and develop new ideas.

If these are problems that you, your company, or your employees or colleagues deal with, a shorter workweek might be worth exploring.

While most of the companies that have already moved to four-day weeks or shorter workdays are clustered in a few industries, don't think *My industry can't do this.* A few years ago there were no restaurants opening only four days a week, no cosmetics makers, no financial services firms, no call centers doing this. Someone's got to be first. Many of the companies that have already made the shift didn't have any models to draw on: they were the first in their industries, or the first in their countries, or no one of their size had tried it. And as we'll see, a design thinking approach to shorter hours helps identify ways to reduce the initial risks, learn quickly from successes and missteps, and iterate and adapt.

Ready to make the leap? Time to break the news and make a plan.

3

Ideate

In the ideate phase of the design thinking process, designers begin to explore how a product or organization could be redesigned. They've reframed the problem, done enough research to have an idea of how to proceed, and have a feel for what will define the new product, what key features it should have, and what emotions it should stir. Now it's time to start sketching out some concepts.

For companies that want to move to shorter hours, this is the phase where you start to seriously consider the steps the organization needs to take first to move to a four-day week. It's where you all start to look for inefficiencies in how the company runs, how it spends its employees' time, what tasks could be automated, and what tasks could be eliminated. It's where you think together about the problems the company might encounter. It's where you start to consider what new cultural norms and behavioral changes need to be cultivated to make shorter hours work.

Perhaps most important, it's the phase where thinking about these issues expands from a small circle of decision makers to the entire group. Opening up deliberation and discussion at this stage is absolutely essential. The company has to think about very practical and mundane issues, like how to cover the phones and how to manage deadlines, and very profound ones, like how the benefits of increased productivity are to be shared, and it needs leaders and employees to think about these questions together.

Leaders make the decision to try a four-day week, but everyone has to play a role in figuring out how to actually make it work. And that requires getting everyone together to think about how they're going to get started.

TANNER STREET, LONDON, ENGLAND

"I started The Mix in 2012 to understand human behavior, and from the start, we knew that we wanted to approach the business in a way that allows for lots of experimentation, trialing new things, doing things differently," Tash Walker tells me. We're sitting in the meeting room in The Mix's offices in Bermondsey, a southeastern London neighborhood whose Victorian-era mercantile exchanges and warehouses are now filled with creative workers. "The starting point of our business is 'How can you understand people better?' If you are at all interested in behavioral economics, which we are"—I glance over at the wall, at a picture of Princeton economist Daniel Kahneman photoshopped into a religious icon—"you will get fascinated by 'Why do people do certain things? Why do they like certain things? What do they do when they go out into the markets?'

"Our whole business is about understanding people, and finding new ways of doing that that are allowing us to explore the edges of what it is to be a person in the world today," she continues. "And so as a business, we've always been set up with people as our focus, because in business, sometimes that gets a little lost. And it makes us think about what **we** do at The Mix, and how **we** are as people internally. And so I think that we have always had a sense of encouraging people **here** to try and find ways of working that express their humanity."

Tash had spent almost seven years in advertising before founding The Mix in 2012. The company has built up an impressive client list of brands like Purina, Nescafé, Smirnoff, and Polo. But "running a business is hard work," she says. "It's stressful. I read that the likelihood of entrepreneurs suffering from mental breakdowns is exceedingly high. And I felt personally a year and a half ago, by the time you spent almost four or five years setting up a business, **tired**. And the more you talk about it with other people, the more you realize that trying to juggle all of the things that you have going on in your life today is a really hard thing. I find it hard, I see it in the office, in our clients, and in our customers.

"But I own the business, we can try things, and there's no sense of carrying on blindly, working hard and harder and harder, if it isn't delivering something back personally." Tash, cofounder Austin Ellwood, and managing director Gemma Mitchell started asking the same questions about their company that they ask in their research. "And so we ended up having this conversation about 'Hang on a minute, how do we want to work? Maybe there's a different way, maybe we should look at a different way of working.' Because if one of our values is to be human, and to retain our own humanity, then we can't also be working fifty- to sixty-hour weeks and at the same time claim to be great at that stuff." They spent several months looking at different models: taking a half day off now and then, working from home, flexible working hours.

At the end of the process, "we ended up with three options," she tells me. "One which was just allowing people to be more flexible; one which was having a half day on Friday; and one which was a four-day week. And I was nervous, I really was nervous, because I thought, 'Well, a four-day week, that's quite radical for a business.' You know, I run a business and I want it to be commercially successful. And that's a risk, that's a big risk. But everything we looked at, aside from a four-day week, felt like a half measure. And so whilst it was a risk, we decided that the four-day week was the right way to go, the risk worth taking, because it was radical enough. And that was important to me: it had to be disruptive enough that it wasn't just about business as usual but in less time. And that was the point at which we decided to think about doing that differently and embarking on the process of 'Okay we're serious about this, let's do it properly, not do a half measure.'"

They took the idea to the board and got approval to trial a four-day workweek. Tash then rolled it out at a company-wide meeting.

"The four-day week was announced during a session where we were talking about different project ideas that we had, and about what works and what doesn't work," designer David Scott recalls.

"We didn't know how it would go" with staff, Gemma Mitchell says, "so we announced it to the team a month before we put it into practice."

"If I'm really honest, I was expecting whoops of enthusiasm" at the news, "of people high-fiving and, you know, just genuine excitement," Tash says. "That isn't what happened."

"There was skepticism," David says.

"I think," Tash says, "people were just like, 'Hang on a minute, I just need to take a moment to work out if this is for real, and what this really means.'"

FIRST IMPRESSIONS

Disbelief and skepticism are actually pretty common among employees when they first hear the news that their companies are going to trial a four-day workweek. Some news reports describe unbridled enthusiasm when companies announce they're shortening the workweek, but at most places, first impressions are more reserved or uncertain.

Two weeks after taking over Bielefeld, Germany–based design and digital strategy firm Rheingans Digital Enabler, Lasse Rheingans announced at an all-hands meeting that the company would be trialing a five-hour day. "They thought maybe I was making fun of them," he recalls. "There was this moment of awkward silence where they didn't know if they should laugh, or cry, or be just happy. But I was pretty serious about it, and I told them, 'No, I'm serious here, I'm up for an experiment where we can all work five hours a day and nothing changes—you will get the same salary, the days off are the same. We would just like test it out for a couple months as an experiment.'" That broke the ice. "I think everyone reads about these crazy ideas about changing the work environment and that sort of thing, and they were happy to have this new boss who is freaky enough to try these things out."

At Radioactive PR, Rich Leigh announced the four-day trial in a memo to the staff. "I always find I think best when I write," he says, and this gave him a chance to explain his thinking and answer some basic questions. After he finished the document, he emailed the staff:

From: Rich Leigh
Sent: 14 June 2018 15:22
To: Team
Subject: Something a bit different

Alrighterrr, have a read of the attached when you get a sec, and then join me downstairs in the meeting room pretty please once you have, so we can all discuss it. I have a feeling you'll want to. . . .

Rich headed downstairs, and a few minutes later everybody else followed. He says, "The first question was 'Is this a joke?' And I say, 'Nope. Any others?'"

At Norwich, England–based design-led marketing agency flocc, director Mark Merrywest announced at an all-hands retreat that the company would trial a six-hour day. (The company was founded as Made, and changed its name in 2019.) During an exercise in which people suggested changes to how the company worked, he recalls, he wrote on the board: *We're working for six hours, and here are the times.*

"There was a sense of disbelief about the room. It was quiet, it was calm, and they were kind of looking at it, staring at it," he tells me.

"What's the matter?" Mark asked the room. "What are your thoughts?"

Someone raised their hand. "You're kidding, are you?"

Mark replied, "No. Why? What's the problem? Do we not want to do this?"

At other companies, people wonder if their salaries will drop along with their working hours, or if the reduction is a sign that the company is in trouble. Because employees will immediately start playing through these issues, "it's really important to be transparent about the four-day week because it comes with pressure and it comes with a sense of expectation," Tash Walker says. "So we had to be really clear straightaway with everyone that it wasn't about, for example, reducing their salaries. It's not about cost-cutting measures. You are going to get paid the same, that's really important."

Emily West, flocc's business development director, explains, "There was a worry that we wouldn't get enough done, that clients would get angry and people would feel stressed because they wouldn't have enough time, but it just didn't work out that way." But people were also curious, Mark says, and wanted to know "How do we get to do that? Where do we need to go? What do we need to do together to be able to get to do that?"

The reservations employees raise point to another issue. Lots of people find meaning in their work, or have friends at work, while people who are unemployed or retired are more prone to depression. So if you cut the workweek by 20 or 25 percent, do you risk reducing happiness by 20 or 25 percent? Unemployment is certainly bad for people's health and pocketbooks, and people who are on part-time or zero-hour contracts tend to be more stressed than people who are working full-time. People who are out of work don't spend their days in carefree leisure; they tend to sleep more, watch a lot of TV, and are more likely to show symptoms of depression. Even some retirees find that not working has its downsides: they miss the absence of a routine, regular contact with people, and the sense of purpose that work can bring.

But is there a linear relationship between your sense of meaningfulness and well-being, and your working hours? Fortunately, a group at Cambridge University has been studying exactly this question. Working with data from the UK Household Longitudinal Study, they looked at the relationship between hours of employment and levels of happiness and well-being. Since the study had over 70,000 people and extended over ten years, some people were working full-time, some part-time, some were employed throughout, and many people got or lost jobs during the study.

What the researchers found was that happiness and well-being peak at around eight hours of employment per week and do not rise higher when people add more hours to their workweek. Having a job reduces a person's risk of developing mental health issues, but working forty hours won't make you twice as happy as working twenty (after controlling for the impact of income on well being). So reducing the workweek to thirty or thirty-two hours presents little risk of decreasing happiness.

After the initial meeting announcing a four-day week, the leadership at The Mix gave themselves a month to work out the details, Gemma Mitchell ran a series of meetings to think about how to put a four-day week into practice, which also provided a chance for people to raise their concerns about the transition. "You assume that the workload of five days is somehow going to have to be managed within four days," David Scott explains, "which I think puts a lot of people off."

The work of going through the issues, raising and dealing with problems, also serves to reassure everyone that their worst fears aren't going to be realized. Tash Walker recalls that at first, "people worried about getting everything done." She got a lot of questions. "Is it going to be more stress, less stress? I know how to do what we do now in five days; how do I do it in four days? What are you getting from this? Are you real about the salary thing? Is there going to be something else that we don't know about?" Thinking through how the workday was currently structured, identifying sources of friction or inefficiency, and thinking through how they could eliminate inefficiencies helped turn the four-day week from something to be wary of to something that they looked forward to. "It took a few weeks of just discussing it before we started the process to make sure that everyone felt comfortable," Tash says.

Gemma Mitchell recalls, "We got together as one team, and where we were able to do almost a bit of a SWOT analysis. We asked, 'What does this mean for us as an organization?' as much as 'What does it mean for us as individuals?' We ran four sessions across the four weeks in the buildup, looking at what the risks were, how we can work together better as a team to manage those risks, what was kind of exciting and what was more challenging, in case there was any additional elements that we need to put into practice."

One question that often comes up is "What do you do with people who WANT to work normal hours?" There are a couple companies where one person who prefers to work a five-day week is allowed to. At Pursuit Marketing, people who really want to blow through their quotas and earn some more bonus money might put in some Fridays, and no one stops them. But elsewhere, and especially in larger companies, everyone moves to the new schedule. The organizational benefits of the four-day workweek can't be realized if people don't actually work four days.

And to be fair, the shift can require a little adjustment. When the Australian restaurant Attica moved to a four-day week, "we literally had to police it," chef Ben Shewry said at the 2018 MAD Symposium, an annual conference for chefs and restaurateurs held in Copenhagen, Denmark. At first, staff would show up two hours early and Shewry would send them away: "Go away, have a coffee, I don't care," he told them. But having worked seventy-hour weeks since he was fourteen, he understood their confusion: "It was a really big cultural shift for them as well, because they'd never ever worked like this." Bong-Jin Kim likewise had to send people away from Woowa Brothers the first few Monday mornings after they moved to a four-and-a-half-day week.

Younger employees in particular can come into a job expecting to work long hours. They may have friends who are putting in lots of overtime, and they all see it as a way—**the** way—to quickly get more experience, get noticed by their bosses, and get ahead. And as Natasha Gillezeau put it in the *Australian Financial Review*, "Unlike previous generations, most Millennials have never known a division between work and the rest of their lives thanks to the ubiquity of smartphones." The challenge is to help them learn how to switch off, and to think differently about how to harness their passion for their work, not to divert it. We all go into these experiments with a shared belief, ingrained in us after years or decades, that long hours are a rite of passage or a way of life.

This can be a big challenge. In fact, one company I visited, the Tourism Marketing Agency in Glasgow, Scotland, ended its six-hour day largely at the request of younger employees. When it was first founded by Chris Torres (under the name Senshi Digital), the company had done a mix of online marketing for travel businesses and website development; when it went to a six-hour day, it adapted techniques like Pomodoro from the software industry. In 2018, the web development side of the business was split off and the company was renamed the Tourism Marketing Agency. The remaining employees, who were mainly younger workers new to marketing, asked to return to an eight-hour day so they could have a more relaxed workday.

CHOOSING WHICH DAY TO ELIMINATE FROM THE WORKWEEK

The first big operational question companies have to answer is "Which day should we take off?" Companies follow a number of paths to make the choice, but they all choose based on one of two factors:

1. What is the company's slowest, least productive day?
2. What day off would provide the greatest benefit?

If there's one day that's your slowest—that generates the least profit, has lower productivity, or would be least disruptive to clients—then that's the obvious day to eliminate. Most of the companies that shorten their hours adopt a four-day week, and for most of them, the easiest day to eliminate is Fridays. For them, it's the slowest day of the week, and customers are least likely to call with problems. One London agency veteran tells me that in public relations, people go out on Thursday night, show up at work Friday morning with hangovers, push some papers around until lunch at the pub, then do some more work until the office beer trolley arrives in the afternoon. This reflects the rhythm of the news cycle. Clients are least likely to call and "journalists are time poor on Fridays, and they're difficult to get hold of," PR veteran Rich Leigh explains, so "nothing proactive goes out on a Friday."

• •

On Choosing a Day Off

Tash Walker, The Mix:

Friday, for most of our clients, is a down day, or a day where they're working from home, or a day where they have no meetings. It's the day of the week when you're least likely to be called upon in a very urgent situation, so it's the day we can afford to not be in contact with them the most.

Spencer Kimball, Cockroach Labs:

At Google in Mountain View, they had a "Thank God It's Friday" event where they gave you company updates and people drank beers and hung out. Often people went out after with their coworkers. But in New York, Google immediately discovered that nobody stuck around on a Friday. In the summer, people were like, "I've got to get out to the Hamptons" or "Why would I want to be at work on a Friday afternoon at five drinking beer? I've got other things to do that are far more important." That was just a New York attitude. And so it made sense to think about, okay, what really is done on Fridays? In the summer, I'd say very little, and if it's not the summer, Friday is still your least productive day. So if you think about giving people 20 percent of their time, you might as well put it on the day where people are just naturally doing less work or heading off to a three-day weekend. We also wanted to avoid the 120 percent time problem, and it was easy to do by saying if it's a single day, and it's well-defined, then people will take it, and people do take it.

Mark Merrywest, flocc:

We looked at the four-day workweek, and there were two reasons why we don't do that. Firstly is coverage. I think over time, client coverage, as more people are doing it, I think that will become better. But at the moment, we can make sure we have our phone calls answered nine to twelve, and one to four—there's never really a time when clients can't get hold of us. There might be a time when they have to call back, or we have to do something else, but we have voicemail, we have email, and most of the week, things are covered.

Second, I want my team to be working absolutely as hard as they can, for six hours, and when they're done they go home. And when you look at them, after they've worked hard for six hours, you can tell in their eyes and their postures that they've been working hard, their concentration is done, and we couldn't do that for longer. So if we did four days a week for eight hours, we wouldn't get the same level of concentration for the eight hours as we do for the six. I can't see four lots of eight hours being as productive as five blocks of six hours, because there is a daily limit to how long a human can be fully, properly concentrating.

• •

For manufacturers and online retailers, Friday is also a logical day to take off. John Sloyan, managing director of UK metalworks AE Harris, observed before moving to a four-day workweek that there was little advantage to sending out goods on Fridays, since customers were not open to receive shipments on the weekend. (See Company Profile.) On the other side of the world in Australia, Kester Black founder Anna Ross reports that with a four-day week, "all of our packing and dispatch is done by the Thursday of each week. This means our products are getting to the customers faster, rather than only getting picked up on a Friday and spending the weekend in a mail sorting office."

In other companies, most of the work is finished by Thursday. When Pursuit Marketing was thinking about moving to a four-day week, Patrick Byrne looked at when his salespeople made their weekly quotas. Call centers know a lot about the performance of their employees, and he saw that "ninety percent of people hit that target by Thursday, and most of the remaining ten percent actually didn't hit their target by coming in on a Friday." Keeping the office open on Friday didn't help the sales staff make their numbers or do much for the company's profitability.

When they were planning their shift to a four-day week at ELSE, the employees quickly realized that since they work on projects that last weeks or months, the office could close any day without inconveniencing clients. But they decided they wanted to all take the same day off. They wanted to "make sure that the team is together" the rest of the week, Warren Hutchinson explains. Some people already spent lots of time off-site with clients, and no one wanted the office to turn into a ghost town. By taking the same day off, "you can just guarantee people are going to be together" part of the week, Warren says, "and I felt that was important." People also worried that if they shortened the workday, they would be less likely to spend time on professional development, and that "working at home on Friday on something they wanted to do was the best way to commit to it and for it to happen." So it was also a way of getting more out of Friday, which was their long-standing least productive day.

If you don't have a slowest day, ask yourself, What day off will bring the greatest benefit? For lots of companies, closing on Friday is appealing because it gives employees the most recovery time. Jade Johnston, the general manager at Aizle, says, "When you don't really see daytime except from outside the restaurant windows, two days off is not enough. For the staff, there's no time outside of work in your five days: you go home, you go to sleep, and you come back to work. So you need the three days to actually see your family, see your friends."

Some companies choose to close midweek to avoid the disruptions of a three-day weekend, to give people a midweek break, and to stay closer to clients. London behavior change consultancy Kin&Co started taking Wednesday afternoons off in late 2016. CEO Rosie Warin argues that it lets employees recharge without losing momentum on projects. Since implementing the change, the firm's worked with clients like Danone, O2, and the World Wildlife Fund, run a widely popular Remain campaign (We Are Europe), and reported 50 percent year-over-year growth. Seventy-four percent of Kin&Co's workers report that they're very productive on Thursdays and Fridays; project manager Jhanvi Gudka says, "it transformed our culture." When Kin&Co surveyed five hundred CEOs about implementing a shorter workweek, she found that while 52 percent thought "a four-day week would not benefit their company," 80 percent could see the benefit to workers of Wednesday afternoons off, and 70 percent could see trying it themselves. Jumping straight to a four-day week is "a big step for a lot of big organizations," Rosie argues, and for them, closing on Wednesday afternoons "might be more realistic."

Things are a little more complex at companies that have to operate on a five-day schedule and need to coordinate internally between team members and externally with clients.

For example, Synergy Vision has a stable of longtime clients who are used to being able to get quick turnaround on editorial or design changes, so Ffyona Dawber felt that the company had to remain open five days a week, even when employees adopted a four-day workweek. Employees have to change the days they take off depending on deadlines, production schedules, and coworkers' schedules. "If you always want a Friday, that's not going to happen," Ffyona says, but Mondays and Wednesdays have also proved popular. Likewise, at Wildbit, members of the support team take either Monday or Friday off; this way, the help lines are covered during normal business hours but everyone gets a three-day weekend.

Another model is to reduce working hours for employees while expanding operating hours. When Sweden's Toyota Center Gothenburg shifted to six-hour shifts for its mechanics, it also opened earlier and closed later. During the 6+6 Plan experiments in the late 1990s, Finnish municipalities both shortened working hours for individuals from eight to six hours and lengthened opening hours for city offices from eight to twelve hours. This allows workers to enjoy a shorter workweek without creating an inconvenience for customers—something that users of essential services are especially sensitive to.

When he implemented a thirty-five-hour week at Woowa Brothers, Bong-Jin Kim decided to open late on Monday rather than close early on Friday for a couple reasons. First, he wanted to make sure that his best workers would get a break. "Employees who are good workers usually get a lot of work," he says, "so they end up not getting time off on Wednesday or Friday," the other days he considered closing. It's harder to think about taking time off when you've still got things on your weekly to-do list. Also, Bong-Jin continues, "in Korean society, people usually cannot rest during the weekend, because they have to go to weddings, first birthday parties, or church." Taking Monday mornings off gives everyone a chance to recover from the social demands of a busy weekend and some "time for themselves to think. Because you are a writer," he tells me, "you must understand how that time of being alone is important." I nod in agreement. "Monday morning is good for people here too, because they can use the time to read and think." Finally, starting late eliminates the "Monday morning blues."

There's one other reason to choose to take one day off, rather than shorten the workday: it's a more radical move. Remember Tash Walker's words: "Everything we looked at, aside from a four-day week, felt like a half measure. It felt like, 'We're gonna, you know, we're going to do a *bit*, we're gonna have *sort* of a go, we're gonna give you a pat on the back rather than go, *This is about doing it differently*.'"

So the choice for companies of what day to close, or how to give employees a day off, is defined in part by the flow of time in their industries, the schedules and needs of their clients, the rhythm of the work. It's also determined by internal needs: whether they want the new schedule to be radically different (as at The Mix) or not (as at Kin&Co); how much employees and leaders value a three-day weekend; what part of the week offers the best chance of recovery (think of Woowa Brothers' late Mondays); and what kind of extra time they want to give employees.

• •

Company Profile

AE Harris

Founded in Birmingham, England, in 1880, AE Harris metalworks has been run by the founder's grandson, Russell Luckock, since 1979 and has operated on a four-day week for more than a decade. "Metal-bashing" has always been a cyclical business, and normally a Midlands indus-try's implementing a four-day week signaled trouble: it was a way to cut production and expenses while waiting out a downturn in business and was often a prelude to layoffs or permanent factory closures. Harris had survived the mandatory three-day week of the 1970s (it "was devastat-ing to cashflow," Luckock said years later), but in the 1990s rising com-petition from China and slowing orders had forced Luckock to reduce his workforce from 175 to 40, and in the mid-2000s he worried that another recession was on the horizon.

Meanwhile, managing director John Sloyan was looking at the com-pany's operations. He noticed that "very little left the site because log-ically our clients would not be taking delivery of goods on a Saturday or Sunday," he told me by email. "On a financial basis I was wondering how the half day on a Friday was financially viable, with heating & lighting a site but shipping & selling nothing."

Luckock and Sloyan began talking about moving to a four-day, nine-hour workweek in 2006. By working more hours Monday through Thurs-day, they could keep wages the same but save the company 20 percent on heating the workshops and increase efficiency by reducing the ratio of machine startup time (the presses needed to be warmed every morning) to operating time. (Harris is not the only manufacturer for whom a four-day week is attractive because of the energy saved in startup costs. In the 1960s and 1970s, a number of American factories experimented with a four-day week as a way to reduce losses from startup and shut-down time. And it's not just durable goods or metalworks that bear these costs: Estonian chocolatier AS Kalev has operated on a four-day, ten-hour workweek since the mid-2000s, to save energy warming the choc-olate.) When they put it to a vote, 90 percent of the workforce agreed to the shift.

Three months later, after informing clients, Harris went to a four-day workweek. "To our amazement," John recalls, "the staff took to it without any hitch." Absenteeism fell because workers took fewer sick days and could schedule life admin during Fridays, and workers "really enjoyed the long weekends, especially in the spring and summer," Luckock wrote. At first, the front office stayed open on Friday to field calls, but "as time rolled by," Luckock says, "our customers and suppliers, realizing that we were not fully operational on a Friday, just did not bother to get in touch." They missed a few incoming calls, but because "the bulk of the calls were people trying to sell to us rather than buying," John says, even that wasn't a problem.

Reducing costs and lowering turnover has also allowed them to move into market niches in which there's little competition. In traditional metalworks, bigger orders are better, thanks to their higher setup costs; smaller, trickier pieces that require more creativity are too expensive for them to consider. With their lower costs and more skilled workforce, AE Harris can "focus more on low volume and custom and bespoke engineering," John tells me, and "make money making the things that others turn away."

• •

What if you're in a business that really can't close? Everyone likes to think they're indispensable and that their businesses are moving at light speed, but some organizations really do have to operate 24/7. Nurses, police officers, air traffic controllers, and first responders must always be available, either because their services are always needed or because you never know when they're going to be needed. So if you shorten working hours or shift lengths at a hospital or fire station, you simply have to hire more people to keep it open twenty-four hours a day. You can't fit eight hours of nursing into six hours.

But there can be substantial returns from shortening working hours even in organizations that run 24/7. The Glebe, a nursing home in Virginia, pays nurse's aides who work thirty hours a ten-hour bonus if they show up on time, don't call in sick, and meet other goals. It calculates that it spends $145,023 per year on its 30/40 program, but it saves much of that thanks to less spending on recruiting, overtime, and temp workers, so the net cost is actually closer to $23,000. And this doesn't factor in less spending on drugs and skilled nursing care for patients who've injured themselves because there weren't enough nurse's aides to prevent an accident.

Likewise, there are direct costs but indirect benefits in shortening shift times in law enforcement. We know that fatigue and sleep deprivation erode our capacity to make good judgments and make us more irritable, less capable of dealing with stresses, and even more likely to cheat. Thanks to a macho culture that treats sleep deprivation as part of the job, low wages that force many officers to take second jobs, shift work, and mandatory overtime, police have "the worst fatigue and sleep conditions of any profession in our society," Stanford professor William Dement said in 2000. Sleep-deprived officers have worse reaction times, impaired decision-making ability, and are more likely to be involved in serious traffic accidents or have long-term disabilities or chronic health issues. Officers who show signs of burnout are also more likely to be verbally or physically aggressive on the job. If shorter shifts cost a department several hundred thousand dollars a year but result in one less multimillion-dollar lawsuit resulting from a bad decision made at the end of a double shift, or one less officer falling asleep at the wheel after a night of surveillance, or lower health insurance costs, they could easily pay for themselves.

The same holds true for shortening and stabilizing schedules for doctors and nurses in hospitals. It costs money when you hire more people, but some of that is money you would normally spend on temporary agency hires or recruiting fees, or indirectly in the form of higher turnover. Finally, state agencies that have moved to four-day weeks have reported saving money on utilities. In 2008, Utah governor Jon Huntsman moved state government offices to a four-day, ten-hour-day workweek, and they operated on a four-day week until September 2011, when a new governor took over. During those three years, the state saved just over $500,000 in utilities bills, state government energy use dropped by 13 percent, and the state's 18,000 government workers saved an estimated $6 million in gas per year—the equivalent of giving the entire state civil service an annual raise of over $100. (The state also generated 12,000 fewer tons of carbon dioxide.)

FREE FRIDAYS

Another option that companies choose is to remain open five days a week, but to set aside one day a week for professional development. These go by different names at different companies: Cockroach Labs calls them "Free Fridays," thoughtbot calls them "investment time," and ELSE calls them "play days." But the basic intent is the same: spend four days on clients and regular work, and spend the fifth day tinkering, exploring new ideas, reading up on industry trends, or playing around with new technologies and products.

Cockroach Labs' Free Fridays drew on CEO Spencer Kimball's experience at Google with "20 percent time," a policy designed to give engineers free time to work on their own projects. Twenty percent time "got me working on distributed systems" when he was at Google, but at Cockroach Labs (whose cloud-native SQL database software evolved out of that 20 percent time exploration) he wanted a program that had more structure and was designed so that people automatically used the time, rather than had to fight for it.

At thoughtbot, investment time is a way to encourage continuous improvement, Chad Pytel explains. The company has tried different versions of investment time—for example, setting aside several consecutive days every month—but a weekly schedule felt more in keeping with the spirit of continuous improvement.

At ELSE, employees spend every other Friday working on their own projects; the remaining Fridays are officially "yay days" when they're completely off. "The only thing we ask is that there's a bit of a monthly rhythm: you set yourself a brief at the beginning of the month, you give it some air time, and then at the end of the month, you decide if you're going to carry on," Warren Hutchinson says. "So someone might do a dozen individual research projects that don't really go anywhere, or they might strike gold in month three and continue that for the rest of the year."

Free Fridays offer opportunities for professional development. Software engineering is fast-changing and has lots of people who are self-trained or learned on the job; for them, continuous self-directed learning is both a professional necessity and an expression of "deep curiosity," *New York Times* and *Wired* magazine technology writer Clive Thompson tells me. Lots of programmers get hooked by a "'hello world' moment where they got the machine to do something for the first time. There's something spellbinding about that—the sense of creativity, and control, and bringing something to life, that was so much fun." Most jobs, however, require that they specialize and focus on immediate problems, which are less rewarding. When you're "the database person, or the front-end person, or the security person," your job is to maintain stability and avoid surprises, and there aren't a lot of "hello world" moments. So "when they're offered twenty percent time within their actual company, this is just like the best of all possible worlds," Thompson says. In fact, he continues, "I talk to vanishingly few coders who do not do their own coding projects on top of their work at home and on the weekends." So Free Fridays "really, really plugs into that fun of the blank page, and being able to make something from scratch, and recapturing that joy they had the first time they got the computer to say 'hello world' back to them."

Free Fridays encourage people to develop an instinct for good problems and to explore new areas that deserve further attention—skills that benefit both themselves and their employers. "I want them to develop the skills to identify topic areas, lean into them, start attacking them, and work out whether there's something there or not," Warren Hutchinson says. Lots of successful products, features, or fixes have their origins in programmers' free time: Google AdWords and Gmail started off as 20 percent time projects, Dropbox's sync functionality was first prototyped during a weekend hackathon, and Spencer Kimball started working on Cockroach Labs' own cloud-based SQL database "as a nights-and-weekends thing."

Free Fridays help companies work more thoughtfully and sustainably. "When we started Cockroach Labs, I didn't want it to be one of those startups where there are foosball tables," Spencer Kimball says, "and I certainly didn't want it to be a company that preferred people to be at the office at all hours, as opposed to having a better work-life balance." Chad Pytel tells a similar story: "It's important to us as a team to have time to be able to go home and have families and have life outside of work, and to work in a very sustainable way." At the same time, he expects people to constantly learn and give back to the profession.

A formal program also creates an institutional bias for exploration that benefits companies and individuals. It bakes time for creative tinkering into the company calendar and makes it something that employees can look forward to every week, not something that you have to find time for. (Imagine how valuable that can be in weeks when you're doing essential but routine work, or have to dive into a long list of tasks that are important for the business but tedious.) It's a welcome example of how everyone can benefit when companies create a social norm around creative use of free time and start to think differently about the relationship between productivity and time. Free Fridays don't just give people time for prototyping. They **are** a prototype, an illustration of what can happen when you start to redesign time in your organization.

SHORTER HOURS VERSUS FLEXIBLE TIME

What about flexible hours instead of shorter hours? They look like similar options, and both offer employees greater autonomy and time management, but in practice they work quite differently.

Companies that have successful flexible hours programs can build on their experience to ease the transition to a four-day workweek. "We've always had flexible working hours or remote working" at ELSE, Warren Hutchinson says, so by the time the entire company started its first trial of a four-day week, "we'd already sort of been experimenting with it, so we knew we could do it. It was just a question of changing the format and making it so that everybody could participate."

For other companies, coordinating teams working in different cities and time zones gives them a level of expertise with scheduling that helps them redesign the workday. At the Hong Kong offices of talent development consultancy atrain, for example, "because we have flexible time and remote work, . . . self-managed work [is] quite the norm in the organization," Grace Lau says. As a result, "moving to four days was not a big jump for us."

But there are important differences between how flexible work and shorter workweeks play out for people and organizations. Flexible hours place the burden of scheduling, and coordinating with colleagues who are working to different schedules, squarely on the individual. Flexible work policies do little to counter presenteeism or the perception among unmarried colleagues that parents who leave promptly at 5:01 aren't pulling their weight. As many employees will testify, "flexible" hours easily morph from moving working hours to simply working more. Remote workers are more likely to be always on and attend meetings at odd hours of the day, and are even **more** likely to neglect family commitments in order to keep up with the office. Shorter hours, in contrast, succeed through company-wide and normative changes. Not only do parents have more time for children; everyone has more time. By encouraging concentration and focused working hours, shorter hours diffuse the potential conflicts and organizational challenges that come when colleagues are on different schedules. And predictability creates what Skift CEO Rafat Ali calls "the flexibility of being able to get in and out," which appeals to employees with significant outside interests or commitments.

Indeed, companies that haven't had positive experiences with flexible hours may choose a shorter workweek to give everyone more time, while avoiding the disruption of multiple conflicting schedules. Australian digital marketer VERSA tried flexible schedules, but, CEO Kath Blackham said, "people [were] taking so many different days off that it became impossible" to work effectively. Giving everyone Wednesday off put the whole company back on the same schedule, made it easier to arrange meetings, and made client communication more reliable.

• •

Company Profile

Icelab: Using Flexible Work as a Foundation for the Four-Day Workweek

Michael Honey cofounded Canberra, Australia–based Icelab in 2006 after working in conventional advertising agencies for a decade. The company—which builds interactive products, apps, and websites—has offices in Canberra and Melbourne, but many of the fourteen staff work remotely. "One of the key things that I wanted to do" when he started the company, he tells me, "was to not have that deadline-driven reactive sort of culture; I wanted to have a more relaxed, more contemplative sort of working environment." A couple years after launching, they tried a four-day workweek. "My desire wasn't so much for reduced hours," he says, "as for having the extra day off." Further, "the transition from five days to four days is only a twenty percent decrease in the number of days that you work, but you get an extra fifty percent of weekend, so mathematically it's quite a good deal."

At first they worked four ten-hour days. "Working a ten-hour day is not impossible—I can work a ten-hour day anytime—but we have relation-ships, and we go to work early and come home late and miss cooking dinner and stuff like that, and working that constantly was just difficult," Michael says. "And we just didn't feel that we were getting that much extra productivity out of those extra couple of hours each day. So after two or three months, we just said, 'Nah, let's just work a standard day, and we'll see how we go.'"

Michael thinks there are some tradeoffs in overall productivity when working a four-day week—"the five-day week is maybe ten or fifteen percent more productive than the four-day week, but it's definitely not twenty percent more"—but "there are some significant advantages. There's only four times that you have to spin up and spin down—that is, come in and have coffee, and then pack up and leave. I like that the number of times that you do that each week is less."

For years, the company has had a significant percentage of people working remotely, sometimes from as far away as Europe. "Seventy-five percent of the company is on the other side of Slack or Basecamp, not across the room," Michael says. That experience with remote work helped ease the transition to the four-day workweek: when they dropped a day they didn't have to eliminate many meetings or dramatically change their processes, and their employees were already used to thinking about how to use technology to stay connected to colleagues and keep projects on track. "If they do have to crunch on something, they use tools like Pomodoro and go on Slack and say, 'I'm going to be working on this all afternoon, don't bother me.' And we try to be respectful of each other when we do that." Their experience shows that "while there's an ambient distraction possibility with Slack or Basecamp, there are ways they can be used to support both collaborative, bounce-things-off-each-other exploratory work and work which involves putting your head down and crunching through some stuff."

Michael also observes that companies that work remotely have structural advantages in moving to a four-day workweek. They're normally bootstrapped, so they're not being told by venture capitalists to work long hours to deliver a 10x return. They're run by founders who are looking for a balanced life, and have people who know how to work in-dependently. And it changes the cost profile of the company: if you're spending less on rent, you have less overhead to worry about.

• •

METRICS AND KEY PERFORMANCE INDICATORS

The philosophy most companies follow when tracking and measuring four-day workweek trials can be summed up as "Measure what matters, using familiar tools." You need to know that projects and products are being delivered, customers aren't being alienated, and people are figuring out how to do their jobs in fewer days. But many founders have bigger, long-term goals—to decrease turnover, to make the company and careers more sustainable, to foster an environment that's more creative—that won't be achieved during a trial phase. So during the trial, leaders rely on familiar measurements to make sure business and productivity aren't suffering, and they don't adopt new tools or KPIs.

This doesn't mean that the only companies that experiment with four-day workweeks are in fields with soft, subjective performance measures. At Glasgow call center Pursuit Marketing, everything is quantified: it if matters, it's measured. "In our business, everything is performance driven, there's data to support every department of the business," Lorraine Gray tells me. "So it was very easy for us to see the real impact the four-day week had on the bottom line." Data manager Sam Werngren explains how they measure performance. "Everything's logged automatically in the system," he says: the number of calls per day, how many minutes each call lasts, revenues generated, and so on. Sales calls ascend five stages. Things start to get interesting in stage three, when callers have a "meaningful conversation"—they get through to someone with purchasing power. If the caller has "a meaningful conversation and there is an opportunity, that's stage four," Sam says. "And closed is stage five." Sam can pull reports for individuals, or the company as a whole, and see "the quality of the leads we get, the actual final output, how much money is being generated, and tie that back to members of staff."

Later, when Patrick Byrne and Lorraine show me around downstairs, they point out several large monitors on the walls, showing dashboards of the company's recent performance. When they moved to a four-day workweek, Pursuit Marketing didn't create new metrics; they didn't need to. In fact, their existing ability to measure everything gave them the confidence to trial a four-day workweek: when they looked at revenues generated over the course of a week and saw that 90 percent of employees hit their weekly sales targets by Thursday, they realized that they could close on Friday without great risk to their bottom line.

One of the longest experiments with thirty-hour weeks has been conducted at a company with clear performance measures. The Toyota repair center in Gothenburg, Sweden, moved to a six-hour day in 2003. At the time, the center was struggling with long wait times, growing customer dissatisfaction, and a team of mechanics who were under pressure to work ever-longer hours, which increased the odds that they'd make mistakes or quit. "We were in a bad situation," CEO Martin Banck explained in a talk at Woohoo's International Conference on Happiness at Work in Copenhagen in 2015. Clearly, something had to change.

At first, they considered expanding the center, but that "would mean halting work and even more dissatisfied customers. It felt like the wrong solution." Banck then looked at the workdays of mechanics. He realized there was "a lot of stop, start, stop, start" for lunch, breaks, and to lay out and put away tools. Further, mechanics "do heavy work and work with expensive machines," and after six hours they became less efficient.

Banck introduced two major changes. First, he cut the mechanics' workweek from thirty-eight hours to thirty. In the new system, they'd work in shifts from 6:00 am to 12:30 pm, or 11:55 am to 6:00 pm, with the occasional four-hour Saturday or Sunday shift. Second, he changed the center's hours to 6:00 am to 6:00 pm on weekdays and 1:00 to 5:00 on weekends. The combination of shorter shifts and longer operating times made them more efficient and profitable. It dramatically cut waiting times; instead of waiting for weeks for service, customers could now bring their cars in "at six am and still be at work at eight or nine," Banck told the conference.

By lengthening operating hours, cutting breaks, and only working mechanics during those hours when they're most productive, the facility has been able to dramatically improve productivity and efficiency. Each repair station—stocked with expensive tools, diagnostic equipment, and hydraulic lifts—handles more cars per day. When they opened a second location, they "could build a much smaller facility" because they "designed it specifically for 6-hour days." In 2014, more than a decade after the trial started, mechanics worked "42,248 hours and billed 63,641 hours. That's an efficiency factor of 1.40. If you look at the industry average, they work 8 hours and bill 7.36 hours. In our 6-hour work days, we bill

8.40 hours. You're probably thinking we're overpaid," getting 40 hours' pay for 32 hours' work, "but we're just very efficient. So we can bill 1.04 hours more in a 6-hour work day than they do in 8 hours. That's fourteen percent better. Naturally, we are very happy with that."

Other companies continue to use their existing tools to measure traditional performance indicators during and after

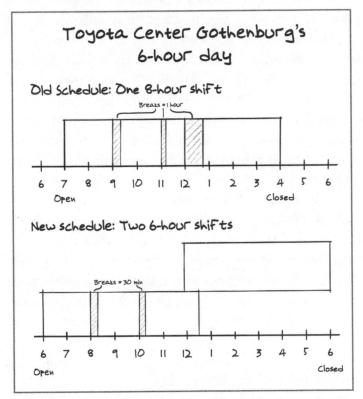

Toyota Center Gothenburg shifted its mechanics to six-hour shifts in 2003. Far from making them less productive, it allowed the facility to lengthen its operating hours (from between 7:00 am and 4:00 pm on weekdays to between 6:00 am and 6:00 pm), made mechanics and the facility more productive, cut customer wait times, and improved retention of mechanics.

trials. When Australian travel insurance company Insured by Us adopted a four-day workweek, they relied on familiar software to track productivity. In particular, since "everyone's activity feeds into Slack, there's always a way to monitor what people are doing," cofounder and CEO Ben Webster says. At UK accounting firm Farnell Clarke, the inflexibility of the tax calendar provides everyone with unambiguous milestones. "Accounts and taxes is a very deadline-heavy industry," managing director James Kay tells me. Farnell Clarke provides clients with financial advice as well as tax preparation, so "we have everything from daily deadlines up to annual deadlines." Further, because they use online accounting tools that are tied into their clients' financial systems—or even help clients put their own financials online—they already had a workforce used to staying in close contact with clients, and had reporting tools to assess those contacts.

Some companies don't abandon their traditional performance measures, but they don't assess the success or failure of a four-day workweek with those tools. At software company Wildbit, Natalie Nagele says, "the most important KPI was, how's everybody personally feeling? Because one of my biggest concerns was the added pressure on an incredible team of people who truly care about their customers and the work that we do." At flocc, "as long as our clients and team are happy and we make our deadlines, we can be confident in what we're doing," Emily West says.

Some CEOs even express philosophical reasons for not measuring trials too closely. "We're dedicated to developing ideas and innovation, so any practices around efficiency and measurement of hours and all that stuff—that's not suitable," Warren Hutchinson tells me. "Innovation is not efficient by nature. It's very wasteful." Bong-Jin Kim makes a different case. "Immanuel Kant once said that you have to treat a human being not as means but as an end," he tells me. (I didn't expect a Japanese dinner in Korea would include a discussion of the second categorical imperative in the *Grounding for the Metaphysics of Morals*, but this is the world we live in.) Consequently, he continues, "to treat employees merely as means to productivity is not right. Their personal happiness has to be respected too."

So measure what matters, but don't try to apply new metrics or new tools. Chad Pytel advises, "Don't put too many KPIs around it." Instead, he says, "get a group understanding of what the purpose of this time is, and where it should be oriented. Have managers work with people to make sure that they're spending their time the way that is most fulfilling to them, but don't put much more structure or measurement around it."

FAQS, SCENARIOS, AND CONTINGENCY PLANS

Pytel's advice points to another feature of four-day workweek trials. They're a time when everyone will be figuring out how to work in a new way. At the outset, nobody—not even management—really knows how to do this. So while it can be reassuring to have some familiar quantitative measures to signal if things are going wrong, it's more important for everyone to understand the larger aims of the four-day workweek and have enough guidance to confidently make decisions about how to work.

Before launching a trial, many companies find it helpful to put together a document summarizing their objectives and contingency plans and answering questions that employees have. An FAQ or manifesto can help set a benchmark for a company's thinking and objectives and provide some guidance for everyone as they experiment with this new way of working. The work of creating the document—not just the writing, but getting people together to surface issues, talk about concerns, explore contingencies, and so on—forces you to think about what's important to achieve, what could go wrong, and how to deal with different scenarios. Planning documents help clarify what **hasn't** been decided, what people will have to figure out for themselves, and gives workers a sense of how much autonomy they'll have to develop their own solutions. They can also serve as a social contract, establishing what management and labor are getting from a shorter workday, what each side is trading and gaining.

It's also a good way to make clear that everyone shares responsibility for making the new workweek a success. One purpose of the planning phase is to create consensus around the company's new path and a collective agreement to make it work. "Everyone should sit down together and collectively build those community agreements," says Joi Foley, communications manager at the Rockwood Leadership Institute, an Oakland, California, nonprofit that has operated a four-day week since 2008. "Say, 'Here's how we're going to do it,' leaving room for people to live their lives outside of work, but also creating structure so that nobody's left hanging."

This planning period is important because it provides a chance to start working out the details of how the trial will actually work, to widen the circle of people involved in the planning, and to provide a reality check for leaders who are enthusiastic about running a trial but haven't yet gotten into the weeds. At Synergy Vision, after announcing the four-day-week trial, Ffyona Dawber "asked each of the leadership departments to nominate one or two people" to a planning team. "We had a meeting every week from October to December," she recalls. "The first meeting was kind of a brainstorm, and afterwards I thought, *This isn't as easy as I thought.*" Events, client projects, vacation policy, project management, people juggling multiple projects—the company had spent years working out its existing processes, and now it had given itself months to revise them.

But the team quickly proved its worth and identified both problems and, more important, solutions that Dawber hadn't. Part of the reason was that it was a diverse group. Because it included people from across the company, "the team came up with a lot of things I wouldn't have come up with just talking to the writers," Ffyona says. "It was really good to have different levels of input, to have a multidisciplinary team."

The team's first product was a three-page document structured as an FAQ that explained the thinking behind the four-day week and provided some guidance about how to implement it. (I've reproduced a few of the questions and answers on page 106.) As is typical for companies that create these documents, it's written in the spirit of meeting notes, not the *Communist Manifesto.* It's meant as a record of internal deliberations, a reflection of the thinking of the moment, and to provide guidance to workers as they embarked on trials. These documents are also often not very comprehensive, because if things go well, they'll be made obsolete as people and teams work out new practices, implement their own solutions to issues, figure out which technologies work best for their needs, and develop strategies for dealing with clients.

• •

Excerpt from Synergy Vision's FAQ

Why are SV trialling this?

We have decided to trial a 4-day working week with reduced hours of 36 hours a week; there is evidence to show there is a huge advantage to individuals' work-life balance and to society as a whole, by people working a 4-day week with 3 days off.

We want to be an employer of choice and we want Synergy Vision to be an even greater place to work.

When will this start?

We will start this trial on Monday 03 December.

Between now and then we would like your feedback on the proposal and any suggestions you may have on how we can best make this work.

If I'm working 10% less time, am I getting 10% less pay?

No, your pay will remain the same during the trial period and beyond, if this is made permanent.

. . . .

What if a client contacts me on my day off?

Where relevant, you should let clients know in advance when you are off and put your out of office on. If a client does call you on your day off, you can let them know who in the office can deal with it or when you will return (or if it is quick, just deal with it). There will need to be some pragmatism around this whilst also ensuring clients are clear on when you are completely unavailable.

How do we maintain productivity as a business?

The reduction in working hours will, of course, mean a reduction in billable hours for each person—we plan to recruit accordingly to ensure we have enough working time on each project. We also believe that focusing on people's work-life balance will increase wellbeing and thus productivity.

In parallel with this trial over the next 6 months, we are having a thorough review of the systems we use internally to minimize time spent on admin and to ensure we are working as smartly as we can.

This is something we want your input on and will be discussing further at the November team day so have a think about systems you are aware of.

What if an urgent email comes through on my day off?

To make this work, we will need to look at alternative ways of working such as shared mailboxes for project teams. We are currently doing a system review to enable people to work smarter, but none of this is set in stone and we would like feedback from the team on how this will work best for them.

· ·

In some firms, the creation of a social contract or general rules for shorter workdays is explicit and comes at the end of a formal process; in others, it happens more informally and continuously. At The Mix, "after the three months trial, when we decided to go for it, we wrote it into everyone's contracts and made it very official that this is what we do," Gemma Mitchell says.

However they do it, companies find that norms are just as important as formal rules for guiding individual behavior, interaction between colleagues, and relations between workers and managers, helping the trial succeed.

Why is that? No set of rules can anticipate every contingency. Workers must be able to extend policies and create new rules for new situations, and to resolve tensions between competing interests. They need the freedom to do this, and confidence that they'll be able to make choices that their peers will accept. This, in turn, requires understanding norms, not just following rules. Advocates of shorter working days all want workers who can self-manage and construct organizations with fairly flat hierarchies. In an environment where people are called upon to exercise self-discipline, to be thoughtful about when they should interrupt colleagues and claim someone else's attention for their own, to adjust to new ways of working, and to be more productive while maintaining high standards, it's not enough for employees to follow the strict letter of the law, they have to understand the logic and spirit behind a policy as well.

The planning and trial phases require time, but with few exceptions, they don't cost much money. Companies spend very little during their trial. Some will buy relatively inexpensive things, like noise-cancelling headphones and do-not-disturb lights for people's desks. But does anyone buy new IT or redo the office? No. Even several years later, most don't seem to spend a lot on virtual or physical infrastructure.

The big exception is restaurants. They may change the dining area to accommodate more covers or expand their kitchen to help cooks be more efficient when they go to four-day weeks. At Aizle, they added tables and installed a bigger stove so Stuart Ralston could cook more efficiently and the staff could serve more customers.

That said, you might want to set aside some money to support people who want to conduct their own experiments with new collaboration tools or apps designed to help people focus, or who want to hack together systems to make meetings shorter. At IIH Nordic and ELSE, lots of popular tools are discovered by individuals and then diffused to the group. It's better to support these small bottom-up experiments that actually verify that a tool will fit in the new workplace you're trying to create than to buy something based on a vendor's promises and try to impose it from the top down. And putting your money where your mouth is shows that the company is serious about making this work and empowering people to make it a success.

Most companies I've studied move everyone to a shorter workweek at the same time. But there are a few exceptions. In late 2018, two offices within Korean *chaebol* SK Group started operating on a four-day week. SK Group consists of ninety-five companies making everything from petroleum and semiconductors to consumer electronics, so it would have been impractical to move all 80,000 employees to a four-day week at once; instead, they're betting that lessons from small trials will inform changes in larger units. (Ford Motor Company switched everyone to a forty-hour week in 1926, but only after four years of experiments in different divisions.) In the United States, there are retirement homes that have implemented six-hour days for nurse's aides, who assist doctors and nurses and work closely with patients, but not for other kinds of hourly workers like kitchen or custodial staff, and other people who work closely with residents, like physical therapists and doctors, are on unchanged schedules. But if the entire staff doesn't move to a shorter workday, everyone in a particular role does.

It's not uncommon for different people in companies today to have different work schedules. Think about hospitals: nurses, lab techs, residents, and senior doctors can all work different shifts. In the energy and mining industry, some people will have nine-to-five jobs while people working in mines or at sea often alternate weeks in the field and weeks at home. (No one commutes every day to oil rigs in the North Sea or Gulf of Mexico!) Midsize tech companies will often have IT people who are on duty at nights or sleep with a pager that alerts them if a server goes down.

Sometimes organizations decide not to change their schedules because they worry it wouldn't work for everyone. The Wellcome Trust looked at moving eight hundred employees in their London headquarters to a four-day week in 2019. They're one of the world's largest medical philanthropies, managing a £25.9 billion portfolio, so for them, money wasn't an issue. But they weren't sure how they could make a four-day week work for everyone, or whether a four-day week would actually improve everyone's working life, so they chose to remain on a five-day week.

Having said that, the question "Would it be politically feasible and functionally possible to implement a shorter workweek for some but not all in your organization?" is one you have to answer for yourself, and the answer is going to be different with every organization.

RUN A TRIAL

Even after discussing it with employees, writing up contingency plans, and establishing performance metrics, very few companies make a permanent switch to a shorter workweek immediately. They first start with a trial period during which they give people time to adjust to the new schedule, observe, and solve unexpected problems. They then review the experiment at regular intervals to assess how things are going, absorb new lessons, and make course corrections.

Three months or ninety days is the most popular length for a trial. That is a bit of an artificial date because in most companies, once you begin trying to figure out how to increase efficiency to gain more time, you never stop. At the same time, even if a company manages to keep up that experimental spirit, it's necessary at some point to officially shift working hours, both to clarify organizational policy and for legal purposes.

ELSE took a more phased approach. "We did the first three months and had a bit of a retro," Warren Hutchinson tells me. "We talked about the things people were finding difficult, and we categorized the things we needed to address: making good priority calls, being more productive, and working in a more focused way. So the first three months really are about us realizing, *Oh, actually, I haven't dropped the ball, and this is doable if I start just trimming out all the extraneous stuff, the procrastinating, the working on things that are of low value.*"

"The second three months are about people beginning to understand that they can exercise their own will on the situation," Warren continues. "They can decide what are the highest value things that they're going to work on. They have the autonomy to explore different techniques. Do you want to try working in Pomodoro? Do you want to change the physicality of how you work? Do you want to have a quiet corner for writing? Do you want to go and do meetings down by the river, or go for a walk?" So six months into the four-day workweek, "everyone's sort of doing their own thing," Warren says. "My expectation is, in the next three months, we'll start normalizing what works for us as a team and start gravitating to shared strategies."

---

3 steps to a 4-day week

ACCLIMATIZE. Adjust to a more compressed schedule.

CUSTOMIZE. Develop your own new practices and tools.

SOCIALIZE. Share best practices, set new standards for your workplace.

A three-step process based on ELSE's experience moving to a four-day week. Other companies report moving through similar phases.

In effect, ELSE has followed a three-step process in which workers first acclimatize to the new environment of the four-day week, customize practices to improve individual performance, and finally socialize them, sharing and adopting new tools and practices across the office.

In addition to practical reasons, calling the first phase an experimental trial period is important for subtler reasons.

First, it makes clear that shorter hours are not a privilege. They're a tool to improve processes, increase productivity and creativity, and spur better leadership and innovation, and if they don't work, the tool can be discarded.

Second, calling it an experiment encourages a mindset that emphasizes reflection on how people are working, a degree of skepticism about your current way of working, and a willingness to try new things. You succeed by asking questions, looking for inefficiencies, thinking about improvements, trying them out, and being unafraid to change things or fail.

Third, it reassures everyone that they'll rein in the experiment before things go off the rails. "I think it's important" to have an experimental phase, Warren Hutchinson tells me, because it sends the message that "we're going to try this out, and we're going to do it in a safe way." As enticing as the idea of a permanent three-day weekend is, it's also an unknown, and transitioning to it is filled with uncertainties. You're asking busy people to take on the personal challenge of reinventing the way they work and deal with colleagues in the pursuit of something that could turn into an existential threat to the company. An experimental phase makes the risks feel more manageable and minimizes the downside.

• •

On Trials and Experiments

Bong-Jin Kim, Woowa Brothers:

It's important to do a beta version, for at least six months, where you make a promise to employees that if it is successful we will keep on doing it, and if it doesn't work out we'll stop.

Natalie Nagele, Wildbit:

The first thing we did was say, "We're calling this an experiment." Calling it an experiment was very beneficial for our team because it didn't immediately just become our new normal. That took some of the pressure off me and the team. It gave us a chance to really understand our pain points and where—as an individual company, in our business, with our customers and our products—we're going to run into issues.

David Rhoads, Blue Street Capital:

Call it a test period. Say, "We're going to try it over the next quarter, and ideally, if it works, we'll continue it." But we really were steadfast and said, "Hey, we really want to do this, we think it can work, but we're just going to do a beta and see how we do with it." That was an easy way to do it but not have that full commitment.

Jonathan Elliot, Collins SBA:

I think what made the trial successful was giving people six weeks' notice that we're going to do a trial, and giving people clarity by saying, "Here are the rules that need to apply during the trial." It gave us the opportunity to coach people, to change their mindset and shift their thinking before we started the trial so they had a belief that it could work. Some people initially thought, "It's not going to work for me, it's a good idea but it won't work," so we had an opportunity to coach people into a positive mindset before the trial.

One of our team members asked me, "So if this trial works and we are more productive in less time, are you going to revert back to the old eight-hour day and require the higher productivity?" That was a great question, and I said, "To me, that would be like killing the golden goose. If we can get the same or better productivity in a shorter work day, I'd attribute that to people being motivated by the shorter work day. If we go back to our old hours, then where's the motivation to maintain or improve?"

• •

Like with any other experiment, there's always the chance that a shorter-hours trial will fail. But because people are likely to resent having newly won free time taken away from them, it needs to be clear that an experiment with a shorter workday is exactly that, and that early results will determine whether the four-day workweek will become a permanent part of life at your company.

GETTING STARTED

"The first thing I would say is, spend less time figuring out what could go wrong and just jump right in as fast as you can," Natalie Nagele says. She and her husband, Chris, run Wildbit, a thirty-person Philadelphia-based software company that has been working a four-day week since 2017. Our conversation is winding down, and I've asked her what advice she would give to companies that want to try a four-day week themselves.

"You **can** anticipate the obvious things," Natalie continues. "As a company, figuring out customer support was big. Personally, one of my biggest concerns was the added pressure of a four-day week: I have an incredible team of people, we truly care about our customers, and about the work we do." It was important that nobody felt overwhelmed or that they had chosen an unrealistic goal. "So I decided my most important KPI was, how's everybody personally feeling?"

"Calling it an experiment was also very beneficial for our team, because it didn't immediately just become our new normal," Natalie says. "That took some of the pressure off, and it gave us a chance to really understand our pain points and where we were going to run into issues in our business, with our customers and our products."

"So my advice is to jump into it, and then just talk about it like crazy with your team, with your cofounders, with whoever else is helping you run the company," Natalie concludes.

"The faster you can jump into it and really experiment, the faster you'll understand what really is a problem and what isn't. It's superexciting, and as long as you leave your mind open to it and have clear, clear communication across your team about what's working and what isn't, I think it's totally doable."

When I put the same question to Tash Walker, she starts by saying, "I think the first thing is to recognize that it's not about doing five days in four days," or getting people to work faster. "You're trying to think about different ways of working that allow you to work more efficiently, so you don't need the fifth day."

Next, she continues, "you need to talk about it with your teams, because it's on them to figure out a better way of doing things. It starts with a decision at the top, but the teams have to be fully bought into."

Both entrepreneurship and design have long shared a fascination with heroic leaders whose genius and charisma set them apart from the masses. But Natalie and Tash see the move to four-day weeks as a collective enterprise, not an exercise in a bold visionary imposing their will on an ignorant world. Leaders may start the fight for a four-day week, but everybody finishes it.

When you start, begin with a trial phase. "It affords you the luxury of experimenting with different ways of working," Tash explains. "We've had to move around a couple of times to get things just the way that we want. So give yourself time to experiment. That's important.

"It's also important to measure it," she says. "We've learned a lot from looking back and getting feedback from people about what works and what doesn't work, and what the business performance has been. And that's been really good motivation to carry on and try something different." For The Mix, KPIs let everyone assess the health of the company—which helps provide a sense of certainty as they embark on an uncertain exercise—and provides information for course corrections and improvements.

Finally, she says, "talking about it to people outside the organization is crucial. It's a bit like if you're starting a diet or you're trying to stop drinking. You can't do it alone, you have to build networks around you to support you."

I hadn't brought it up in either conversation, but both Natalie and Tash outlined a process that followed the stages of design thinking. Start by identifying what really matters. Brainstorm with the whole team to guarantee that everyone understands the goal, everyone's concerns are heard, and the plan draws on as wide a range of expertise as possible. (Empathy isn't just a feel-good ingredient; it's a shrewd way to produce smarter designs.) Figure out what a successful experiment looks like, how you measure it, and how long you need to test it.

In the next chapter, we'll see how to build a functional prototype of the four-day week. It doesn't have to be perfect. In fact, imperfection creates opportunity. It gives everyone a chance to iterate and improve on the prototype, to tweak the schedule, create new tools and processes, and figure out how plans for a four-day week can be refined and improved.

AT THIS STAGE . . .

- **Share the idea internally.** Listen to initial reaction and ease skepticism or worries on the part of your employees (or, in some cases, your boss).

- **Decide on your time reductions.** The choice of whether to go to a four-day week, Free Fridays, or a six- or five-hour day requires balancing several considerations, but it comes down to two big questions: *What's your least productive day?* and *What day off would have the biggest positive impact?* To answer these questions, you need to think about when clients or customers need you to be at work, what employees need as parents and people, whether the work requires your presence for a minimum number of hours per day or days per week, and whether one type of time reduction would work best with your culture.

- **Develop an inclusive planning process.** This is important even if your company normally operates in a more top-down fashion. Good ideas can come from anywhere in an organization, people are experts about their own jobs, and an inclusive process gives everyone a sense of ownership. For employees, the planning process is an opportunity to raise concerns, share ideas about how to move forward, and push the company toward a future everyone can look forward to.

- **Create scenarios and contingency plans.** The planning process needs to generate contingency plans to deal with situations you can anticipate and lay out more general guidelines to help people deal intelligently with conflicting goals or unexpected problems (and there will always be unexpected problems). Devolving responsibility for scenarios and contingency planning will get everyone thinking about how they can start redesigning their jobs, let them apply their knowledge and expertise, and start working out together how to compress the workweek. (It'll probably also be necessary to come up with new policies about vacations, overtime, and family leave that don't run afoul of labor regulations.) For employees, it's a chance to think deeply about how work is completed now, what factors shape their daily work and schedule, and how the four-day week can be used to find better ways of working. As the great futurist (and my mentor) Russ Ackoff said, plan or be planned for.

- **Set a trial period and start date.** Most companies declare a ninety-day experimental period, with the understanding that if things don't work out, the company will return to normal operations hours.
- **Set clear aims.** It's important for the immediate success of the experiment and the good of the organization that everyone knows how the trial will be judged. At the same time, stay open to the possibility that valuable indirect benefits of shortening the workweek may emerge. Focusing too narrowly on your initial metrics could lead you to overlook those other benefits or underestimate their value.
- **Recognize that the trial is not the end.** Even if it goes well, the ninety-day trial is just the start of a continuous process of experimentation and improvement.

Once the planning phase is done, you can get to building. It's time to start prototyping a new day.

4

Prototype

Now it's time to take the plans, build a working model, and start to see how it performs. In the prototyping phase of the design thinking process, the action picks up: you move from ideas and ideals to org charts and actions.

You've thought through the general shape your four-day work-week will take (or one of the alternatives, like a six-hour day or thirty-five-hour week), made some contingency plans and guide-lines, and decided how and how closely to measure the results, so our focus now shifts to designing days and optimizing for flow. The challenge now is to build routines, cultural norms, organizations, and technologies that will support more focused ways of working and more effective ways of collaborating.

In this phase, the circle expands yet again, from leaders and workers to companies and their clients. As your company figures out how to make a four-day workweek actually work, it's time to start sharing the news with clients. It's a chance to explain what you're doing and position the trial to be well received.

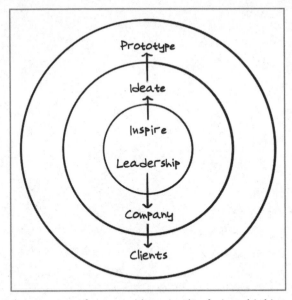

As you move from one phase in the design thinking process to the next, you also move from a narrower to a wider circle.

As they work with it and respond to it, you'll start to see how users react to the design. You'll get a better idea of whether it's really functional, whether it works for them, and whether they'll embrace it and make it their own or reject it and demand something different.

ARTILLERIVEJ, COPENHAGEN, DENMARK

The headquarters of IIH Nordic are located in a converted industrial building in the southern part of Copenhagen, Denmark, on the border of a quiet suburb and the university district. Visiting there one autumn morning, I was struck by how I could have been in Silicon Valley or Singapore: the search engine optimization company's office had the same mix of open floor plan, exposed brick, and minimalist décor; glassed-in conference rooms; and modern kitchen favored by startups the world over.

But unlike most tech companies, IIH Nordic has been relentless in its efforts to shorten working hours for its employees. It started experimenting with four-day weeks in 2014 and made them permanent after a two-year trial phase. The results were visible in small artifacts meant to support the company's distinctive way of working. Clocks in the conference rooms that counted out twenty minutes (the new default length of meetings). Noise-cancelling headphones everywhere. Red lights on every desk. Email inboxes filled with punchy headings and short bodies. Bowls of fruit and vegetables in the kitchen, rather than chips and cookies.

For cofounder and CEO Henrik Stenmann, it all comes down to being able to take more coffee breaks.

When he was a student, one of his professors advised him, "Henrik, be excellent in Excel and you can get lots of coffee breaks." Excel is ubiquitous in the business world, but most users never bother to exploit its more powerful capabilities or learn how to automate recurring tasks. Henrik realized that his professor's advice didn't just apply to spreadsheets. "When you use tools intelligently and change your behavior," he realized, "you can create and save time." However, few people bother to think about how to use tools smarter because they have little motivation to do so. In most businesses, the value created by efficiencies are captured by owners, not workers. Make the system more efficient and the system benefits. Under these circumstances, most of us would prefer to match the tasks we have to the time we have to do them, rather than learn to do them faster, work more effectively, and risk increasing our workloads.

Henrik returned to this problem at IIH Nordic in 2014. A time-use study had revealed that workers were spending up to 60 percent of their time on email and meetings, and supervisors had an average of seventeen hours of meetings per week. At the same time, headhunters were circling; as one of the first online marketing and data analytics companies in Scandinavia, IIH Nordic was rich with talent that recruiters were keen to tap. The company had software tools that could "really save us time" and make the company "more effective and increase our productivity" if used properly, but motivating people to adopt and master them was a challenge. How could they get people to focus more effectively, use tools better, and redesign the organization to prioritize work that really mattered without driving people out?

The answer, Henrik realized, was to shorten the work-week. Giving his employees Fridays off would motivate them to master their most important tools and create an incentive to be more focused, more efficient, and more productive. It would encourage workers to experiment with new technologies and ways of working and to share those with their colleagues. And it was a benefit that none of his competitors were offering.

They eased into a four-day week: for several months they took one Friday off per month, then added "Innovation Days" when people could work on their own projects, and finally reached four-day weeks every week.

Once they started implementing it in 2015, though, the company quickly realized that "the four-day workweek is like an iceberg: the four days is just the tip of the iceberg, and under the iceberg, it's actually a change in our way of working, our way of thinking, our way of problem solving," Henrik says. "A lot of the thinking behind how we work is from the Industrial Age, and it's not been updated."

Some of those changes involved rethinking how they used familiar tools. "No one asks, 'How good are you at handling email?'" Henrik says; you just assume people are knowledgeable users. "But in reality, people are utterly ineffective. We found we could increase productivity a lot by teaching people how to use a headline, how to not put any quotes in an email."

The difference is visible in lots of little, intentional things. Everyone now has noise-cancelling headphones and a subscription to Focus@Will, a concentration-supporting streaming music service. (Its cofounder was previously a member of the 1990s group Londonbeat.) The red lights and egg timers on their desks are for Pomodoro: wind up the timer, turn on the red light, and it's clear that you're not to be disturbed for the next twenty-five minutes. A hand-crafted wooden box that reads "Thank you for not using your cell phone during this meeting" sits on one conference table. Meetings begin and end with a minute of silence, to give everyone a chance to center themselves and focus on the task at hand. The fruit and vegetables replaced higher-calorie snacks that tempted, then slowed down, people.

Other significant changes are invisible. Employees are encouraged to divide tasks into three categories—A and B, which are essential and create value, and C, which are more routine—and either automate C tasks or delegate them to a team of virtual assistants in the Philippines. There are lots of custom-made tools that automatically create reminders from emails, automate basic research functions, and create reports for customers. The company surveys employee mood every week. New employees are given an app to help guide them through the onboarding process.

REDESIGN THE WORKDAY

In the 1960s and 1970s, a number of US factories experimented with a four-day, ten-hour-day workweek. Factory lines stand idle at the beginning and end of the day as machines are started up and shut down, and managers calculated that they could boost output by running lines longer for four days and avoiding the fifth day's idle time; they would also save money on heating and cooling costs for buildings. Today's experiments with four-day workweeks are also concerned with energy; but this time, it's the energy of *people* that companies want to conserve and use more efficiently. Agencies and software firms want to maximize the creativity and concentration of designers and developers and minimize the amount of time they spend in time-wasting or unproductive activities. Restaurants want to avoid overworking line chefs and servers. Call centers don't want marketers working on days when there's little money to be made. Companies that shorten their working hours might save some money on their utilities or other fixed costs, but almost no one talks about it as a factor they consider when deciding to prototype a four-day week. This time, it's all about people.

When redesigning the workweek, companies do several things to help people and organizations be more efficient. This means streamlining or eliminating unproductive tasks: reducing the number of meetings, automating some kinds of work, and encouraging people to ignore distractions. It means reworking daily schedules to create preserves of unbroken, uninterrupted time in which people can focus hard on their most important tasks—and breaks when people can be social. It means using technology in ways that help people be more productive and minimize interruptions and distractions.

More subtly, redesigning the workday also requires changing company culture to respect everyone's attention and to treat focus and concentration as social resources, not just personal ones. And it means setting goals for employees, but leaving it to them to figure out how to implement them.

REDESIGN MEETINGS

Companies that move to four-day workweeks reduce the total number of meetings they hold, shorten meetings, and keep them focused and purposeful. Indeed, meetings are a great place to start when redesigning the workday.

Why start with meetings? Most people really enjoy killing—or at least aggressively pruning—them. "I swear, I wish I'd done this ten years ago" at UK marketing and branding agency Goodall Group, founder Steve Goodall tells me. "When I think about all the time, every week for the last ten to fifteen years, that we just wasted . . . " he trails off. At atrain, Grace Lau and her cofounder already "both hated meetings, so since day one, it's been in the DNA of the company" to keep them short. When they moved to a four-day workweek, it was an easy decision to eliminate everything but one Monday lunchtime meeting.

Few people like meetings, they're easy to see as a waste of time, and efforts to make them shorter and more effective are always popular. They're an effective example of how companies can improve processes and give time back to people, and of how these kinds of time reductions are social phenomena that require people to work together and respect cultural norms.

So what are these companies doing to make meetings more effective?

Make Meetings Shorter

At IIH Nordic, most meetings have been cut from sixty minutes to twenty, or ninety minutes to forty-five. "The average office worker spends forty to sixty percent of their time in email and meetings," Henrik Stenmann says, "and the average leader spends seventeen hours a week in meetings, so that was one area we wanted to focus on" when the company began experimenting with ways to shorten its hours. Before Zozo moved to a thirty-hour week, imagination strategy office head Takayuki Umezawa recalls, "meetings were these things that we just scheduled for an hour without really thinking about it." After the change, people became more deliberate about the length and scheduling of meetings, and as a result they dropped to thirty to forty-five minutes. At other companies, internal meetings are capped at twenty to thirty minutes, and meetings with clients at forty-five minutes. Holding walking or standing meetings is another popular way of keeping them short.

One common refrain I heard when talking to founders and employees is that most businesses are used to scheduling hour-long meetings, that this is a subtle but powerful default setting in our workdays, and that breaking and resetting the default is an early example of how you can rethink your workday and escape constraints you hadn't even noticed before.

At Planio, Jan Schulz-Hofen says, they tried resetting the default meeting length to ten minutes and discovered that if they are careful about who is invited—asking, "Who is really necessary to solve that problem?" rather than inviting an entire team or management layer—they could "actually get the work done in that time." Better to have too few people at a ten-minute meeting and need a second one than to have lots of people wondering, "Why am I here, and when is this over?" They also tried something like a flipped classroom model for meetings: rather than use meetings to discuss how they might solve a problem, people try to solve problems first, then share their solutions with others.

Make Meetings More Focused

The campaign to make meetings shorter and less frequent doesn't just include weekly meetings or hour-long discussions that could be handled in a few minutes. Informal meetings are eliminated too. "The single biggest thing we did as a business—and this may sound very simple but it really changed the way we operate on a day-to-day—was get rid of the 'Got a minute?' meetings as much as we possibly could," says Blue Street Capital CEO David Rhoads. "Those interruptions—'Hey, got a minute?' 'Hey, got a second?'— never end up being just a minute, and by the time you get back to your task, it's a half hour or forty minutes later. So we really were steadfast in getting rid of those." Alex Gafford agrees that "the way we do meetings are very efficient now" compared to when he was working eight- or nine-hour days.

Other companies develop new practices to make meetings more focused. Most require precirculated agendas and goals, or share background material beforehand. When Zozo moved to a thirty-hour week, CEO Yusaku Maezawa waved away bulky slide decks. "Those are unnecessary. Just explain it to me in person," he would tell subordinates.

Use Technology to Enforce Rules

Companies are careful to make sure that conference-call phones and other tech are running smoothly before a meeting is scheduled to start, so staff don't spend the first ten minutes looking for dry-erase markers or punching in conference codes. They also adopt new tools to signal when meeting times are up, or when the group only has a few minutes left. The most popular tools are simple kitchen timers (they're cheap and everyone knows how to use them), but a couple have taken a more high-tech approach, using Philips Hue lightbulbs and some locally sourced code to have the room itself signal when you should start wrapping up.

I first heard about this tool at IIH Nordic, but others have created versions of it too. Philadelphia design firm O3 World created a Roombot app that connects the company's calendar API and smart lightbulb API and warns participants when a meeting time is about to end by flashing the conference room lights. If another group is scheduled to use the space, it gets more aggressive: "Seriously, get outta here," a voice warns. "You see those other people out there? That's my ass on the line. Roombot's getting angry!" That personality is perfectly suited to the city that gave us the *Rocky* movies and the sports mascot Gritty, but in other cities a gentler version might still work as an effective nudge to keep meetings from running late.

Hold Meetings with Purpose

Another common refrain is that standing weekly meetings are eliminated, and that meetings only happen if they have a specific decision that needs to be made, information that can't be shared another way, or another clear purpose. At Administrate, "We share best practice around things like making sure you have a clear agenda, making sure that the only people in the meeting are ones who really need to be there, and questioning whether you actually need to have a meeting in the first place," Jen Anderson says.

Restrict Meetings to Specific Periods of the Day

Another very popular practice is to confine meetings to specific parts of the day, most often the afternoon. At IIH Nordic, "one of the rules is that a meeting is only after lunch," Henrik Stenmann tells me, to keep the rest of the day clear for focused work. And "if I get a meeting invitation without an agenda," he adds, "I have the ability to reject it."

For companies with remote workforces, thinking about when to hold meetings may end with meetings being almost entirely eliminated. Wildbit has employees in several time zones, and when the company moved to the four-day week, Natalie Nagele says, they shifted to more asynchronous communication. "A meeting at the beginning of my day is fine, but if it's the middle of the day for somebody else, that'll just rip their whole day apart."

"We have very few scheduled meetings" at Normally, co-founder and design leader Chris Downs says, and when they do, "we'll have the meeting until what needs to get done is done." Clients, in contrast, "set a meeting for an hour, chat about the weekend at the beginning, get to work and make a decision, then chat more at the end to pad out the hour." Collective Campus founder Steve Glaveski schedules fifteen minute long meetings, partly to nudge other executives to question the assumption that meetings need to be an hour long.

SHORTER MEETINGS PROTOTYPE SHORTER WORKWEEKS

At many companies, the hour-long meeting becomes a symbol of how unchallenged default practices can take over your day and consume your time. Shortening meetings helps companies become more aware of how business culture and normally invisible constraints can block change. At ELSE, Warren Hutchinson encourages people to hold meetings "to answer this question, and this question, and once we've answered this question, we're done," he says. Despite this internal drive to short, sharp meetings, "there's still a bit of that 'We have this meeting so I booked an hour' because we interface with clients all the time, and that's their culture affecting ours."

Some companies encounter technical obstacles to shortening meetings. At IIH Nordic, when they shortened their standard meeting time from one hour to twenty minutes, their calendar software fought back. "The default setting for a meeting in our system is an hour," Henrik Stenmann tells me, "and it was very, very difficult for us to change the setting." This is a small but telling example of how everyday tools can play an unexpected role in reinforcing old habits and get in the way of our ability to make changes.

These are good practices, but it takes time for them to become habits. Still, it's liberating to start questioning why meetings take up so much of our working lives and to ask simple questions like "Who decided that meetings have to be an hour long?" "Why can't they be just a few minutes long?" or "Who really wants to work this way?" Changing meetings opens the door to asking other questions about how we work, and how we could work better. They're also valuable because they illustrate how wasting and saving time is a collective, social affair: it's easy to see how everyone's time is wasted in a meeting if one person doesn't set a clear agenda or if someone rambles on.

Redesigning meetings teaches skills you can then use to redesign the rest of your day. It's a great example of how we can become more effective by doing "less"—in this case, less sitting in conference rooms. And it clears space in everyone's calendar to experiment with other time savings and to bundle formerly broken pieces of time into continuous periods of unbroken, high-quality focused time.

DEFRAGMENT THE WORKDAY

Once meetings have been shortened, the next step is to consolidate the workday, in order to create larger reserves of time during which people can work without distraction. Business writers and productivity experts have long argued that we do better work, and get more done, if we prioritize quality time over quantity of time. Companies that have adopted the four-day workweek show just how true this is.

Some companies map their time over a week or two to see where there are additional conflicts or inefficiencies. At Planio, for example, "the first thing we did was look into how we use the time in our day," Jan Schulz-Hofen says. "It became very obvious really quickly that we were not organizing our time so well." In particular, two of the key jobs—working on the software and interacting with customers—conflicted with each other. (Everyone at the company, including developers and product managers, spends time responding to customer queries.) "We would have a lot of time during the week where we would try to get focused work done, but calls from clients or emails would interrupt our flow. Whenever you shift from one task to another, it takes a little time to refocus and to change context, and that adds up to a lot of lost time."

To solve this, they created support shifts, "when people can take calls or emails. Then, when they're not on their shift, it is clear that they cannot be interrupted doing concentrated work. That really helped get our focus back." For software companies, creating an environment that's focus-rich is especially important, as people often work on very complex problems that require long periods of intense concentration.

• •

Planio Founder Jan Schulz-Hofen on Why
Flow Is Important in Software

As you work on code, you're constantly getting deeper into layers of the problem that you're working on. That means that if you develop a feature, or if you try to fix a bug, you find something on the surface that is not working and then you dig one layer deeper to find the root cause, only to find out that it's actually not there, and you have to go even deeper into another part of the software, or open up another component and see what's going on over there. And this can go down many, many layers. It's like a rabbit hole, basically.

But as you work on this, all the time as you go through all the layers you need to remember through all the layers that you went through already, where you started. Because once you've fixed the root cause, maybe buried deep down in a core part of the software that you don't know really well, you still need to dig your way back up, revisiting everything that you've done from the beginning. And that means that as you're working, you need to remember all these different steps that you've already taken—and that requires a large amount of concentration.

I think that is the hardest part about being a software engineer. You need to keep all these things in mind all at the same time, because software consists of many moving parts, all working together.

And so whenever I work at my computer, I have this stack of all the different layers in the back of my head, and when somebody pops into my office, or gives me a call, or an email comes in, I feel like this stack is crumbling down. It takes a lot of time—thirty minutes to an hour—to find my focus and build the stack back up, and to really get back to the problem that I was working on.

• •

CARVE OUT BLOCKS OF FOCUSED TIME

Having cut down on meetings and identified other sources of inefficiency, the next step is to design a schedule that lets people work more effectively on their key tasks—and, often, lets them get more done in four days than in five.

At companies where focus is critical for productivity, they block off times of day for serious work. At IIH Nordic, programmers are regularly running Pomodoro sessions, twenty-five-minute periods of intensive sprints followed by a five-minute rest. When Swedish game company Filimundus implemented a six-hour workday, it divided the day into two three-hour focused periods, with an hour's break for lunch.

At other companies, scheduling focused time is done more formally. Flocc divided the day into "red time," "amber time," and "green time," ninety-minute periods representing different levels of focus and quiet.

A typical day at flocc starts with a brief meeting, then ninety minutes of high-intensive red time. Mark Merrywest explains the idea behind red time. "We talked about the fact that we needed time when we could say, 'Look, unless it's

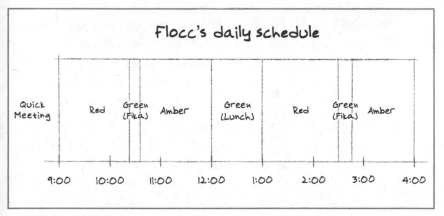

flocc's daily schedule.

really, really important, just don't disturb me. I'm really trying to focus on getting this bit of work done, just leave me
alone if you can.' And that's to our colleagues, but also to
emails, and phones, and other distractions, everything." That
period is followed by ten to fifteen minutes of green time, a
midmorning *fika* (the Swedish term for coffee break). The
rest of the morning is amber time, when meetings are held,
calls returned, email zeroed out, and the like. After an hour
of green time for lunch and errands, the pattern repeats in
the afternoon: periods of focused red time and less intense
amber time, broken by green time *fika*.

As I explain in my book *Rest*, there's a good reason to
front-load important work at the beginning of the day: people have more energy and capacity to focus in the morning
than in the afternoon. Traditionally, businesses organize the
working day with the tacit assumption that our energy and
attention levels don't vary throughout the day, and that every
hour is essentially interchangeable. It's an approach to work
time that borrows from the factory, where workers would be
expected to do the same job for an entire shift. But psychologists and sleep researchers have found that our ability to
focus and to work on cognitive tasks varies throughout the
day, depending on our energy levels, alertness, and attention.
Research on ultradian rhythms shows that most people can
sustain intensive focus for about 90 to 120 minutes before
attention falters. Very creative people often discover these
rhythms and design their days accordingly: they front-load
their most important work in the mornings, so they're guar-
anteed several hours of undisturbed time. Ernest Heming-
way, Toni Morrison, Stephen King, and many other novelists
have done the bulk of their writing in the morning.

Companies shortening their workweeks pursue a similar strategy. They sync their daily schedules to human circadian and ultradian rhythms, guaranteeing that people are free to do their most intensive work at the time they're best able to focus.

RESPECT EVERYONE'S TIME

It's necessary to encourage workers to both take greater control over their time and treat their colleagues' time as just as valuable as their own. When you're redesigning the day, people can't just follow business as usual; they need autonomy to experiment, prioritize, and spend their time as effectively as possible. But this control has to be tempered by mutual respect and a recognition that within organizations time is a collective resource. No one gets to take Friday off unless everyone is done, and everyone's ability to finish their work depends on everyone else's willingness to respect their time.

Woowa Brothers has changed its culture to balance these two imperatives. "We have a campaign to not say, 'Goodbye, see you tomorrow' before you leave. You just leave," Bong-Jin Kim points out. At Korean companies, the ritual of saying good night reinforces hierarchies within the office and makes employees "feel bad leaving work before their managers do," explains Yeon-ju Ahn, director of the People Team at Woowa Brothers. While this is a particularly Asian issue, studies of social life in Western companies reveal that especially in open offices, people are likely to notice and judge people who leave early.

One of the People Team's most visible works is a poster listing "11 Ways to Work Well" that I see on many of the walls. The first principle is rather cryptic: "9:01 is not 9:00."

It expresses two rather substantive ideas, vice president of public relations Jin Ryu explains: respect for each other's time, and that autonomy can only be successful if it balances flexibility and discipline.

"In Korean tech culture, companies emphasize flexibility, and people can come to the office at 10:00 or 11:00," he says. "Some companies allow the employees even not to come to the company at all; they can just stay at home as long as they do their job right. But that kind of atmosphere, that kind of environment can lead to a lack of discipline. Here, work starts at 9:00, so you should be here by 9:00, not 9:01 or 9:02. And if you have a meeting with someone, you do your best to keep your promise to them."

Respect for the clock—and through it, for other people's time—is a foundational piece of discipline at many companies that shorten their working hours. At London game studio Big Potato, for example, the adoption of a four-day week "was helped by the introduction of hard rules to encourage people to get into the office," according to *Wired* magazine. At Woowa Brothers, being punctual shows that you can manage yourself in the interest of conserving your—and just as important, your colleagues'—time. It also indicates that when faced with the challenge of figuring out how to do a job, you'll be able to balance autonomy and discipline. "What sets Woowa Brothers apart from the other startup companies is that our employees know that the flexibility comes with abiding by the rules first," says Hanna Na, a member of the People Team. Flexibility without discipline and responsibility leads to chaos; it also can unintentionally hinder the careers of individuals by letting them drift out of sync with the company's needs. And in the absence of strong formal rules, you need strong cultural norms, a sense of mutual obligation, and

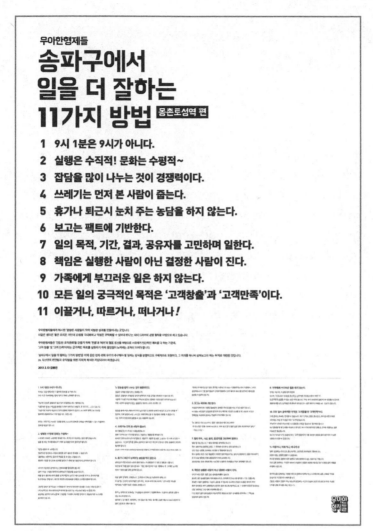

Woowa Brothers poster of "11 Ways to Work Well." The admonition "9:01 is not 9:00" is first on the list. Others include "Vertical execution with horizontal culture" (no. 2), "Report only based on facts" (no. 6), and "Lead, follow, or get out of the way" (no. 11).

a recognition that you and your coworkers have to cooperate in order to make challenges like the four-day week succeed.

REDESIGN TECHNOLOGY

Having formally or informally broken the day into periods of focused and more casual work, the next task is to adopt technologies to support more intensive focus, better collaboration, and improved time management. For some companies, using existing tools more intelligently, automating time-consuming tasks, and learning to use collaborative tools to work together more effectively is an important factor in making shorter hours a success. IIH Nordic, for example, has built a number of tools or scripts that automate reporting for clients, or allow clients to build their own reports, thanks to Henrik Stenmann's interest in labor-saving technology and the company's tech focus.

These technologies operate at several layers. Project management and collaboration tools help groups or the company work more effectively. Automated systems can help employees or enterprises with particular tasks. Finally, some tools and practices are adopted to reduce distraction.

PROJECT MANAGEMENT AND COLLABORATION TOOLS

Moving to shorter workdays provides an incentive for companies to improve their project management tools, or develop new ones. At flocc, trialing a six-hour workday revealed the need to improve their internal processes and technology infrastructure. Before, the company was "using very up-to-date technology for our clients, but we didn't have many of our own structures and processes in place," Emily West tells me. They went from "writing things down with pen and paper, believe it or not," to adopting Google Drive and other tools that allow the designers and developers to coordinate more easily. "Not only is the communication better," she says, "we also work better as a team."

At Synergy Vision, every project now has its own dedicated email account that automatically forwards to team members, to improve communication between teams and clients. "We encourage clients to always copy in that account, so if somebody isn't here it's copied into the general inbox and somebody can pick it up," Ffyona Dawber says. "We also have a number of Slack channels, and communicating internally with Slack has cut down on emails."

At Blue Street Capital, the implementation of DocuSign, a service that allows contracts to be signed electronically, greatly sped up their work. If a startup on the West Coast was getting financing from a bank in the South, contracts and notarized documents could fly back and forth for days or weeks before they were finalized. Implementing DocuSign "took a long time because we have different underwriters, and some liked it and others did not," Alex Gafford says. But its impact has been "huge in our industry," reducing the amount of work needed to send contracts to different parties and the time required to collect signatures.

AUTOMATING WORK

Using tools to automate or speed up time-consuming tasks is an important source of time savings at some firms. For example, Radioactive PR uses automated services to cut the amount of time they need to spend gathering press clippings.

"Say you get a couple hundred pieces of coverage for a campaign, which is really good going. That's going to take you a **day** to clip and send to the client," Rich Leigh explains. "Now you can pay for online monitoring services and tools that help with cutting those. You just copy and paste the URL, and the service pulls full-screen grabs, domain authority, likely circulation, whether there's ink [i.e., a print version]. What used to take eight hours now takes three minutes." Just by using this service Radioactive PR can buy enough time to take Fridays off.

Automation can help shorten the workday, and shortening the workday can create an incentive to automate. At Collins SBA, a couple months before the five-hour workday trial, they introduced software that would speed production of a client deliverable called the Statement of Advice. Before the trial, uptake was slow and grudging. Once people saw that they could move to a five-hour workday if they learned how to use the software, adoption jumped to 100 percent. Clients saw an immediate benefit too: rather than taking days to write it up, advisors could now "produce a financial plan in front of our client, during the meeting, in twenty minutes."

Farnell Clarke was able to shift to a six-hour day because it had adopted cloud-based accounting, which made many of its processes and client communications easier (see Company Profile). For them, moving to a shorter workday didn't require adopting new tools, but rather exploiting the potential of a platform that they had used for years.

One important thing to note here is that most of the automation is done by workers themselves, not by management. This means that these companies aren't pitting technology against people; instead, people are using the technology to make *themselves* more effective, and make themselves more valuable. Without intending it, companies shortening the workweek provide a showcase of how technologies can be used to augment workers' abilities and skills, rather than automate them out of existence.

• •

Company Profile

Farnell Clarke and Cloud-Based Accounting

We tend not to think of accounting as a high-tech business, but Norwich, England–based Farnell Clarke shows that cloud computing, mobile devices, and Big Data can enable shorter days in even the most traditional industries.

Farnell Clarke opened in 2009. Like many startups, it first operated out of cofounder Will Farnell's garage, and over the next decade grew to a staff of forty-two. Most of their employees are in their twenties and thirties, and their clients are younger firms in technology or creative industries. The company had expanded rapidly during the 2010s, adding clients and staff and moving to larger offices, but an exodus of people in 2016 served as a wake-up call that they had outgrown their old processes and managerial habits and needed to make some big changes. "We didn't really make sure that we had the right staff and the processes internally to cope" as they grew, client relationship director Frances Kay tells me. They hired James Kay (Frances's husband) as managing director, and he got to work implementing "the right processes to allow us to track what those people are doing and to track the satisfaction of our clients," and changing their hiring practices "to make sure that we're confident that we've got the right team," he says.

Farnell Clarke was an early adopter of cloud-based accounting software, which allows them to access their clients' data in real time rather than annually, supports automating various kinds of reporting, and also allows the firm to replace traditional bookkeeping with a range of more technical and advisory services: integrating expense tracking software with accounting systems, for example, or working with clients to build dashboards of their financial health.

James explains, "Traditionally, you have massive paper files" and accountants spent the bulk of their time wrangling documents rather than advising clients. Computers helped streamline some of that labor, but "with accounting software, it was always a case of, you have to have fourteen backups and you have to pick the right one and load up the correct data before you can do any work." In contrast, cloud-based accounting systems eliminate version control problems, give accountants the ability to automatically generate reports on a company's financial health, and let them more easily customize services to suit a client's needs: a trucking company whose drivers work nonstandard shifts, for example, or a small company that needs to manage tax obligations in several countries. It also frees accountants to work "from a coffee shop or from home or whatever," wherever they can find internet access. And it's let them shift from hourly billing to charging clients "a fixed fee every single month, just like your TV bill," Frances says.

Automation at Farnell Clarke is "not about lowering fees" or reducing head count, James explains. They want to create more time for "getting to know the client, understanding their business, helping them, and ultimately providing them more services that have an advisory nature. Hot word, advisory, at the moment." The work of moving clients to an online platform, and figuring out what processes can be safely automated, is also a good way to get to know them better. Taking charge of that process also means that clients adapt to Farnell Clarke's systems, "and that helps us be as efficient as we possibly can be," James says.

The company began thinking about how these tools could be used to shorten the workweek a couple years ago. Will Farnell reported in a 2017 interview, "we're doing lots of stuff around system development . . . to be really flexible over how our staff work." They wanted to shift managerial focus to output rather than input, and that required having better tools. Visibility and flexibility were connected: in order to see that shorter hours were working, they needed to be able to see people's output and step in if things started to go wrong. They also surveyed the staff at the end of 2016 about whether they thought a shorter day was feasible; most of the staff said, "Actually, yeah, I could do the job I'm currently doing in seven and a half hours in six hours," James recalls. They now had a company-wide goal, and flexible work and a six-hour day became the endpoints that justified learning new tools, developing new habits and processes, and accepting a greater degree of oversight.

The company spent the next two years preparing. Recruiting and training people who could work in the way the company envisioned proved "the biggest challenge and the reason it's taken two years," James says. In December 2018, "there was a massive push up until Christmas to get procedures and processes in place, documented so that everyone knows how the work flows, where to go for what, and so on and so forth," James says. They had been experimenting with Slack for internal communications and to keep track of people's locations; they added private channels that clients could also use, started using status messages to keep track of each other's schedules and availability, and made more use of features like video chat. (Being cloud-based has made Farnell Clarke appealing to younger tech companies, so their newer employees and clients are "all sort of tech whizzes.") They added new tools that measure email response times and the firm's Net Promoter Score with clients. (A widely used tool among Fortune 1000 companies, NPS measures customer loyalty and satisfaction by asking how likely they would be to recommend the company to someone else.) A new vacation tracking system let them forecast and avoid problems with clients being unable to get help.

Finally, in February 2019, satisfied that they had the systems to keep the company on track and a workforce that could handle it, the company implemented a six-hour day.

• •

USE TECHNOLOGY TO REDUCE DISTRACTION

Finally, a range of technology initiatives are devoted to reducing distractions and helping people and groups concentrate. Noise-cancelling headphones are common in offices that shorten their workweeks, because they give people privacy and signal to colleagues that they shouldn't be disturbed. Synergy Vision installed a white-noise machine that "completely changes the atmosphere" of the office, according to Ffyona Dawber. IIH Nordic and Cockroach Labs equip desks with red and green LED lights that indicate if employees are interruptible or not. At ELSE, each desk has an hourglass, and "if you've got one turned up, no one's allowed to talk to you unless it's really, really important," Warren Hutchinson tells me. One of the designers at ELSE also built an "On Air" button for the open-plan office. "It's a system which works like a radio station," Warren explains. "It's linked to our calendar, and when a meeting starts, it lights up an 'On Air' sign, turns the studio music down, and draws everyone's attention to the fact there is a client call on."

Other changes focus on using technology more mindfully. Many companies encourage workers to check email or Slack at specific times of day, rather than continuously. At Rheingans Digital Enabler, which implemented a five-hour workday in late 2017, employees check email twice: in the morning while planning the day's work, and again in the afternoon when laying out the next day's tasks. A number of companies discourage people from sending or checking email on the weekends. "We try to reduce the amount of out-of-work communication," Bong-Jin Kim tells me, "especially for the lower-ranking employees." But like every tech company, Woowa Brothers has some mission-critical functions like servers and the company website that need to be monitored 24/7, and "higher-ranking employees have to respond to emergency situations."

These practices improve employees' ability to choose where to direct their attention and energy, and to keep it there for longer periods: UC Irvine informatics professor Gloria Mark and colleagues found that workers who were allowed to turn off email stayed on task longer, were able to focus more, and multitasked or self-distracted less. Creating a workplace norm is also important because recent studies indicate that company expectations around connectivity shape user behavior even more strongly than friends' expectations.

REDESIGN SOCIABILITY

The emphasis on increased productivity and focus shouldn't come entirely at the expense of sociability, and it doesn't have to.

For a few weeks in late 2016, after Pursuit Marketing moved to a four-day workweek, Lorraine Gray noticed a few workers were still coming into the office on Fridays for an hour or two, then disappearing. She soon found out why. "They hadn't told their wives about the four-day week," she says, "so they were coming in, doing a few hours, going to the pub together, then going home at five."

The story illustrates an important point: lots of us have friends at work. In a 2018 survey of US tech workers, 60 percent of female respondents and 56 percent of male respondents said that a coworker was one of their best friends. And while work helps us make friends, friends help us work better. Having close friends among your colleagues makes you happier and more engaged with your work, boosts your personal productivity, and improves your ability to cooperate with others on difficult challenges or during trying times. If shortening the workday or workweek accidentally loosens those bonds, both people and companies lose.

In response, many companies that shift to four-day workweeks organize social events. In Tokyo, employees at Zozo and Cybozu can get financial assistance for company clubs and interest groups organized around everything from sports to Nintendo DS to K-pop to gel nails. The clubs also connect people from different parts of the company and foster a sense of camaraderie and informal connection and widen employees' social networks. Los Angeles–based organic skin-care company SkinOwl organizes monthly activities that range from spa days to days spent volunteering at animal shelters; other companies sponsor workout classes, weekly talks, or regular happy hours.

Sponsored events remind employees that even companies that prioritize hard work and free time outside the office—as companies that shift to four-day workweeks obviously do—understand the value of friendships and sociability in the office. At Wildbit, Natalie Nagele recognizes that "one of the biggest risks of this focus-focus-focus work, where everything's asynchronous, is we never see each other's faces, and we very much care for each other." Companies struggle to make focused time at the office feel more like going to the movies—a time where friends gather, sit together, but also appreciate not having their attention disrupted during the movie—rather than something that weakens friendships. In fact, at least one company that trialed a four-day workweek gave it up because it had a detrimental effect on office social life (see Company Profile).

• •

Company Profile

APV and the Perils of Losing Office Friendships

Losing the sense of sociability and camaraderie in the office made Hong Kong video production company APV abandon its four-day workweek after four months in 2018. Founder Mark Erder had read about the four-day week at Perpetual Guardian, and "I just sprung it on everybody at a Monday morning meeting," he says. "I decided that if we did talk about it, we'd talk to death, and I wanted to make it work." Video production is the kind of business that attracts highly creative people and keeps the ones who learn to be highly collaborative and work together under tough deadlines and pressures, so he was confident that his team would take it seriously.

The company decided that everyone would still attend the traditional Monday morning meeting, but people could choose which day they'd take off. Closing the whole office for one day would be too disruptive for clients, every week's time demands were different, and people needed to be available for shoots, client pitches, and production meetings. "One of the only rules we had was, on your day off, you're not taking half the day, you're not working from home," Mark says. "You're spending time with your family, or giving back to your community, or working for a charity, or doing something else that you really enjoy doing that is of great value to you. I wanted people to take a full day, to really focus on not being at work. And in that time, if you're doing something that's creative, ideas do come to you. They can then be applied to your work."

After four months, the financial side, client satisfaction, and quality of work were all fine. But, Mark tells me, "because we're a small company, when a couple of people were off for their four-day week, somebody was on holiday, somebody else was out sick, and crews were out shooting," the office could be a ghost town. "That didn't just happen one day a week; that could have happened a few days a week. It damaged a sense of sociability, conviviality, collaboration, joy over being at work—all those things that make working here fun. Everybody liked the idea of having one day off, they liked it when they were away. But they didn't like it so much when they were here and other people were away." As a result, at the end of the trial, they decided to go back to a five-day week.

When I ask what Mark would advise other companies do to avoid the pitfalls that brought down APV's four-day week, he answers, "I would say, 'Choose a day,' rather than make it scattershot as we did. Choose a Friday or Monday and have everyone take a three-day weekend." He thinks that they might try a four-day week again one day, because Mark still believes that reorganizing the workweek to give his employees more time off is worthwhile. "Especially if you're in a creative business, you have to take that day off," he says. "I think that with the kinds of stress that we're all under, this is almost as inevitable as the five-day week was once upon a time."

• •

Companies also recognize that group activities are more memorable than rewards that go to individuals. Pursuit Marketing, for example, has started taking the entire office on vacation during the depths of the Scottish winter. "We did a winter holiday to Tenerife that cost £400 per head," Lorraine

Gray tells me. "If you gave everyone in the company a £400 bonus, it would be spent and it would be forgotten. But because everyone went away on a little holiday, they still talk about it."

Workers drive lots of the new initiatives in companies, but many of them also socialize on their own. The most important thing they do is the easiest: they start eating lunch together. Lunch emerges as an important time for socialization and bonding and a break from the demands of being highly focused during the morning.

Before they moved to a six-hour day, lunch at Filimundus "was really dispersed," CEO Linus Feldt recalled: some people would go out for lunch, others would pack a lunch at home, and others would "sit in front of the computer and eat in ten minutes." After they implemented the six-hour workday, employees spontaneously "started to bring food to the office and they sat together for a full hour, socializing," he says. "On their own initiative, they compensated for the social stuff we had removed. That social bonding is what companies long for, and they did it themselves."

Encouraging time off for meals can be an important signal that the culture of a company is changing. Feeding people is a powerful way for bosses to make their roles as providers and leaders visible. It marks a break with that style of leadership that demands you suppress even your own bodily needs in favor of the workplace's demands. When Noma reopened and moved to a four-day week, chef Rene Redzepi also started a group lunch. He had spent years "eating out of a plastic container while standing next to my section," and "I don't want my cooks getting accustomed to the same thing." He wanted to demonstrate that as a head chef your duty is to shape the culture and care for those under you.

And for chef-owners brought up in a culture of long hours and deprivation, carving out time for real meals offers a simple but powerful way of showing their employees—and the next generation of chefs—that it's possible to build a better culture in the kitchen, and that you don't have to create an abusive culture to do great work. In other companies people skip lunch or eat at their desks because they worry that eating out signals a lack of commitment. And in many places they're right: a 2018 survey of American and Canadian managers found that a third of bosses consider in performance reviews whether employees take lunch breaks, and nearly a quarter believe that employees who take lunch breaks are less hardworking than those who don't. In this context, encouraging people to stop and eat together is a way for leaders to signal that they treat employees like people, that they recognize the value of taking care of yourself, and that having a body that needs fuel won't be held against you.

Shared meals also make organizations better places to work, and better at their work. They let people get to know each other, allow newcomers to learn about a company's culture, give youngsters a chance to hear old hands tell stories, and let people bond in all the subtle ways that turn individuals into teams. In fact, studies of firefighters show that shifts that eat together are more cohesive and perform better than those whose members eat separately: they get higher marks from their supervisors, and individuals say they feel more like a family. At a firehouse, everybody chips in to pay for the food, they work out a schedule of who cooks and cleans up, they agree on menus, and cooking provides a way for people to establish their value and identity within a group. And after a stressful day, cooking can be therapeutic.

• •

The Importance of Lunch at flocc

Emily West, flocc:

We wanted to be more collaborative as a team, but also get to know each other better. And when twelve o'clock came around, generally people didn't really want to go outside in the winter, so people just sat together on the sofa and got to know each other naturally more. When you know someone better, it's much easier to work with them, and it's been very key for us. And again it's attracted so many people who want to work for flocc purely because of our team.

Because we're not talking to each other in work time casually about this, that, and the other, when we're together at lunchtime we're not distracted by work, and we have the funniest conversations, the best conversations you'd have with friends. That hour lunch break has been really pivotal for communication in the office. It's an incredible way to get to know people, because it is more meaningful in that sort of space of time than chitchat in the office. And then we get back into work again, and it's all right not to talk.

Mark Merrywest, flocc:

Before the six-hour day, people coming in late and leaving late, having lunch at different times, it was quite difficult for us to ever get meetings together, for me to manage people's time, for me to manage people's workflows.

Lunchtime is an hour with my whole team, pretty much all together, bonding. They're not at work, they can do what they like, but they're all here. I've gotten to know my team as people better, and they know each other so very well because they spend that social time together outside of the periods when they're concentrating on their work. And it's, like, the teamwork and the understanding between them that time together builds? You can't buy that.

• •

REDESIGN SPACE

After redesigning their workday, introducing new tools to help people collaborate and focus, and creating new rules around office sociability, companies often find that they have to change their physical space to accommodate new ways of working and socializing.

In most cases, this means carving out different spaces for focus, collaboration, and informal get-togethers. This mirrors the clearer daily breakdown between work time and social time. When I visit ELSE's office in the Metropolitan Wharf, a converted Victorian warehouse on the north bank of the Thames River, Warren Hutchinson points out the staff kitchen in the back, a couple sofas and overstuffed chairs in the center of the office for client meetings and breaks, and a small table and hard chairs in one corner for quick "single-question meetings." Meetings stay focused and short, he says, because "no one wants to sit in those chairs very much." When flocc moved into its new offices in 2019, they built a glass conference room near the front of the office where they could meet with clients without disturbing red time, and a second, more private staff room in the rear for lunch and *fika*.

In other companies, space is redesigned to promote collaboration and focus. When Big Potato Games moved to a four-day week in 2019, they set up a quiet room in their

Shoreditch, London, office, and a second room where the staff can all make sales calls together. Up the street at Normally, "we have whiteboards around every surface of the studio, and standing tables near the whiteboards," Chris Downs explains. "So if we look around in the studio, if we see two people at a standing table next to a whiteboard, and if one of them is at the whiteboard, then we know work is being done. That's what work being done looks like: two people talking and writing on the wall." Nobody has their own desk, but the abundance of collaborative spaces creates "efficiencies in the physical environment" and nudges people to be more productive. "Everyone comes in in the morning and, more often than not, congregates wherever their project feels it needs to be that day."

These changes often come at the insistence of employees, and that has a subtle but important benefit. Giving people more control over the physical design of their workplaces increases their job satisfaction and productivity. In one experiment, researchers put people in one of three offices: a bare-bones minimalist office, an office that had been decorated for them with some plants and pictures, and an office that they could decorate themselves. They found that people who got to decorate their own offices felt better about their employers, said they were more physically comfortable, had higher rates of job satisfaction, and were more productive than the other groups. The presence of decor had a slight positive effect on productivity, but being able to decorate your space had an even bigger effect. It didn't matter so much whether your office looked like a picture in an architectural magazine or a dorm room during finals: control over your space had a real impact on productivity. Then they conducted one more experiment: they first let people decorate their spaces, then told them that the arrangement wasn't suitable and changed it around. In that case, productivity plummeted.

Interestingly, six months into their trial with a four-day workweek, Hutchinson told his employees, "Over the next three months, my challenge to you is to try and make it"—the four-day workweek—"visible. I want to feel and see it. I want to be able to point to the difference between being a four-day company and not, so when someone comes into the studio, I can say, 'That exists, and this stuff exists, because of our four-day week.' That might be as simple as rearranging the furniture a bit, more walking meetings, some stand-up desks over there for calls, a quiet area designed for reading."

GIVE EMPLOYEES CONTROL

Warren's challenge highlights another important feature of the drive to shorten the workday. "A four-day week is a leadership-instigated change," he tells me, "but what you really need is for everyone to take ownership of it. As the leader, you open the floodgates and say, 'Right, we're now going to do this.' But you need everyone to find their own rhythm and their own way of embracing it. I'm very mindful of letting the team develop its own answer."

In companies that shift to a four-day workweek, a good leader defines the broad goal and milestones, such as reaching a four-day week or six-hour day without sacrificing client satisfaction, productivity, or revenues. A great leader, though, will intentionally leave it to employees to figure out how to reach those goals.

"Giving autonomy to workers to work as they see fit, and giving them a bubble to do it, but having a culture of honesty on top of it, is a major thing," says Amritan Walia, business operations director at Type A Media, a London-based SEO consultancy. Mark Merrywest agrees. "Micromanaging won't make you more efficient, particularly with developers," he says. "But when you give them breaks and the regularity that they need, they're actually much better at coding and much more efficient at bug fixing and everything else. And they can't do that if you're micromanaging them."

Why does an employee-driven approach to shorter hours deliver benefits? For one thing, employees know their jobs better than their bosses, so they're in a better position to really understand how to translate the ideal of a four-day workweek into action.

At Synergy Vision, employee-staffed planning groups came up with some of the most important tools now used by the company. "We had one very junior person straight out of uni, we're his first job, and he was brilliant, very hands-on and practical," Ffyona Dawber tells me. The company's experience also illustrates how bringing a variety of perspectives and roles into the planning process is important for generating novel solutions. For example, "the idea of creating email addresses for each project came from a group that does events, and the work they do is very different from the medical writers.'" The project teams also figured out that "a complex Excel spreadsheet" to manage absences and make sure essential functions were covered five days a week wouldn't work as well as "just talking to each other." "It has to be the project teams" that came up with this solution, Ffyona says. "I wouldn't have enough details to know how to do that."

People are also more likely to make rules that work for them, and follow rules that they make. IIH Nordic's experience shows that employee engagement generates rules and tools that are more popular and successful. Many of the tools the company has adopted were discovered, tested, and validated by the employees themselves: widely adopted tools are supported by in-house, local knowledge, not the opinions of outside consultants or so-called experts. By giving people the freedom to figure out how to make the experiment succeed, they get the satisfaction of solving what looked like an impossible challenge.

Having to change how you work, learn new systems, and replace familiar ways of working with something new is never easy. Shorter days make change easier by creating a new incentive structure around innovation.

In a shorter workweek, feedback on good new ideas is immediate and tangible: finish the work more quickly and you can leave. In most workplaces, they're also more social: everyone can leave if everyone pitches in. Shorter hours turn innovation from a zero-sum game in which workers lose while the company benefits into a win-win-win: higher productivity and more efficient work gives workers more time, gives businesses more output, and gives customers faster work.

Under normal circumstances, Collius SBA CEO Jonathan Elliot notes, when companies introduce new tools, workers bear the burden of having to learn and adjust to it while managers and clients reap the benefits. "This is the conundrum of a lot of business owners. We tell our employees, 'Hey, team, here's a great tool that's going to make your job more efficient, we're going to get a thirty percent increase in productivity, here, go and run with it,'" he explains. "When we do that as business owners, we're getting something out of it: we're getting an increase in productivity. Our clients may benefit because they get better, faster outcomes.

"But the people using that tool? There's nothing in it for them because they're still there eight hours a day. There's not really anything motivating them to get the most out of that tool." When workers get a direct benefit in the form of more time, they have a reason to do it. The shorter workday serves as a social contract that allows workers to immediately enjoy the benefits of increasing productivity.

Giving people the power to redesign their work also boosts company loyalty and job satisfaction. People value things that they build more than things they don't. Duke University psychology professor Dan Ariely once ran an experiment in which one group assembled a cardboard box while a second group was given a preassembled cardboard box. When each group was asked how much they liked the box and how valuable they thought it was, the "builder" group liked their boxes more and thought they were more valuable than the "inspector" group. They dubbed this the "IKEA effect," and it's one that scientists and marketers have observed in lots of contexts. It's why cake mixes that require an egg and oil are rated by their makers as better-tasting than cakes made from mixes that just require water. It's why yogurt shops that let you add your own toppings can charge a premium price and why a stuffed bear whose features you choose costs more than an off-the-shelf toy. Making something yourself, even if you're only following some instruction, makes it more valuable to you.

Whether consciously or not, Warren Hutchinson applies the same principle by letting people find their own ways to make a four-day workweek succeed. "When I see things not working as quickly as I would hope, or I see someone struggling, it's kind of challenging for me right now to help them solve that," he says. "I don't want to tell them that they should try this or that. They've got to come through that process on their own. So all I can do really is to stimulate the conversation about who the four-day week is working for, what ways of working have they adopted, and what can we transfer to the rest of the team." That extends from small personal things to company-wide ones. "I'm a list maker, so I like products like Trello, but that's not for everyone. Some people are very physical. There's someone in our studio who loves Post-it notes around their screen, because they can see it and they like clearing it down. So there's a lot of things in play at the moment, and we share a lot about what's working for me, what's working for you, just encouraging people to adopt it."

Having a sense of control over how you work also has benefits. A study of Royal Air Force and Luftwaffe air crews during World War II and American air crews during Vietnam found that high-performing crews felt they had the freedom to determine how their orders would be carried out. Autonomy gives teams space to succeed.

For small companies working in an unconventional industry, choosing people who can work in an environment where "everyone's kind of their own boss" is essential, SkinOwl CEO Annie Tevelin says. As the head of a six person company with a global online fan base and retail partners in the United States, Hong Kong, Australia, Canada, South Africa, and Lebanon, a podcast, and a series of events about self-care, Tevelin has to deal with everything from product development to sourcing ingredients to marketing. As a result, "I don't want to micromanage people, and I'm not able to."

People like having autonomy over their work and control of their environments, and place greater value on things that they build. So it makes sense that giving employees the opportunity to redesign their workdays, and to take charge of the changes necessary to make a transition to a shorter workweek, would increase their sense of loyalty to the organization and give them a greater interest in seeing the experiment succeed. This, in turn, raises the odds that a trial will have a positive outcome. Kester Black founder Anna Ross puts it this way: "Your staff have all the answers when you're trying to change company culture."

TELLING CLIENTS

One of the biggest obstacles to moving to four days is the belief that clients would never stand for it. Leaders regularly tell me about imagining disaster striking after telling clients that they were experimenting with shorter workweeks. At The Mix, "I was so nervous" about the reaction of clients after moving to a four-day week, Tash Walker says. "I was wondering, 'Could this work?' Were people going to call me and be like, 'Where the hell are you? We need this work done!'"

Most leaders take pains to explain to clients why they're trying shortened hours, what they expect to get out of it, and what features of the relationship are not changing. Seeing that you've thought about how to design the experiment to maintain your relationships, continue doing great work, keep hitting your deadlines, and remain available during emergencies communicates to clients that you treat those things seriously.

When you're a company that already has relationships built around novelty, introducing a change in your schedule becomes easier. "People who choose to work with Kin&Co want something different," Rosie Warin says. Taking

Wednesday afternoons off in order to give employees time to recharge showed clients that "we stand by our principles." For a firm that helps companies define and publicize their own values, this was a powerful piece of messaging. Further, because "we could say, 'We believe in this, the psychology is there, the evidence is there,'" the trial became an illustration of their ability to translate science into action.

At The Mix, they were "very clear with clients in explaining the why of doing it," Gemma Mitchell says, "and to position it not as a threat but as a benefit. We worked really hard on that language to make sure everyone understands why you're doing it, because obviously it can be seen that you're just trying to cut costs. Everyone stayed on exactly the same salary they were on, and that was something that was really important to us to communicate—that it's a sign of the health of the business, it's a sign of us wanting to do something differently."

For advertising agency Type A Media, eliminating Fridays was a way of giving clients higher-value time. "Do clients want to buy our Friday hours," when people are already hungover and the day is broken up by pub lunches and drinks trolleys, "or our Monday hours?" founder Ross Tavendale asks rhetorically. Shortening the workweek was a way to give clients more Monday hours.

When clients worried that a four-day week would affect ELSE's ability to respond to emergencies, Warren Hutchinson pointed out, "we don't really do anything that's just in time like that, so that's probably not going to happen." Further, the consultancy would now "deliver on a Thursday, so everything's been delivered a day early." Still, for one client they agreed "that there will be some prearranged remote support if needed" on Fridays.

The anxiety is understandable. After all, "without happy clients, we don't have all this," Rich Leigh tells me, waving a hand around the meeting room in Radioactive PR's office.

UPGRADING WORK AT IIH NORDIC

Henrik Stenmann estimates that at IIH Nordic they've conducted as many as three hundred different experiments to automate routine tasks, encourage focus, discourage distraction, surface critical tasks and submerge the less important. At this point, they're not just questioning habits and practices from the five-day week, they're reevaluating things they implemented in the early days of the four-day week. For example, the company first implemented a practice of spending ten minutes a day on training—watching instructional videos or TED talks—but it proved hard to build the habit. They replaced the daily practice with a weekly "Tech Tuesday" and an optional Friday hackathon.

Most of the experiments have been proposed and conducted by employees themselves. The upside of that approach is that it gives everyone a chance to become involved, to reflect on how they work, to try new things, and to learn from experience and each other. The downside is that some techniques that are "very, very interesting, that really can improve our productivity" don't always get the attention they deserve, or are treated as optional rather than essential. "We have implemented so many tools, and people are really using those tools differently," Henrik tells me.

So in late 2018, they decided it was time to roll out IIH Nordic 2.0, "to take what really works and make that required across the company," Henrik explains. "We have to make sure people are on the same level, and we want everyone to have the same concept and have everyone understand what is the four-day workweek now." Everyone, from the newest to the most senior employees, would go through onboarding again, to guarantee that everyone was familiar with the most valuable tools and practices. "There are some things we need to require that everyone knows how to do," he says, "because it is really important for the company and the working culture."

AT THIS STAGE . . .

Making a four-day week work isn't just about finding ways to work faster, as Henrik says. Of course, whether you're the boss or a team member, you have to think about how to be more effective, how to be politely ruthless with your time, and how you can get your work done by Thursday. But there are also cultural and cognitive changes you have to make. It helps to see time as something that you can design and the workday as something you can prototype, just like you'd prototype a new piece of hardware or experience.

The idea of time as designable isn't one of those abstract concepts that you can learn in a textbook. It's more like a formation in a team sport, or a linguistic rule: it's something that you learn through practice. So how do you practice it? For leaders and companies, you learn it by doing these things:

- **Make meetings shorter, smaller, and sharper.** Reducing and redesigning meetings is a good early goal. The goal is not to eliminate meetings entirely, but to get them under control, to treat them like the tool they are, and then to make that tool as useful as possible. Meetings should be no longer than necessary, no bigger than necessary, and have as clear a purpose as possible—in other words, be short, small, and sharp.

- **Redesign the day.** Once meeting time has been converted into free time, the next step is to create blocks of time when people can concentrate on high-value work without distraction. Make clear that during these periods, people can focus on key tasks to the exclusion of other, less important things, that they can ignore emails or other distractions. At the company-wide level, this may mean mandating certain times of day for meetings or setting down new norms around interruptions, messaging, and email.
- **Craft an experimental process for redesigning jobs and testing new tools.** We often give surprisingly little thought to how we work or how we use technologies (or, as behavioral economists have shown, how we make a variety of decisions). This is as true for companies as it is for people. It's valuable to articulate a process for how to individually or collectively test promising technologies, whether they're personal tools or enterprise-level systems.
- **Have a story for clients.** Being able to explain to clients and customers why you're shifting working hours can help them understand why you're embracing such a dramatic change. Anticipating and answering their concerns shows that you value them enough to make them part of your plans and makes it more likely that they'll be supporters rather than critics.

Workers also discover that redesigning the workday isn't something that you do by yourself. It's not just about your own personal productivity or designing a schedule that works best for you.

- **Time and attention are social resources.** Your ability to focus depends on others' ability to respect your attention. What this means is that you can't just concentrate on making yourself more productive; when you're redesigning the workday, you need to pay attention to building and following social norms that help everyone be more productive.
- **Share what works.** During a trial phase, everyone is adjusting and trying new things. Don't keep those experiments to yourself. It's in your interest to share what you've learned—both what works and what doesn't.
- **Share other things too.** One of the pleasures of work is that it provides us with social connections. These don't have to be lost when you focus and work harder. One of the good things about a more focused workday is that it can actually create time for better social interactions— real lunches and conversations, rather than just text messages. Treat the social life of the office as something you can redesign along with everything else.

A prototype can help clarify your thinking about a challenge and give you a chance to think and play creatively with ways of meeting it. But as designers will tell you, it's not enough to design and build a prototype; to see if it really works, and how it can be improved, you have to test it.

5

Test

In the test phase of the design thinking process, you gather data on the performance of your prototype and use it to improve your plans and guide the next prototype. At its simplest and briefest, product design is an iterative process, with groups moving through several generations of ideas, prototypes, and testing before delivering a final product.

In our world, designing the workday is a continuous, open-ended process. It never really ends. Clients change, employees come and go, new technologies emerge that can help you automate tasks or augment workers' abilities, and they all present opportunities to improve your workday.

Here, though, we'll only follow one cycle of the phase. We'll see the impact the four-day workweek has on productivity and prof-itability. We'll see how it affects recruitment and turnover. We'll examine some of the subtler and sometimes unintended effects it can have on creativity, the lives and careers of working mothers, the health and well-being of employees, the spirit of innovation in a company, and the quality of leadership. And of course, we'll see how clients react. (Spoiler alert: if the previous phase went well, the reaction should be positive.)

SCRUTTON STREET, LONDON, ENGLAND

"We are experimental by nature. We always ask ourselves, 'Why does something exist? Why is it so? Could it be different?'" Marei Wollersberger says. Marei is a cofounder of design agency Normally, and I'm sitting with her and Chris Downs in the conference room of their offices in the fashionable London neighborhood of Shoreditch. "And one of the things we thought could be different is working hours and how the workweek is structured. And so for us it was an experiment: let's see if we can work a shorter week."

Marei and Chris started Normally with two other friends in 2014. The agency works with clients like Facebook and the BBC, and most of their projects live at the intersection of strategy, design, and data. *We think there's an opportunity in this market,* clients will say. *Can you help us build a new product to service it?* Before founding Normally, Chris and Marei spent their careers in other agencies and freelancing in the United Kingdom and Europe. They're "recovering workaholics," as Marei puts it; she "always worked crazy hours, even on the weekend," because "I thought it was the only way to hold the level that I thought was acceptable." But both became disillusioned with conventional agencies' hours and career prospects and saw a chance to create something different at Normally.

Early in his career, Chris worked in agencies where "we'd work weekends, we'd work through the evening, we often worked all night." When he had the chance to take the occasional weekday off, though, "I realized that the weeks that had that day off were weeks where I was way more productive." At about the same time, he recalls, "my parents had recently reached retirement age" and saw their generation retiring after "working very hard, and sacrificing a lot, and then not being able to enjoy it because their health was struggling, and their financial situation wasn't what they expected because of the market crashes."

The two experiences made him rethink whether he should defer happiness and toil away in unsustainable environments for a future that didn't look very appealing. "So I wanted to know, could we bring parts of retirement forward?" he asked. "Could I work a little bit less now and enjoy the benefits of having the time when my body's relatively capable of doing things I enjoy—being outdoors, doing sports, spending time with my children? That led us to the question of 'Given these problems, what can we do that's different?'"

Marei started questioning her assumptions about work after having her first child. "I realized that being a parent was completely incompatible with the job I had at the time," she says, so she moved to a job where she worked three days a week. With a child at home, "I needed to be done at a certain time; for the first time in my life, I could not work open-ended." But to her surprise, she found she could work normal hours and get just as much done.

"I think if you ask any part-time working parent, they'll probably tell you exactly the same thing: they thought they would do less" at work once they became a parent, "and they ended up doing just as much or even more. And then Chris said, 'This should be a company policy. We should all work four days.'"

So how does Normally manage a four-day workweek? "Productivity is absolutely at the core of the culture, to the

DNA of the organization. Everything else forms around it," Chris says. "And then we look for efficiencies in the physical environment, in how the studio is set up, to give people the most efficient working environment." Unlike other organizations, though, Normally pursues productivity improvements to enable a shorter workweek, not to wring even more out of people in a conventional day.

"The software tools that we use are almost all collaborative tools," Chris says, "We're very rarely using a piece of software that only one of us can see at any one time." This makes it easier for teams to work together, and increases accountability.

They've also shaken up the traditional design process, which moves from research to strategy to prototyping to building. In contrast, "everyone at Normally is a hybrid, so they cover two roles," he continues, so workers form small teams that "research, design, and build all at the same time. Our teams can build something more quickly than most people can specify it." Further, "we build efficiencies into our management style and management structure, and we give our teams a lot of autonomy."

Not many people can work this way. "Everyone works at such a high level, they're so productive, so focused for four days, no one here could possibly sustain it for five," Chris says. The combination of working hard on challenging problems in a multidisciplinary way puts lots of demands on people. "Especially when you work on complex problems, you sometimes need a bit of time off to think about them from a different perspective," Marei says.

You might think it would be hard to find people who are intellectual hybrids, who know how to focus, work in autonomous small teams, and can appreciate the value of the four-day workweek. But the industry creates a surplus of people who fit this profile yet aren't always a fit in a more traditional firm. Some are introverts. "In our industry, there's a culture that rewards extroversion and presenting yourself," Marei says. "Those character traits are usually perceived as being correlated with success, management, and leadership." Other people are older, or parents. In particular, "there are a few women with children here for whom a five-day week is just not possible," Chris says, who "cannot reenter the world of work at the level we're at and maintain their careers at other companies because they have children." But they fit right in at Normally.

So how do clients react to the company's four-day work-week, I ask?

"When we started out as a business, frankly, we were concerned," Chris says. "Part of our experiment was, will clients accept our four-day week? And some remarkable things have happened. First of all, we've never had a client say no to our four-day week, which, looking at that now, is amazing."

"It is amazing," Marei continues. "I did think it was going to be problematic, but there's been no effect."

"In fact, you find a different level of respect from the client," Chris says. "They really respect that we have some values, and that we're prepared to stick by them, and we're willing to put them ahead of our commercial opportunity."

"Most clients will genuinely get it," Marei says. "I think, actually, most people get that it's a good idea. They lament that it's not personally available to them. But I'm sure most of our clients would prefer to work a four-day week, and so the first reaction is almost always a positive one, which we didn't expect it to be."

"Yeah, we thought they might say, 'Well, that won't work for us, we'll need you on call,'" Chris says. "But they're always like, 'That's amazing that you guys can do that, and we'd love to learn more about how you do it, we'd love to implement that here.'"

"Absolutely," Marei says. "The second thing that usually happens is they forget about it when we start work. Because ultimately we are measured by the results of the work, rather than by how we organize ourselves internally. So, usually, they forget about the four-day week. But then they see the work, and the quality of the projects is almost always exceeding their expectations because the team is experienced, because they can work efficiently, because they have a longer weekend to think about the really knotty stuff. And when the client sees that, they say, 'I can't believe what you achieved in four days!'"

HOW CLIENTS REACT

The anxiety of leaders that clients will abandon them over the four-day workweek is completely understandable. In a 24/7 global economy, being always on and always accessible seems like a necessity. Many professionals are socialized to "this false belief that our clients expect us to get back within five minutes, otherwise they're going to leave us," as Collective Campus cofounder Steve Glaveski puts it. When working long hours is a mark of seriousness, cutting back risks making you look like a dilettante. In industries where most of your colleagues and all your competition are staying late or working on the weekends, shortening your workweek feels risky and rebellious. For small companies, and especially creative and professional service firms, keeping clients happy is existentially important: lose their business, leaders worry, and you lose your business.

The reactions by Normally's clients—who operate in always-on, hypercompetitive environments—illustrate one of the biggest surprises of my research: almost without exception, clients respond positively. Farnell Clarke managing director James Kay reports that "99.9 percent of clients who responded in any way had positive responses." Kin&Co's clients "love it," Rosie Warin says. "When you're delivering brilliant results and they know you're taking Wednesday afternoons off, they say, 'It's amazing! How do you do that?'"

Positive responses come from clients around the world. London-based Synergy Vision works mainly with pharmaceutical companies in Europe, and "ninety percent of clients have been very positive," Ffyona Dawber tells me. "They said, 'That's amazing,' and that we're a forward-thinking company." At atrain in Hong Kong, "we get really nice comments" about the four-day workweek, Grace Lau says. Anna Ross reports from Melbourne, "We have four hundred wholesale accounts, and not one person has complained that we work four days." Why do clients react positively?

CLIENTS CARE MORE ABOUT WORK THAN TIME

First, most clients are concerned about results, not the hours you put into them. The first client Rich Leigh told about Radioactive PR's new schedule said, "As long as you do the work that we pay you for, and results are as good as they were, or better, we don't care." Formal surveys confirm that clients approve of the work companies do during shorter workweeks. When they trialed their firm's forty-hour week, Weiden+Kennedy's London office only told half their clients about the experiment. Those who were not informed express the same levels of satisfaction with the firm's work as those who were informed. Farnell Clarke measures client satisfaction using the Net Promoter Score, which asks clients how likely (on a scale of 1 to 10) they would be to recommend the company. The percentage of those who respond with a 9 or 10, minus the percentage who respond with a 6 or below, is a company's Net Promoter Score. A positive score is good; a company with a 50 or above is considered excellent, and 70 or above marks you as world-class. In the United Kingdom, John Lewis, Aldi, and Virgin Trains score in the 40s. In the United States, Costco, Apple, and Nordstrom all score above 70. Farnell Clarke had a 79.

CLIENTS BENEFIT FROM SHORTER HOURS

Second, some clients recognize that there's a direct payoff for them. "They realize that you're buying people, and if they're burned out it won't work," Rosie Warin says. Pursuit Marketing's clients "know they're going to get better results because they've got a really motivated and cared-for team," Lorraine Gray says.

A four-day workweek also gives clients a little more free time. Kin&Co's Wednesday afternoons off "give clients better work-life balance," Rosie Warin says. Architecture firm Bauman Lyons found that being out "on a Friday can be advantageous to our employers & collaborators," as one designer wrote, since it gave them a chance to get caught up with their own work. In an age when everyone wants everything right now, not bothering people can feel like a gift.

CLIENTS LIKE WORKING WITH INNOVATORS

Pursuit Marketing "works with some of the top technology companies worldwide," Lorraine Gray tells me. "In the technology industry, there are people who are used to remote working, and people who are working longer hours for fewer days a week." Because of their own experience, they tend to be "very advanced culturally, and they were really accepting of" the four-day workweek. And even if they're skeptical, Lorraine says, "once a client's come in and visited us, they meet the team and see the operation, they get it."

YOU'RE PROTOTYPING THEIR FUTURE

Clients may see four-day workweek trials yielding lessons that they can try themselves. Clients themselves are probably working 24/7 and know all about overwork and burnout. Some have their own struggles with flexible work or work-life balance and are sympathetic to big efforts to find a solution. Supporting a company that develops an innovative new approach to dealing with these problems gives them hope that they can change too.

Like other positive client reactions, this is something companies around the world report. "A lot of the startup clients that we work with" at thoughtbot "specifically choose to work with us because they want to instill their company with the culture and values that match ours," Chad Pytel says. In Australia, Michael Honey reports that most Icelab clients "think that it's cool, and they are excited about the idea because they themselves would like to do something like that, and they can see the value in it. And they liked the idea of working with a team of people who are, you know, well-rounded human beings." In Hong Kong, clients ask "how we make it work, and then the conversation becomes how can they make it work," atrain's Grace Lau says. And it's one thing to cite experiments in other countries or industries when making the case for a big change in your own company; it's more persuasive to see these innovations in your own ecosystem, led by companies you know and have worked with for years, who've earned your trust, and who share your culture and outlook.

In fact, some clients are so interested in the experiment, they even help companies keep their four-day weeks on track. If an email goes out from Normally on a Friday, they'll get replies saying, *Aren't you supposed to be off today?* Likewise at The Mix, Tash Walker tells me, "Occasionally, I might send an email on a Friday, and a client will go, 'Why send me an email? You're supposed to be having a day off.' It's a really good relationship when they support us to have our four-day week." Overall, she says, "clients are really supportive. They find it's a great thing, they really enjoy it, and they hold you to account. If you talk about it and they get it and they buy into it, then they, on the whole, respect that and you will get fewer emails and calls on a Friday and they will help you achieve four-day weeks."

• •

On Telling Clients

Emily West, flocc:

We try to be as open and honest as possible, set those expectations, say this is how we work, this is what we do, and it attracts a lot of clients and a lot of people who want to work with us. When you really explain to them why we're doing it, they completely understand. There's not one client that's come to us and said, "You haven't gotten back to me" or "I need an answer ASAP." A lot of people have been really interested, and one has said, "I'm going to take this back to my board."

Tash Walker, The Mix:

At the end of the three months, I called a bunch of people, sent a bunch of emails to clients, to tell them what we had done and to ask for their feedback. And universally, people were surprised and amazed. They hadn't noticed, and they were unbelievably supportive and excited for us. We had really amazing reactions from people who are, you know, sending us crazy, crazy emails of enthusiasm, and I think even envy. We have a couple of companies who said internally they were talking about it.

And I realized straightaway that regardless of what we thought, there was a big world out there of people who were almost wanting other people to do stuff, and use them as role models for their own working practices. So, for example, lots of our clients either work part-time, or have worked in a flexible way, but feel very unsupported by their organizations; they saw us almost as a coconspirator, as another person who could understand where they were coming from. And we had lots of conversations about that, and those people have been particularly supportive, whether it was returning moms or people who worked flexibly for various reasons, they were looking for other people to be buddies with. And I think that was really evident when we reached out and said, "This is what we're doing," and they immediately came back like, "This is amazing, it's great that other people are doing that stuff, can we talk about it." So people didn't notice during the trial, and they were universally supportive after we told them.

• •

FOUR-DAY WEEKS IMPROVE PERFORMANCE

By several measures, companies that move to shorter hours are able to maintain levels of performance equal to or better than before.

Companies report that the four-day week encourages greater cooperation within the organization. "It commits us much more to a team mentality" at The Mix, Tash Walker says. "It really inhibits the idea of individuals succeeding over the team. There's a collective sense that we are all in this to-gether to get a four-day week out of it, and so we have to collaborate better. No one can get their stuff done in isolation in a four-day week; you have to rely on your team members to help you get there. And so it encourages, at its basic form, more collaboration fundamentally." "In a five-hour day, peo-ple *have* to be team members," Jonathan Elliot says. "Creat-ing accountability between people and fostering team-work was really important, because you can't have people leaving after five hours and dumping work on others."

Shortening the workweek also encourages companies to adopt some tools that won't make individuals more produc-tive in the short run, but will make the company as a whole more efficient. At flocc, they now build components libraries based on projects they do for new clients. It takes a couple extra days to properly write and document new programs, but it saves developers time in the long run.

People can also work more intensely. At Maaemo, a three-star Michelin restaurant in Oslo, Norway, "people were more happy, energized, [and] excited" after moving to a four-day workweek, Esben Holmboe Bang said at the Food on the Edge 2017 symposium in Galway, Ireland. He then went to a three-day workweek. "Chefs working three days a week are like Duracell bunnies," he reported.

As we've already seen, many companies report higher profits after adopting shorter hours. Some of these increases are quite dramatic. Korean organic cosmetics maker Enesti began experimenting with a four-day workweek in 2010 and made it standard for all workers in 2013; in the three years since, its revenues rose from ₩6 billion to ₩10 billion in 2016, and the workforce has grown from thirty-two to fifty people. After implementing six-hour days, Swedish startup

Bråth saw its revenues double every year between 2012 and 2015. SkinOwl's business has doubled every year since its founding in 2013, and its products are now sold in retail stores in the United States, Hong Kong, Australia, and Lebanon, as well as online. In the first year after the company went to a four-day week, at The Mix revenues rose 57 percent; in the same period at VERSA, revenue rose 46 percent and profits tripled.

Companies have also managed to secure venture capital despite rejecting normal startup working hours. Zipdoc received ₩1.5 billion in investments in its first two years. Cockroach Labs has had three successful fundraising rounds that have yielded a total of $53.5 million. Administrate received a $2.5 million investment from Scottish venture capitalists and the Scottish Investment Bank in late 2015, and another $4.6 million in early 2019. Woowa Brothers closed a $320 million round of venture capital funding in December 2018, with investors from Korea, Singapore, and the United States. Venture capitalists have a well-deserved reputation for encouraging the technology industry's culture of overwork. Yet even they will invest in companies that work shorter hours when those firms have great products and lots of potential.

FOUR-DAY WEEKS IMPROVE RECRUITMENT

Not surprisingly, the four-day workweek has a positive effect on recruitment. Several companies that have been profiled in the media for their four-day weeks report a bump in applications, but it's easy to tell who just wants to work shorter hours and who is genuinely intrigued by the idea of redesigning the workday. As a result, even leaving aside the slackers, companies raise their profile in the marketplace. More important, though, they get more senior and experienced applicants, and make themselves more competitive against companies offering higher salaries or located in big cities or industry centers.

The four-day week also helps small companies and startups compete with large companies with bigger checkbooks. When hiring at Normally, "Our competitors are Google, Facebook, Apple, and we cannot always compete with them on financial benefits—you know, we don't have stock to give away," Chris Downs says. Despite the competitiveness of the market in Edinburgh for tech talent, John Peebles tells me, "a four-day, thirty-two-hour workweek has let Adminstrate grow and attract talent we otherwise wouldn't be able to access."

It's not just companies in big cities like New York and London, or newer tech hubs like Edinburgh, that are able to use shorter hours to attract more experienced workers. Being "based in Gloucestershire, not traditionally the PR hub of the UK," might look like a minus, Rich Leigh says, but he's figured out how to leverage it to Radioactive PR's advantage. "I've done my time in London, I know the industry very, very well, and I know that people tend to move here once they've done ten years-ish in London," he confides. "People move to Cheltenham, Gloucester, the Cotswolds, Bath, and the surrounding areas, because it's nice and they want to get out of the hustle and bustle." As a result, "there's a phenomenal roster of talent out there at the more senior level" right in his backyard—people who want to stay active in the profession, would love a shorter commute, don't want to go back to sixty-hour weeks, and find Radioactive PR's schedule and approach very appealing. Likewise, a five-hour workday gets Collins SBA attention from applicants who are fielding offers from big accounting firms in Sydney and Melbourne and otherwise wouldn't look at a small firm in Hobart, Tasmania, 370 miles south of Melbourne.

The four-day workweek makes small, self-funded companies attractive to older, more experienced workers who probably wouldn't otherwise consider leaving larger, better-paying firms. Like founders, these workers aren't slackers, but veterans looking to apply their experience and often substantial talents in environments that don't take their sacrifices for granted. Type A Media looks for "people at the top of their game at big networks, but who are jaded," founder Ross Tavendale says. Their ideal candidate? "You have an expense account, but they treat you like shit." Accounting firm Farnell Clarke hears from junior people who've finished their training at larger firms but won't be brought onto the partner track, or more senior people who have "been there ten to fifteen years and they're in touching distance of partnership or directorship," Frances Kay tells me. Lots of Normally's designers had become disillusioned with the culture of overwork in most agencies and "were waiting for the workplace to catch up with reality," Marei Wollersberger says. Just like founders, these workers have become disenchanted with the idea of treating long hours as normal, are not impressed by perks like free massages and on-site dry cleaning, and see the value of simple benefits like three-day weekends and boundaries. They value their own time and have enough experience to appreciate what the four-day workweek says about how the company is run and where it directs its ambition. For them, a shorter workweek can be just as appealing as a higher salary.

FOUR-DAY WEEKS DECREASE TURNOVER

After they implemented a four-day week in 2015, Pursuit Marketing's annual turnover rate dropped to 2 percent, a remarkably low figure in an industry where job-hopping is common. Not only has that helped keep productivity high and justified their higher-than-average investment in employee training, it's also saved the company more than a quarter million pounds on recruitment. In Glasgow, corporate recruiters usually charge about £4,000 to hire a single telemarketer; thanks to the four-day week, the company was able to grow from 50 to 120 people without paying any recruitment fees at all. The four-day workweek also makes it easier to recruit people, and it makes it harder for other companies to steal them. "I've had competitors try to steal my people," Goodall Group founder Steve Goodall says, "and the four-day week has kept them."

Most of the companies that have implemented shorter workweeks for a few years report a drop in turnover. At Japanese groupware company Cybozu, turnover dropped from 28 percent to 4 percent after introducing a flexible work system that offered a four-day workweek. At IIH Nordic, turnover dropped by 20 percent after the introduction of the four-day workweek. And several nursing homes have successfully used shorter hours as a way to cut turnover among skilled nurse's aides (see Company Profile on page 184). Restaurants also see turnover drop dramatically. At Aizle, "we retain staff better" working a four-day workweek, chef Stuart Ralston says. "The front of house staff have been the same staff now for over a year, so I think that's prolonged their lifespan in the restaurant." At Maaemo in Oslo,

Norway, turnover dropped to zero after the three-star Michelin restaurant shifted to a four-day workweek in 2016. There is one exception to the lower turnover rule: a few people will quit rather than work a shorter day. When the five-hour day was announced at Blue Street Capital, Alex Gafford says, "there were some people who were like, 'This is awesome, let's try it!' but they just never could get it to work because they just couldn't focus, they couldn't get rid of distractions and multitasking." However, those departures created room for "some amazing people who love where they are and are really doing great things for us," Blue Street Capital CEO David Rhoads adds. At Collins SBA, "we're much more discerning about who we take on" after moving to a five-hour day, Jonathan Elliot says. "What we're doing is very generous and we're not just going to give it to anyone. We need a certain caliber of person to be on the team." After replacing less enthusiastic workers and hiring more selectively, Elliot feels he has a much stronger workforce. "If you asked me a year ago 'Would you reemploy everyone in your business if you started from scratch?' I'd have said no," he says. "Now, I can say 'Yes, I would.'" The workforce builds the shorter workweek, and in turn the shorter workweek builds a better workforce.

So how do you filter out the slackers who just want to work less? Stephan Aarstol came up with an elegant way to identify them. Everyone who applies to Tower Paddle Boards has to "send in a two- to three-minute video cover letter before we bring them in for an interview," he tells me. "Half of them are saying, 'I'm one of those people who does three times the work of everybody in the office that I'm in, and this sounds like that's what I'm doing.' So it definitely attracts those high-performing people. But it also attracts, I don't know what to call it, like, sloths basically. They're eating Doritos on their couch, saying, 'Yeah, man, I can't believe somebody didn't come up with this a long time ago, I've been saying this *forever*.'" The video literally makes it easy to see who approaches the five-hour workday as a challenge and who only view it as a way to work less.

You might imagine that getting lots of low-quality applicants would be a problem, but it's not. Since announcing Radioactive PR's shift to a four-day workweek, "I can't move for great resumes from great people, and that was a big part of doing it," Rich Leigh tells me a couple months after shortening the workweek. "I want the best people to say, 'Not only do they do great work, not only are they quite noisy in the industry, but nobody else does four days for the same money. Why wouldn't I go at least talk to those people?'" Anna Ross says that "the four-day workweek attracts hard-working people" to Kester Black who are "really intrigued by that kind of work." In Japan, e-commerce company Zozo stopped hiring people straight out of university; for several years they've been able to only hire people who have previous industry experience.

• •

Company Profile

The Glebe: Using Thirty-Hour Weeks to Lower Nursing Turnover and Improve Care

The Glebe is a retirement community outside Roanoke, Virginia, with two hundred residents. Like many modern retirement communities, it's divided into sections that offer different levels of services to residents: independent living for those who are still active, assisted living for those with permanent mobility and memory issues, and skilled nursing for people who are recovering from illnesses.

In the United States, about 1.3 million people live in nursing homes, and certified nursing assistants (CNAs) provide most of their daily care. CNAs help patients in and out of bed, change dressings, assist with feeding, dressing, and bathing, and organize social activities. It's difficult work to "provide care for people who are elderly, falling, have multiple clinical issues and comorbidities," says Jonathan Cook, CEO of LifeSpire, the company that owns the Glebe. In most of the country, it's also not very well paid; assistants "could be making the same amount in fast food, without dealing with bedpans and irate family," says James Berman, a journalist who covers the industry. Many assistants have to juggle two or three jobs to make ends meet. As a result, annual turnover can exceed 100 percent in some facilities. It's costly for nursing homes to have to keep replacing workers, and it disrupts the lives of residents. "Beyond taking care of people at the end of life, there is probably no bigger topic in long-term care than skilled staffing," James tells me.

Despite its rural location, the Glebe has not been immune to problems of recruitment and turnover among its skilled nursing staff. In May 2018, executive director Ellen D'Ardenne started a trial in which certified nursing assistants would receive forty hours' pay for thirty hours' work. The 30/40 program, as they call it, is structured as an incentive program. Workers who are punctual and don't "call off" any shifts that week receive forty hours' pay for thirty hours' work; if you show up late or call in sick, you lose the bonus. The six-hour day also doesn't include time off for meals, which reduces the number of handoffs between staff and time when the facility is shorthanded. The incentive structure makes it formally stricter than shorter-hours experiments in other industries, but even places like EDGE and Woowa Brothers have cultural expectation around punctuality and presence, and of course nurses have to be on-site to do their jobs. Further, last-minute absences are costly to colleagues and facilities, who have to ask employees to work double shifts or hire expensive temporary workers.

The Glebe is not the first nursing home to try such a program. Jonathan Cook first encountered the 30/40 concept in the skilled nursing center at Marquette, a retirement home in Indianapolis. "I was just blown away at how that community was attracting and retaining—retaining being the big word—high-caliber CNAs," he recalls. "We had a waiting list of CNAs who were waiting to come to work at Marquette. We had the choice of the cream of the crop."

To make it work, the Glebe added nine CNAs to their staff of eighteen. This meant more money on salaries, but "based on the amount of money that we put into the ongoing recruitment efforts . . . [and] turnover costs, it was a no-brainer," D'Ardenne told an industry magazine. The program cost $145,023 a year in wages and benefits in the first year, but it saved almost $122,762 in hiring costs, overtime, and payments to staffing services, for a total cost of about $22,261.

What did they get for their money? A year into the program, call bell response times decreased 57 percent and acquired infections dropped 65 percent. Falls and skin tears are down dramatically, indicating that nurses are more reliably available to help patients, and are doing a better job moving them. (Falls are also a leading cause of death among the elderly.) Administration of psychoactive medications is way down, because nurses can spend more time with patients and maintain continuity of care. On the staffing side, annual turnover went from 128 percent to 44 percent, and application traffic increased fourfold.

Similar experiments have been conducted in other countries. In Gothenburg, Sweden, the government-run Svartedalens nursing home conducted a two-year trial in which assistant nurses' shifts were reduced from eight to six hours with no reduction in pay. (The trial was ended by a new, more fiscally conservative center-right government.) They had to hire fifteen more nurses, and labor costs went up by 20 percent, or €700,000 (about $735,000) during the trial; roughly half of that increase, though, was offset by savings that came with a 15 percent decline in sick days and call outs, and by taxes paid by newly employed workers who no longer drew state benefits. Residents also said that care improved when nurses had a six-hour day: nurses organized more activities and were happier and more responsive. Monica Axhede, the director of the home, told a reporter that dementia patients, who can require lots of interaction, were "clearly more peaceful" in the care of better-rested nurses. Compared to a nearby care center that stayed on an eight-hour shift schedule, nurses were healthier and less stressed. "During the trial all the staff had more energy," Svartedalens assistant nurse Emilie Telander told the BBC in 2017. "I could see that everybody was happy."

In health care, it's necessary to look beyond the additional manpower expenses when assessing the total cost of programs to shorten working hours. Not far from the Svartedalens nursing home, the Sahlgrenska University Hospital moved its staff of eighty-nine orthopedic doctors and nurses to a six-hour day in 2015. It isn't cheap—about 1 million kroner per month for an additional twelve staff—but some of those costs are offset by being able to perform more operations and having fewer patients stay in the hospital with complications. They also have dramatically shortened their waiting lists and can treat patients within weeks rather than months of a referral.

• •

FOUR-DAY WEEKS AND WORKING PARENTS

Not surprisingly, some of the people who benefit most from—and are most coveted by—companies working shorter workweeks are working mothers. For companies, the four-day workweek creates opportunities to attract skilled and senior workers whose family commitments would normally not allow them to work at a level that matches their abilities. For parents, shorter workweeks let them spend more time with their children, to avoid the stigma that follows efforts to balance the conflicting demands of work and parenting, and to do a better job at work and home.

When companies implement shorter hours, they quickly discover that skills like the ability to focus, to prioritize, and to maintain boundaries are now more valuable than the stamina to endure long hours. And who has professional experience and those personal skills? "Returning-to-work mums, mums who have been out of the workforce for a while . . . are actually the kinds of people that we want to attract, because they've got skills, they have a lot of experience," Kester Black CEO Anna Ross tells me. In Glasgow, Lorraine Gray says that Pursuit Marketing "got a couple of good members" when it "created term-time roles completely aligned to the school day" that accommodated parents' schedules.

Chris Downs says Normally's four day workweek "makes it possible for brilliant, experienced, super-focused, and productive women to come back into work and not feel any less than anyone else in that situation." But it's also made him aware of just how unfairly most workplaces treats working mothers. "It makes me beyond furious that we've built a society that makes that happen," he says.

For years, companies have struggled with the problem of retaining and supporting working mothers and, to a lesser degree, fathers. For high-stress professions like medicine that already have issues with attrition and burnout, these problems make a bad situation worse. Replacing people who are good performers but are forced out of the profession in their thirties and forties—often when they're nearing the peak of their productivity and profitability—can be very costly: one 2009 report estimated that replacing high-performing attorneys cost big American law firms $20 million a year in "regretted losses."

SHORTER HOURS VERSUS FLEXIBLE WORK

One problem is that relatively few decent jobs have a lot of flexibility. According to a 2015 Timewise study, only 6 percent of advertised roles in the United Kingdom that paid over £20,000 offered a flexible work option; for jobs paying over £100,000, the number fell to 2 percent. In most companies flexibility is an exception, not an option.

But companies may create formal part-time or flexible work tracks, only to find that people don't use them. For example, 90 percent of big American law firms have such programs, but only 4 percent of eligible lawyers take advantage of them.

Why aren't they more popular? Even in forward-thinking offices, workers who take advantage of flexible work options risk what sociologists call the "flexibility stigma." Flexible workers risk being branded as less ambitious and unreliable during crunch times, or are seen as creating extra work for others.

As a result, even when they put in extra effort to make sure that they're not forgotten by their bosses and labor to guarantee that their absence doesn't create problems for colleagues or inconvenience the system, people who opt for flexible schedules are likely to be pushed onto less interesting and lower-profile projects, get promoted more slowly, get smaller raises, and ultimately are more likely to leave their jobs. Professionals who theoretically have lots of control over their time are expected to "choose" to work constantly; even academics find themselves punished if they aren't seen voluntarily spending their free time working.

The flexibility stigma affects women more strongly than men. Women are more likely to need flexibility, and the assumption that women will have to divide their attention between job and family puts them at a disadvantage during hiring and promoting. But men who take advantage of flexible options also risk being seen by their bosses as less ambitious, aggressive, or career focused.

SHORTER HOURS AND RETURNING PARENTS

Those who take time off to raise children face other structural problems. A 2017 KPMG study estimated that worldwide, 96 million working women between the ages of thirty and fifty-four were on career breaks; of them, 55 million had been middle managers, executives, or senior professionals. As many women who've taken time off can testify, going back to work can mean facing a gauntlet of questions about your career choices, your professional commitment, and the likelihood that you'll stay on the job. In the United Kingdom alone, according to a study by PwC, over 400,000 professional women—managers, lawyers, doctors, engineers—were taking voluntary or involuntary career breaks in 2016; if they returned to the job market, more than a quarter million would have to work in lower-skilled positions or work fewer hours than they would like. This would result in "an immediate 12–32% reduction in hourly earnings," and £1.1 billion lost wages annually.

The long-term impacts of career breaks on lifetime earnings can be dramatic. A study of male and female MBAs in the United States found that a decade after graduating, men earned 60 percent more than their female classmates who'd had children, and most of that difference could be explained by women taking time off after a child was born. Even in Denmark, which has a generous paid family leave policy, a recent study found that women with children experience an immediate, sharp drop in their incomes, and even after ten or twenty years are likely to earn 20 percent less than either men or women who do not have children. In contrast, fatherhood has a statistically insignificant effect on earnings.

The four-day workweek changes all that. On average, women MBAs with children work 24 percent fewer weekly

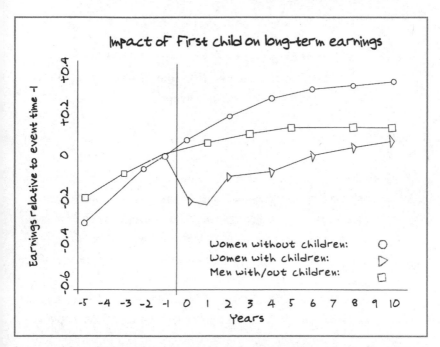

Impact of first child on long-term earnings. Statistics gathered by the Danish government between 1980 and 2013 showed that earnings of new mothers declined sharply, and lagged behind both men—with or without children—and women who did not have children.

hours than men; moving to a shorter workweek precisely closes that gap. It eliminates flexibility stigma and reduces the need for career breaks. By giving everyone more time off, it removes the suspicion and resentment that otherwise attaches to leaving early. Its egalitarian nature means that people don't feel obliged to put in extra hours to make up for the "gift" of flexible work. It makes work-life balance something that everyone aspires to. The fact that companies encourage workers to disconnect after hours and to spend their three days doing restorative activities, professional development, serious hobbies, or self-care means that the boundaries between work and personal time are likely to be stronger.

• •

On Shorter Hours, Flexible Work, and Working Parents

Tash Walker, The Mix:

The challenge of flexible working that I've observed is that it creates a power imbalance in an organization. And in a way, the person who is working flexibly almost has to feel grateful to the organization, which creates the sense of almost being beholden to them. You've got to do the organizing, you've got to make sure that everyone knows your schedule, you've got to do all of this extra stuff—and then work harder, because you've got to prove that flexible working works. So the people working flexibly I talk to almost always end up feeling like they work double the amount of their colleagues, because they're constantly having to prove themselves. And so I think you end up with all these kinds of power inequalities and balances, which means that it's actually quite hard to get stuff done.

Michael Honey, Icelab:

For Icelab, four days a week is full time. But if you work four days in an organization where five days a week is the norm, then you are a deviant employee. You are deficient. And I don't know if it's actually possible to make that go away in conventional organizations, because there are going to be times when you're not in the important meetings or you don't get given the important projects, therefore you can't successfully deliver the important project, therefore you don't get a promotion.

There's an ineradicable problem with working only a fraction of what the other people in the organization work. And that means that for people who want to go part-time—and it's no surprise that a lot of them are women—there is a systematic problem with things like lower lifetime earnings. So from a social justice point of view, just giving people the flexibility to work part-time is not good enough. That's fine from the company's point of view, but for the person who goes part-time, it is more difficult and it has these long-term hidden costs.

Jen Anderson, Administrate:

My understanding from friends who've had kids is that mothers returning after maternity leave often have not been able to get back into the roles they had before or get the days that they were looking to work when they went back. During my time here I've had a child, and I think under normal circumstances, if I had been working five days a week, I would have wanted to come back and work four days a week. I haven't had to change anything about my working life as such, other than the fact I've got a child and all those additional things to think about, so my job is the same and I've not had to take a drop in pay or anything like that. That's worked really well. For me personally, and I know for others with families in the company, it's a huge, huge, huge benefit.

Georgina Robilliard, Insured by Us:

The combination of four days and flexibility has helped us hire those sort of moms and dads who want to take a very active role in their children's lives. So we regularly have people drop kids off at school and daycare and things like that and then use the fifth day to hang out with the kids. So in terms of gender and age, we've kind of got a larger bracket, I suppose, than if we had offered only Sydney and five days a week.

• •

SHORTER WORKWEEKS SUPPORT BETTER PARENTING

A four-day week doesn't just give you more time for parenting; it lets you be a better parent. At Gothenburg, Sweden's Svartedalens nursing home, nurse and single father Arturo Perez said that the six-hour workday made parenting less stressful. "I no longer have to pressure [my children] in the morning to go to school," he told a journalist in 2016. "Everything is much more relaxed. . . . I think I've become a better dad, as well as being a better caregiver."

Parents report that they spend higher-quality time with their kids. Mark Merrywest says that a few weeks after moving to a six-hour day at flocc, one employee told him that because she could leave work earlier, "'I can now get home to see my kids and talk to them before teatime, before they're tired, before they're grumpy. You know, I don't have to just talk to them in the car on the way home, I can interact with my kids again.' And that's just incredible."

Parents at these companies not only have more time with their children, the day they spend with their children is also a day they save money on childcare. This was highlighted to me by several parents working in London, a city where families spend an average of 50 percent of their disposable income on childcare. So moving to a four-day week means saving thousands of dollars per year **and** having hundreds more hours with their child—the very definition of a win-win.

The effects of shorter hours are felt by fathers and mothers alike. Working mothers face plenty of challenges balancing work and parenting, but a growing proportion of fathers in developed economies complain about structural challenges to their being good parents.

At Icelab, shorter hours and remote work "make it possible for a parent to be both a good parent and a good employee. There is no doubt that they are able to be better fathers," Michael Honey says, because it provides more flexibility "for when the children are inevitably sick or they need to do

Working Fathers' attitudes to parenting

UK	Highly involved in parenting:	58%
	Issues with employers over work-parenting balance:	45%
	Impact on mental health:	37%
	Feel guilt about impact of work on spouse:	61%
	Feel guilt about impact of work on kids:	51%
US	Think parenting is important:	57%
	Work-life balance is difficult:	52%
	Spend too little time with kids:	63%

Recent surveys of working fathers show that more men take their roles as fathers seriously and feel that the structure of work today interferes with their ability to be good parents.

something." The four-day workweek also benefits the spouses of Icelab employees "because it makes it possible for them to continue their career. I mentioned that we have quite a few fathers in our organization, and very often it falls upon the mother to be the person whose career is sacrificed. I think this makes it much more possible to have a more equitable parenting arrangement." Several young children whose dads work at Normally are getting "a day a week that they get to know their fathers," Chris Downs says. "That's something that no other organization can give them. Of all the things we've done at Normally, that's my proudest personal achievement."

FOUR-DAY WEEKS BOOST CREATIVITY

In a number of industries, four-day workweeks are appealing because they promise to boost creativity. Creative agencies, software startups, and restaurants are always looking for new ideas, and new ways to come up with ideas, from brainstorming and ideation sessions, to adopting tools to promote flow and concentration, to doing "stagings" at other restaurants. Four-day workweeks boost creativity in several ways: by improving problem-solving capacity, by providing people with more time for creativity boosting experiences, and by fostering an innovation mindset in organizations.

CREATIVITY AT WORK

During working hours, having more time in flow helps people get deeply immersed in problems and able to work on them more intensively. More time off gives people a chance to recover from that kind of intensive work.

Shortening working hours encourages workers to concentrate on their most important problems and spend less time on either diversions or less essential tasks. "On Monday through Thursday, I feel like we have a more focused and engaged workforce, because they say, 'I just need to make sure that I'm getting the things that I need done, done,'" Cockroach Labs CEO Spencer Kimball tells me. "Having shorter time doesn't mean that you're losing creativity," game designer Linus Feldt says, since being "more focused made the staff more creative and better at finding solutions." The four-day workweek at web design firm Reusser Design gives developers "more concentration time, and that, paired with a conscious effort to minimize interruptions, means more productive days" than a five-day week, writes UX designer Andy Welfle. "You wouldn't believe how much we get done" in a compressed week, CEO Nate Reusser told CNN in 2015.

Clearing substantial parts of the day for focused work also delivers big benefits for designers and programmers, who work best when they're able to dive deeply into problems. Cristian Rennella, the founder of software firm el Mejor Trato (which trialed a four-day week in 2015), writes, "A developer needs an average of 4 consecutive hours of uninterrupted work to be able to carry out a good quality job with significant advances." Eliminating the constant barrage of meetings and other distractions doesn't just result in a linear improvement in the quality of a programmer's work; it's more like an exponential increase.

The four-day workweek also improves creativity by giving people more time to recharge the mental and physical batteries they deplete at work. This time for recovery is especially critical to have when working in the more intensive manner demanded by a four-day week or six-hour day. Creative work "is tough on the mind," says Linus Feldt, "and it's hard to sustain a full eight-hour day if you're a creative artist or a programmer. With six hours divided into two shifts, people can maintain focus easily." Maria Bråth, CEO of Swedish SEO company Bråth AB, says that a six-hour day lets her firm maintain a level of focus and creative intensity that helps it compete against larger, more conventionally run competitors, but "we couldn't keep it up for eight hours." Employees at her company can "squeeze in eight hours'" worth of work "in our six hours because we come to work rested, we work, and then we leave."

Programmers also praise the four-day workweek for helping them approach their work with a better-rested, clearer mind. "Creativity flourishes in clear thinking, and the ability to clear your mind in a three-day weekend is just tremendous," Natalie Nagele says. Cockroach Labs' developers work on problems that require "sustained abstract thinking" and can best be solved if approached with "a clear and relaxed mind," not the brute-force method of "fourteen-hour workdays and lots of caffeine," Spencer Kimball says. Of course, everyone benefits from more unstructured time. "Creative brains need time off," W+K London executive creative director Iain Tait says, and their shorter-hours trial was designed "to make sure that we're protecting our people's minds." He knows from personal experience that periods "when my brain's exhausted and I'm whipping it, forcing it to think harder," are "not when good ideas happen."

Shorter workweeks also give people more time and energy to experiment and develop new ideas. Chefs who formerly worked seventy-hour weeks talk about having more time to create new dishes when they move to four-day work-weeks. "With a four-day week, I've had time to do more research and development into products," Stuart Ralston tells me. "I'm definitely spending more time designing the dishes, spending more time with the staff doing the dishes. I think the food's never been better."

At Rheingans Digital Enabler, Lasse Rheingans notes that since moving to a five-hour workday, "one of the things that amazes me most, and one of the findings I see with my team, is that they come into work in the morning and they're very concentrated on the operational work, the tasks they have to do." This heightened focus helps people solve problems faster, but Rheingans observes another way in which shorter hours boost creativity. "Then they go out, do whatever they like to do—some do a little nap, some go to lunch with friends and then go swimming or go on a hike—and suddenly in the moment when you least expect it, the greatest ideas come. I see it with myself. It's something I realize a lot these days." Shorter working hours enhance creativity by providing more time for mind-wandering and casually thinking about problems.

The unexpected insights that Rheingans describes have happened to us all: if you've ever tried but failed to solve a problem, only to have the answer pop into your head a few minutes later when you're thinking about something else, you've experienced an everyday version of the same thing. For nearly a century, psychologists have used a four-stage model to describe the birth of creative ideas. It begins with preparation, a period of conscious investigation and efforts to solve the problem, followed by a period of incubation, then a moment of insight, and finally verification, when the insight's correctness and details are worked out.

That moment of illumination is a familiar but mysterious phenomenon, but recently, neuroscientists have edged close to identifying a process in the brain that helps account for these moments. When we relax our attention, the neural networks that process and interpret the world switch off and are replaced by what scientists call the default mode network. The default mode network links together regions that are associated with (among other things) creative thinking and problem solving. The default mode also appears to gravitate to recent unsolved problems; autobiographical accounts of spontaneous problem solving by figures like nineteenth-century mathematician Henri Poincaré and twentieth-century biologist Barbara McClintock suggest that the default mode works on these problems in proportion to the intensity and conscious effort we devote to them. Unsolved problems that are fresh in our minds get more attention from our creative subconscious than problems we work on casually or tried and failed to solve a long time ago.

This is a model of creativity that blends laboratory research with historical material, so take it with a grain of salt. But if the broad outlines are correct, then shorter workweeks—with their combination of more structured, intensive working hours and long breaks—are almost tailor-made for boosting insight by giving the default mode network material to work on, and then giving it time to work on problems. As Rosie Warin puts it, days off are a way of "building in the space and giving yourself permission to let creative thoughts in."

It helps explain why a number of people I interviewed talk about having ideas after work. "I always find myself enjoying thinking about work" after hours, flocc's Emily West says, but it feels different after a six-hour day. In her previous roles, "when I was not at work, I was constantly thinking, 'Oh I should be doing this.'" Now, though, "because I know I have done what's expected of me during the day and I'm not exhausted, I enjoy thinking about work at home, rather than hate thinking about work at home."

It may sound paradoxical at first that greater creative problem solving during free time would be a benefit of more free time, but most of us would agree that there's a big difference between, say, absentmindedly turning over an idea while out on a hiking trail and grinding away at it while sitting at our desks. Spencer Kimball says, "Friday, I'm going to potentially still be working on" a programming challenge, "just in a more relaxed fashion." Likewise, Anna Ross tells me, "I still work a couple of hours on the Friday, but it's more of a creative process," not an effort to cross another thing off her to-do list.

● ●

On Creativity and Downtime

Mark Merrywest, flocc:

One of the biggest side effects that I've really been pleased with is that people are having the time to think about work outside of work, but not in a stressed way. They'll come back in and say, "Look, you know, I've mulled it over overnight, and this is the best way of looking at it." I'm 90 percent sure it's because they've had time for their brains to relax and to be doing something else that then allowed it to process, whereas if we were really pushing them to the edge of the day, then they'd just want to go home and slump, rather than actually still be thinking about it. So even though they have six hours actually in the office doing the work, I reckon they're working for longer outside it as a natural side effect.

Spencer Kimball, Cockroach Labs:

I often use it to spend more time with my daughter. But when I do work, I actually use that day to approach my work differently. That's actually been the biggest revelation. People aren't having meetings, most people don't come in the office, the email load goes from high to low. So during the week, I've got this problem and I keep getting harried between these meetings, and all these other things. But on Friday, I can just sit down and focus on this problem. And I'm at home in my office and make myself a coffee. And I just approach it differently and often am very surprised at the result, because when you're able to sort of kick back and more leisurely explore a problem, you often get better results. So I can solve things that might have stymied me during the week, partly because I couldn't really focus on them, but also partly because I'm under pressure to get this done now, and that can sometimes be counterproductive. And I've heard similar stories from many of the people who work here.

Lasse Rheingans, Rheingans Digital Enabler:

You can't force creativity. You can't tell the creative guys, "Come up with your best ideas now." But if they have the opportunity to relax and do whatever, they come back and they have twenty or fifty ideas, and all of them are pretty good. This is what happens here. People go off, have great ideas, come back, and they're super-motivated to talk about them with their colleagues, and they empower each other to be better at work. When you give yourself the time off regular work, your brain has the energy to come up with these things.

• •

FOUR-DAY WEEKS CREATE TIME FOR NEW EXPERIENCES

Shorter days also give people time to explore new things and to dive into subjects or activities that enrich their creative and working lives. At Kester Black, Anna Ross says, "When my staff come to the office on Mondays after they've had a day off doing other things, it brings new creative ideas, which only further benefits the brand."

Getting out of the kitchen is essential for today's world-class chefs, for whom great cooking can be less about mastering a canon of recipes or an established method than exploring unfamiliar cuisines, blending ingredients and approaches from different parts of the world, and developing entirely new ways of cooking. Ben Shewry, whose restaurant Attica is best known for introducing indigenous Australian ingredients into fine dining, told an interviewer in 2018 that "most of the innovation I have found in cooking in the past 6 years has been inspired by looking outside of the field of cooking and hospitality." Likewise, Esben Holmboe Bang said in 2017 that a year of working three-day workweeks had allowed the staff at Maaemo time to rest, but also "time off to get better at our jobs."

When W+K London ran its trial to shorten working hours, managing director Helen Andrews tells me via email, one aim was to give everyone "more time to be creative, to be exposed to culture, to have moments of inspiration away from incessant meetings and email interruption." "Our days are filled with rampant collaboration and idea generation," her colleague Iain Tait says. "We need the time and space to be able to process the ideas and stimulation that are generated through the workday. But most of us get far too few periods for silence and reflection."

People don't have to go to art galleries and openings to be exposed to great ideas. Michael Honey says, "I think a lot while running, when I do a trail run. I have insights when I'm doing things which are not in the problem domain—that is, that you find analogs and analogies which are helpful to your thinking. If your entire life is spent in the same domain as the one that you work in, then you don't get that opportunity." At Skift, Rafat Ali tells me, several employees are musicians or improv comedians. The discipline of improvisation teaches that actors can build order (and humor) out of the chaos if they listen actively, think fast, build on other actors' ideas, and work as a team. These are qualities that many organizations would love to cultivate in employees, but Skift's employees develop them on their own.

• •

Company Profile

Baumé: Using a Four-Day Week to Focus on What Matters

The four-day workweek encourages you to concentrate on your most important work and also pushes companies to redesign their culture and schedules to prioritize focus over distraction. This has the benefit of making people more productive, encouraging flow, and creating space for more creative thinking. It also helps companies look for ways to help workers be more efficient and productive. Over the long run, it can also give you the space to focus on what's most important in your life, and to redesign your work to support that.

Bruno Chemel and his wife, Christie, opened Baumé, a restaurant in Palo Alto, California, in 2010. It's located on a pleasant but unassuming street lined with low-slung Cold War-era buildings; it shares the block with a FedEx printing and shipping center, barre and CrossFit gyms, and a smoke shop. A cheap pizza place and a famous dive bar (a dive by Silicon Valley standards, anyway) are nearby. The restaurant won its first Michelin star the year it opened. In 2011, it was awarded a second, which it has retained ever since.

It's a long way from the provincial French restaurant and inn where Bruno first went to work at fifteen, where it was "just me, working with that single chef guy in the kitchen, working a lot of hours," he tells me, his accent and grammar undiminished by years living in the United States. From there, he studied under Guy Savoy in Paris, and at the two-hundred-year-old Le Grand Véfour. He went on to work in kitchens in New York, Tokyo, and Honolulu before meeting Christie in San Francisco and settling down in California. He spent two years as head chef at another restaurant in Silicon Valley before leaving to open Baumé.

Bruno's menu blends elements of classical French cuisine, a Japanese attitude to ingredients, and the precision of molecular gastronomy; the Michelin guide praises Bruno's emphasis on "coaxing flavor to profound levels" from local and seasonal ingredients. (Baumé partners with a local farmer who cultivates hard-to-find vegetables for the restaurant.) When it first opened, Baumé had twenty-four covers, served lunch and dinner, and had a dozen staff in the front and back. But Bruno and Christie disliked the long hours and stress of managing a restaurant that size. With multiple services five days a week, Bruno needed a large brigade, but "because I was trying to catch error of cook or staff, I was not focused on my job, I have a lot of stress, a lot of energy out," he tells me. "I was so tired at the end of the day. And for what?"

They changed the schedule to four days a week, and it was a revelation. "When I was younger, I worry that I get no new ideas, but working six days or seven days a week, I was burned out, and I don't even know. That's why I get no ideas," Bruno tells me. Like many of us, his younger self was better able to sustain the abuse of long hours, but confined to the kitchen, he had fewer opportunities to explore, tinker, and have experiences that could enrich his cooking. Opening only four nights a week has allowed him to spend more time in gardens and farmers' markets, explore the Bay Area's diverse culinary scene, and develop new dishes. "Now I get more ideas because I'm spending less time in the restaurant. Automatically that makes me more creative. And opening four days makes us more efficient, more focused." They kept paring down: they eliminated lunch, reduced the number of covers from twenty-four to nine, and in 2015 made the decision to run the restaurant themselves. Working in the kitchen by himself is "a relief," Bruno says. "I don't need to yell at nobody. I just yell at myself if I want to."

Is the food really better? "Better?" Bruno shrugs. "I don't know, we don't have three stars yet." I don't get the sense that he and Christie are worrying about a third star, though. "It's so much less stressful working four days," Christie says. "You have more time for yourself, time to organize, and time for your family." Neither one of them seems eager to give that up.

Baumé shows that shorter hours can help leaders channel their ambitions and encourage them to focus on things like quality and sustainability, rather than chase more costly and potentially self-destructive kinds of success. For Bruno and Christie, that means not managing a large staff of servers and cooks, keeping the restaurant small enough so they can do all the work themselves, and turning down chances to consult or appear on cooking shows (unlike fellow Guy Savoy alum Gordon Ramsay, the chef who trained Stuart Ralston). It does not mean setting your sights low: Baumé, after all, is one of only four hundred two-star Michelin restaurants in the world. But for most chefs, maintaining that level of quality requires enormous sacrifice, licenses bad behavior in and out of the kitchen, and can take a huge personal toll. After decades of long hours, working a four-day week put Bruno and Christie on a much less stressful and more sustainable path, one that lets them focus on creating incredible food, world-class service, and retaining more control over their business and lives. "The advantage of being such a small business is we don't have stress, and we control everything," Bruno says. "The disadvantage is we don't really make too much money. We will never be the richest people at the cemetery, I can guarantee you that."

"But we're happy," Christie says.

"We're happy and we make enough money at our level to make us happy," Bruno says. "Some people want to make big, big, big money, they want like ten Ferrari in their garage. Me, if I get one Porsche, that's all I want." By Silicon Valley standards, that's positively monastic.

• •

FOUR-DAY WEEKS ENCOURAGE AN INNOVATION MINDSET

"Almost immediately" after shifting the Goodall Group, a marketing and branding agency, to a four-day workweek, "the whole team started to act more like owners," Steve Goodall tells me. He had been happy with their performance—the four-day workweek was a way to give something back and keep his team happy, not a clever ploy to get more work out of them—but paradoxically, when they worked fewer days, "they would take things on that they wouldn't normally take on. I get phone calls and emails on Friday, Saturday, and Sunday from my team now. I never had before. I say to them, 'You don't need to be doing anything, it's Saturday!' And they're like, 'No, no, I was just out shopping, and I thought about this, what about this idea.'" Months into the experiment, he's still shaking his head over it. "They started to feel more like owners," he says. "All I did was give them a day off."

It may seem contradictory that giving people more time off would increase their sense of ownership of their work, but it happens at other companies too. Tash Walker says people at The Mix are more likely to say, "Let's think about how we work. Let's work better, smarter. Let's think about new ways of doing things." Jonathan Elliot loves how the five-hour day has "created a mindset, and it's empowered people throughout the team to think of better ways to do things, to identify frustrations, blockages, and solutions" at Collins SBA. Like Goodall, Elliot observes everyone acting more like founders. Employees are "constantly saying, 'Hey, this could be done better, and this is solution.' I can tell you as a business manager, to have your team come to you and say, 'We've identified this problem, this is a better way, this'll make us more efficient'—I think that is just brilliant."

Why does this happen? A shorter workday creates a clear incentive for individual innovation and great opportunity to benefit directly from improvements you make to a company's efficiency. In traditional companies, the main benefits of innovations go to the company, which then (might) reward the innovator. But shortening the workday isn't like adding to the corporate bottom line: a change you make shows results almost immediately and pays out in the form of time savings that everybody enjoys.

Once that mindset is planted, it becomes self-sustaining and spreads throughout the business. The experience of experimenting with new processes, office designs, or schedules pushes everyone—leaders, workers, the entire organization—into a mode where they're more observant and skeptical, and more likely to notice and look more critically at other everyday assumptions. In a normal workplace, anyone can identify problems (this is always a popular topic around the water cooler). Shorter days require workplaces to be more flexible, to accept changes from below, to embrace things that save workers' time as well as increase company profits. This creates a space for worker-driven innovation.

In fact, once it's started, managers should be prepared for employees to keep asking questions, challenging convention, and pushing for more improvements. "We've improved our processes to be more efficient in a more condensed amount of time" since moving to a five-hour day, Blue Street Capital's Alex Gafford says, "but it's an ongoing thing." In fact, "there's no doubt in my mind that we will continue to improve our process to the point where one day, we'll be working less than five hours a day."

• •

On Shorter Hours as a Stimulus for Innovation

Natalie Nagele, Wildbit:

To keep a four-day workweek, we've got to do the right work, we have to know why we're doing it, and so we constantly have the exercise of asking, "Well, why, why, why, why?" Asking ourselves those questions and trying to get the most out of ourselves and each other has been actually really exciting, and I think has really pushed the team to do super-creative work and thoughtful work.

Patrick Byrne, Pursuit Marketing:

I think that as time moves forward, you see that more and more jobs that are repetitive or process driven are becoming automated, and people talk about machine learning and AI pushing that even further. But the one thing that's not ever going to go away and can't be automated is creativity. So the more we can empower our staff to be creative, to find solutions that are going to deliver more value in a shorter period of time, and to relinquish that need to perform repetitive tasks, the better it's going to be, not just for our business but for the economy as a whole, and actually for society as a whole.

It's about finding new ways to do new things more effectively, more efficiently, and to the benefit of business or society as a whole, which ultimately is the same thing. For us, it's about accepting nothing, questioning everything. That's how we've built this business. When people said, "Why are you going to a four-day week, how's that gonna work? Everyone works a five-day week," I actually asked, "Why? Why do people do things a certain way?" And in every single role that we have within this organization, from finance through to ops director through to CEO to managing director, you should question what is it you do and is there a better way of doing it, is your time being used in a way that's to your own enrichment and to the business's benefit. That's really what this is all about. It's about questioning everything.

• •

FOUR-DAY WEEKS BOOST LONG-TERM HAPPINESS AND JOB SATISFACTION

A century ago at the Hawthorne Works in Illinois, industrial psychologists experimenting with ways of boosting productivity of factory workers thought they found a bunch of changes that increased productivity, but it later turned out that the workers were working harder because they knew they were being observed. Could productivity gains and reports of increased happiness at companies that shorten their workweeks be examples of the Hawthorne effect and thus wear off soon?

Fortunately, some of the companies that switched to four-day weeks have actually measured employee happiness and job satisfaction over time. When I visited Synergy Vision in London, managing director Eileen Gallagher had just compiled the results of their latest job satisfaction survey, which they had conducted throughout the company's six-month trial with four-day weeks. As she pointed out to me, happiness levels started out high, then actually dipped in the second month as people struggled with the reality of figuring out how to make four-day weeks work (something you wouldn't expect to see with the Hawthorne effect). In the third month, happiness bounced back and stayed high. After

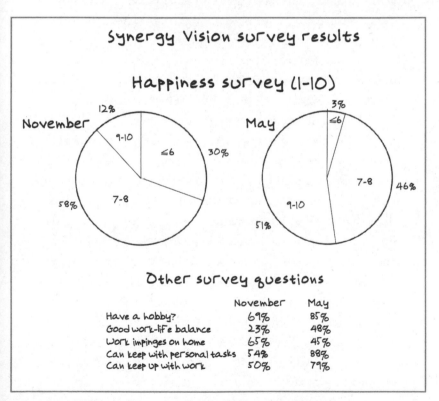

Happiness, work-life balance, and time pressure at Synergy Vision before and after moving to a four-day week.

six months, 97 percent of employees rated their happiness level as 7 or higher on a scale of 10. Even more impressive, the number of very happy people had increased more than fourfold: 12 percent had reported themselves a 9 or 10 at the beginning, but six months later, 51 percent did.

Even more amazing? The percentage of respondents who said they had enough time to get their work done went *up*, from 50 percent to 79 percent. Partly, this reflects more efficient time use, but there's also a psychological explanation: unbroken periods of time and deeper engagement with one's work produce a subjective sense of time passing more slowly. When people are more mindful about how they spend their hours and where they need to focus their attention, their sense of control over their time increases. Getting into the mental state that psychologist Mihaly Csikszentmihalyi calls "flow" also distorts one's sense of time: when you're more absorbed in a problem, time passes more slowly.

As for the productivity gains, some of these companies have been operating shorter workweeks for years now and have seen sustained increases in productivity. At Pursuit Marketing, for example, productivity levels are still higher than they were when the call center operated on a five-day week. Further, when you look inside the companies, it's pretty clear that the increases in productivity don't just result from simple changes imposed from the outside: cutting hours doesn't automatically raise productivity, even temporarily. Employees figure out how to make shorter hours work, and the changes they make aren't a psychological trick.

Finally, a 2017 Swedish study took a rigorous look at the longer-term impact of reduced working hours on happiness and quality of life. They took 636 public-sector workers employed in offices, nursing homes, call centers, and elsewhere and reduced their workweeks (but not salaries) by 25 percent; 75 percent lived with partners, and half were parents. Participants had to spend a week recording how they spent their time in time-use diaries right before the experiment began, nine months into the trial, and again nine months later. The researchers found that after nine months, most people were spending their extra time on domestic duties and relaxing hobbies, not taking second jobs or otherwise "spending" their free time on nonrestorative activities. Researchers also observed improvements in work-life balance, lower levels of work-home conflict, and less time overall spent in paid and unpaid work (in other words, domestic work and childcare didn't swell to take up all their free time). While picking up kids and cleaning the kitchen aren't usually considered restorative activities, the fact that participants had more time to do them, and that they could be completed without rushing, seems to have made even these chores less stressful. "Getting more time for domestic duties," the researchers speculated, "might make it easier to detach from obligations and relax" and "release more time for recovery activities during days off." After eighteen months, the numbers were unchanged: once people settled into their new patterns, they tended to stay there, and they continued to enjoy the same benefits.

FOUR-DAY WEEKS MAKE BETTER LEADERS

Moving to a five-hour workday has allowed Lasse Rheingans "to be the CEO I wanted myself to be for a long time but didn't have the power or the energy or the creativity because I was working all the time," he says. Shortening working hours creates challenges for leaders, but it also gives them space to become better leaders.

LEADERS ARE COACHES, NOT COMMANDERS

The four-day workweek changes the nature of leadership. When you preside over a company whose employees are acting more like owners, who are working more intensively, and who are questioning everything about how the company works, your role shifts from a commander to a coach.

In an interview with a Danish business magazine, Henrik Stenmann compares himself to a coach who schedules rest days for his best players, even though they want to always be on the field. In another interview, he says that the four-day week improves workers' ability to survive in today's fast-paced world. It's not the swiftest animal that survives but the most adaptable, and a four-day week gives workers space to evolve.

Sometimes the coaching is very direct. At Radioactive PR, "if one of the guys are still here at six, I'll go to them and say, 'What are you doing?'" Rich Leigh says. "If you're here now, and it's not an anomalous situation, your time management is off, and if your time management is off, how can I help you fix that?" Again, the phrasing—helping someone fix a problem rather than simply intervening—speaks of a coaching mindset, not a command mindset.

At other times, the coaching is built into the rhythm of the company. At Cockroach Labs, for example, Free Fridays isn't just about giving engineers time to simply play around with technology. "Engineers love to work on these problems," Spencer Kimball says, but because "it's hard to get them to moderate, to take a step back and a deep breath," they'll continue to obsess about problems well after they're sharp enough to solve them. Free Fridays helps them learn about how to better pace themselves when building new, complex technologies, and that even—or especially—when working on difficult problems, it's important to build in time for breaks and avoid burning yourself out.

• •

On Helping People Adjust to Shorter Hours

Lorraine Gray, Pursuit Marketing:

We have to continually reinforce with the team that there is no expectation for them to come in on Fridays at all, and we want them to walk away at half five on Thursday and enjoy those three days off. Everyone knows what success looks like in their own role; whether they're a telemarketer, they're in the IT department, finance department, digital marketing, they all do what's required of them to be profitable to the business and make bonuses and sales, and so they all leave on that Thursday knowing that they've achieved that. There should be no feeling of guilt or doubt that they're going to come in on Monday and be in trouble for not being in on Friday.

• •

As a leader, you have to move away from thinking in terms of getting the most **time** out of people (presumably as a way of wringing the most value out of them) and think instead in terms of getting the most **value** out of people. One of the ways you do that is by modeling good behavior.

"There have been times when I have heard back from other managers that people feel obliged to reply if I or the board email at the weekend," Ffyona Dawber says. "I had to actively stop doing this and put time delays on emails done at the weekend as I know it doesn't set a good example." As the head of Kin&Co, Rosie Warin knows that she sets the tone for her employees, and in a thirty-person organization, what the boss does is as important as what the policy says. Such personal examples are more important in an era when promotion and career advancement are harder and more uncertain, when people have to worry about being a good culture fit or demonstrating enough passion, and when corporate ladders have been broken and recycled into endless rounds of self-branding and freelance work.

FOUR-DAY WEEKS CREATE TIME FOR STRATEGIC THINKING

Implementing a shorter workday or week, moving the company to adopt it, and maintaining an environment in which it can be a benefit rather than a liability also requires leaders to think more clearly about both their own and their company's priorities, and know where the company should go.

At the daily level, this means not letting their inboxes take control of their day, and not letting other people's priorities determine theirs. At the company level, this means putting good work first, being very clear about goals around growth and revenues, and not demanding long hours in pursuit of a dream of market dominance, an IPO, or status as a billion-dollar valuation. Leaders have to have a clear vision of the company's norms and future that reflects their own priorities, not social expectations about how founders should act, or what they should want, or how to measure success. This in turn requires founders to think more about strategy and long-term goals.

Because they have to worry less about hiring and retention, crashed schedules, micromanagement, or emergencies, shorter days create more time for founders to think long term and to be more creative. In typical companies, long-term thinking is something that happens once or twice a year, often during a retreat or formal planning process, and integrating that perspective back into your daily work is a struggle. Monograph.io cofounder Robert Yuen notes that most of his fellow tech founders "take nights and weekends to strategize and do things that don't have immediate ROI." Since his company, which makes project management software for small architecture firms, takes Wednesdays off, "I have time during the week to do that. I don't have to wait till Saturday to ask, 'What happened this week? How do I strategize the next week?'" In a four-day week, you have time throughout the year to reflect and think about new products **and** pay attention to the weak signals that can indicate a downturn in the market or shift in consumer preferences. "When you're in a leadership role in the business, where you're having to constantly improve and change things, having time out when you've got time to just play with ideas in your own head, that's really important," Jonathan Elliot says.

FOUR-DAY WEEKS GIVE LEADERS MORE TIME TO BE CREATIVE

For Anna Ross, having "one day of creative thinking . . . gives me so much clarity around all of the things that I'd like to work on." It gives her time to think through new opportunities that she might not otherwise discover. Kester Black introduces new colors regularly, and Anna learned early on how extra time for reflection can help her be more aware of untapped markets. The company's sales grew substantially after she adjusted her nail polish formula so observant Muslim women could wear it—a change she made after a conversation with a customer about how conventional nail polishes are impervious to water and oil. "I really get to think things through" on her days off, and that gave time for the idea of water- and oil-permeable polish to incubate. (That kind of clarity is good for leaders and companies, but also for the health of workers. In a 2018 survey of tech workers, "poor leadership and unclear direction" was the top cause of burnout.)

Taking Wednesday afternoons off also helps Rosie Warin "be strategic and creative and calm and lead the business in a way that's created a lot of success for us." The habit of building free time into her day, recognizing the value of rest, and taking rest more seriously provides more time to think strategically and creatively. "Do you come up with better ideas at the end of a busy day or first thing in the morning after a walk?" she asks. "Your brain is meant to work more creatively when you're in a calm, rested place."

FOUR-DAY WEEKS BOOST LEADERS' HAPPINESS

Moving to a four-day workweek is also "an awesome challenge as a leader," Natalie Nagele says. "You get to say, 'I'm going to optimize for my team and for our happiness, but still grow the business.' Then you figure out, how can I do that?"

It's not just that the four-day week creates more space for leisure in entrepreneurs' busy weeks; its specific combination of focus, downtime, and control may be especially beneficial for founders. A 2012 study in the Philippines of entrepreneurs' coping strategies compared the value of "active coping"—tackling problems head-on when they come up— and "avoidance coping"—leaving problems and getting out of the office to unwind—to novice and experienced entrepreneurs. It found that experienced entrepreneurs benefited more from "avoidance coping"—for example, getting out of the office or doing things that took their minds off work—than novices. But researchers also found that entrepreneurs who combined active coping—like trying to solve problems—with avoidance coping had higher levels of well-being. Finally, they observed that it took several months for the benefits of combined active-plus-avoidance coping to become clear.

So four-day workweeks create new challenges for leaders and require a style of leadership that's more thoughtful and forward-looking. But they also create space for people to become better, happier leaders.

HOW PEOPLE SPEND THEIR FREE TIME

When I visited The Mix, several people explained how they spend their Fridays. Gemma Mitchell says, "I do all of my life admin. I get through all my laundry, go for a swim. It tends to be a quiet day in my life, and I enjoy that." (The term "life admin" came up in a number of interviews in the United Kingdom and Australia.) Having an extra day to get through your to-do list means that "on Saturday and Sunday I can do what I want rather than stuff that I have to do, which is so much better," says designer Kay Pollingsworth. Tash Walker makes marmalade. "It's a passion point of mine, but it is very time-consuming and very messy, so it's not an endeavor to be taken lightly," she says. "So it's nice to have a Friday to do it, otherwise your kitchen is a disaster zone until Sunday."

At other companies, some people take on side gigs. In Edinburgh, Administrate scrum master (and former rugby player) Iain Brown is becoming a personal trainer. In Sydney,

Insured by Us people and culture head Georgina Robilliard and a friend run a catering business called the Cheese Pair, while Kester Black's graphic designer does freelance work to build her portfolio and aims to launch her own studio. Given that Ross started Kester Black in her bedroom while working another job, she sees the ability to do those kinds of side projects as "a great freedom to pass on to my staff."

At Aizle, people are using their extra day to get back in shape. Stuart Ralston started running. "I've lost, like, twenty pounds already," he tells me. "Every single member of staff has begun to exercise," Jade Johnston says. "You see a big transformation in your life schedule and when you feel motivated and excited, you work so much better." That exercise-related boost in productivity is something that scientists have observed elsewhere. Swedish researchers compared the productivity of workers who reduced their working hours and engaged in mandatory exercise, and a second group that worked shorter hours but did not exercise. They found that both groups had higher productivity compared to colleagues who worked normal hours, but the group that exercised was more productive than the group that did not.

We often underestimate how physically draining knowledge work is, but during periods of deep concentration our brains demand increased quantities of food and oxygen, and stronger cardiovascular systems can better supply the brain. Exercise also reorients our attitude to stress: rather than recoil from it, our bodies and brains are less likely to shrink from stress, but meet it head-on. In almost every company that moves to shorter hours, people say they exercise more, feel better and healthier. At Pursuit Marketing, Sam Werngren has organized Friday walks on Munros, Scottish mountains that are over 3,000 feet tall. "If folk had to give up their Saturday for that, it'd be a lot harder to get any kind of team cohesion," he says, but "on a Friday it's a lot easier to get buy-in from the team, and to become pals outside of work as well as inside work." Henrik Stenmann says that since IIH Nordic moved to a four-day week, "I've lost ten kilograms because I've had time for exercise again. I'm more fresh and open, not so tired in the evening." With more energy and stamina, he marvels, "I work less, but I get more done. That sounds crazy, but it's true."

More exercise can also mean more time for new thinking. A number of founders have taken up running or cycling, because it provides time for reflection or mind-wandering. "I do my best work when I'm on the bike," Jonathan Elliot tells me. On the roads around Hobart, "you're in a meditative space, you've got the endorphins going," and during long rides he often finds answers to problems that eluded solution in the office. The day before we spoke, he says, "I resolved some things and came up with some bright ideas" during a two-hour ride. "If I was sitting in an office behind a computer, I wouldn't have done that."

Giving people more time for exercise also results in a drop in sick leave. "We've seen quite a significant reduction in sick leave" at The Mix, Gemma Mitchell says. "People are just getting a bit more rest, and they're able to be at the top of their game for four days." As a result, absenteeism dropped 75 percent in the first year after they introduced a four-day workweek. Pursuit Marketing's sick days fell from 1.3 days/person in the year before they moved to a four-day week to 0.5 days/person in the first year after. At Icelandic digital marketing consultancy Hugsmidjan, sick days dropped

44 percent after they shifted to a six-hour day in 2016. Less than 2 percent of employees at IIH Nordic now call in sick per year.

At Normally, having a four-day week gives people more time to look after themselves and others, which makes everyone better off. "I think that our four-day week makes us a much smaller burden on social services," Chris Downs says. "We require less National Health, because we are able to look after our mental and physical well-being." Employees spend less on childcare and can spend more time with elderly parents.

Indeed, for most of Normally, free time "is about taking care of someone," Marei Wollersberger says. "That someone can be yourself, and your own health and well-being. It can be children. It can be a parent who gets ill, and the person wants to spend more time with them."

"Absolutely," Chris agrees. "So yeah, if you summarize what people do with their fifth day? They care."

AT THIS STAGE . . .

The test phase gives you a chance to observe how your prototype has done, see how people build on and extend it, then decide whether it's worth further work, or whether you should return to business as usual:

- **Document new cultural and social norms.** People work in different ways when the workweek is shortened and learn to work with each other differently. They develop new rules and norms around things like managing collaborations, responding to interruptions, dealing with emergencies, and having breaks and meals together. It can be valuable to articulate these informal rules: it makes it easier for new hires to acculturate and supports thinking about how those ideas can be extended or modified with time.

- **Create an internal process for sharing new ideas.** Because people will often have their own particular enthusiasms—the person who tries lots of behavioral nudges might not test groupware, and the person who loves timers might not care about office design—it's essential to have a process for sharing experimental results with the company as a whole, whether via regular (brief) meetings, online tools, lunchtime talks, or even a TED-like miniconference of short talks.

- **Check in with clients.** Most people think it's essential to inform clients at the beginning of a trial period; it's often good to make sure you know their opinions of your work and relationship at the end of the trial as well, especially if yours is a business with more episodic contact with clients.

- **Look at your KPIs.** Review your initial KPIs and see how the organization has fared. Sometimes it's clear that the experiment has been a success on its original terms, sometimes there are additional indirect benefits that also weigh in favor of making the shift permanent, and sometimes there are unintended effects (on social life, for example) that weigh against shortening the workweek.

- **Make a decision.** At the end of the trial period, it's important to make a formal decision about whether to permanently adopt a shorter workweek, to have it as an option during summer hours, or to abandon it and return to normal working hours. If you don't adopt it, it's important for everyone to see that the decision is defensible. But a company that stays on shorter hours should continue to iterate and prototype, to test new tools as they become available, and to continue looking for ways to be even more efficient.

Throughout the trial, individuals have been sharing the results of experiments with new tools, worked together to improve group processes, and done the (sometimes difficult) work of redrawing the lines between personal, focused, and social life in the office. But it can also be valuable for people to share how the four-day week is changing their life outside the office.

- **Encourage people to share their stories.** Some larger companies set up internal discussion boards or group chats for workers to share word about what they're doing with their free time; smaller places can do this quickly and informally. These can be useful for organizing informal groups like the Munro climbers, seeing how other people spend their Fridays, or simply reassure people that, contrary to the signals they get from workaholic cultures, it's okay to take time off.

Of course, this is an idealized description of the entire process. In real-world cases, it's both more iterative and more improvisational: there's more back-and-forth between brainstorming, goal setting, prototyping, and testing, and steps can be rearranged and remixed according to a company's or industry's specific needs. Some companies realize early in the experiment that a shorter workweek is too good to abandon, companies vary widely in when they tell clients, and small companies can be more informal about sharing results and trying new things than large firms. It's important to make the process your own, and make it work for you.

6

Share

The last phase of the design thinking process is to tell the story of the process, to give a view of your product's journey. Sharing the story is a way of framing a product for your users and to help fellow designers learn from your experience.

In this chapter, we'll begin by sharing the story of how the four-day workweek has revived an especially unlikely establishment: Jinya, a traditional Japanese inn whose fortunes improved after it shortened its hours. Jinya is notable as a technical innovator, and for its efforts to make this traditional industry appealing to modern workers.

Those efforts point to an important part of the story of companies moving to four-day workweeks. Their solutions turn out to hold the seeds of a business revolution, a paradigm shift in how we think about work, productivity, time, and technology.

That paradigm shift, as we'll see in the final section, holds the promise of a better future of work. It could contribute to solving looming problems with an aging workforce, climate change, and automation and AI.

TSURUMAKIKITA, HADANO, JAPAN

The Jinya *ryokan* is a small inn located in Kanagawa prefecture, about an hour outside Tokyo. A ryokan is a traditionally styled guesthouse: think futons on tatami mats, hot-spring baths, multicourse kaiseki meals, and well-tended gardens. Some ryokans aren't just traditional but genuinely medieval: the oldest ryokan has been operating for 1,300 years. Jinya isn't quite that old; the property and oldest buildings only date from the twelfth century.

Owners Tomio and Tomoko Miyazaki have run the inn since 2009, when Tomio inherited it from his father. Tomio had grown up there, but neither he nor Tomoko had experience working in the hospitality industry when they took it over. The first year was hard: the inn was heavily in debt, operating expenses were weighing down the balance sheet, and the payroll had a hundred part-time employees. A couple months after they moved in, the global financial crisis started to hit the industry. Revenues at Jinya dropped 40 percent in the first year.

But the inn also had plenty going for it. Originally built for a prominent samurai family, it had all the ingredients for a great guest experience: an outstanding location near Tokyo and Yokohama, a grand hall for special events that was built in the late 1800s for a visit from Emperor Meiji, a picturesque Shinto shrine, and eight acres of inspiring garden and grounds. (As a child, Tomio's cousin Hayao played in a large camphor tree in the garden; it later inspired the magical tree in the classic animated film *My Neighbor Totoro*.) The Miyazakis stabilized the inn's finances over the next couple years and began modernizing operations.

"The whole environment was very analog" when they took over, Tomio says. "Only one person knew how to use

a computer." Reservations were still recorded in a big led-
ger. "When someone else was using the book, we couldn't
write down new reservations," Tomoko recalled in 2017,
and Tomio's mother kept track of return guests in her head.
Bookkeeping was a mess. Internal communication across
the eight-acre spread was patchy, and guests frequently complained about slow service. The fact that the entire ryokan
was operating in a pre-digital age meant that there was an
enormous amount of work to be done, but it also meant that
Tomio could put everything from reservations to internal
communication to billing on a single digital platform.

The problem was there was no such platform. Ryokans
aren't large enough to attract the attention of big IT companies, and most are family-run businesses that are traditional
and not very tech-savvy. So Tomio, who had studied engineering at Keio University and was a fuel cell researcher before he became an innkeeper, set out to create one. He built
a web-based app atop Salesforce Connect that combines accounting and inventory, online reservations and customer
information, billing, and a chat function. Staff could access
it through tablet computers and smartphones. Some employees struggled with the new system, but after integrating payroll and requiring everyone to log their hours on it, adoption
skyrocketed.

The impact on both management and customer service
was immediate. Tomio and Tomoko could monitor reservations and sales and get a near real-time sense of the inn's financial health. The online chat system eliminated the need
for all but very occasional staff meetings. Customer requests
could be queued and shared with the entire staff (an especially
useful feature, it turned out, for foreign guests who couldn't
communicate in Japanese). Dinner reservations and special
requests could be recorded during encounters with guests in

the hallway or during strolls in the garden. Information about guest allergies or food preferences was displayed on a monitor in the kitchen, so chefs could prepare custom meals.

Further, because they could communicate in real time, it was possible for staff to take on a wider variety of roles, which allowed the inn to consolidate some part-time jobs into full-time positions. At the same time, the Miyazakis didn't want the system to centralize decision-making. Traditionally, inns are run as matriarchies: employees wait to be told what to do, roles are tightly proscribed, and initiative is discouraged. The Miyazakis, in contrast, wanted a more distributed system in which employees could exercise their own judgment and work together to address guest requests. They soon realized that Tomio's system captured information about each guest's preferences and experiences, which they could use to improve service for return visitors. Less time delivering messages and performing formerly time-consuming duties also meant that staff could spend more time interacting with guests or handling special requests.

In Japan, there's a concept called *omotenashi*, which means anticipating a guest's needs and fulfilling them without being asked. By routing intelligence about guest needs between staff in real time and creating an institutional memory of each guest's stay, the digital platform was augmenting the inn's ability to deliver omotenashi.

Stabilizing the inn's fortunes, training staff on the new system, and improving service was hard work, and after several years, Tomoko, who had taken charge of daily operations, was feeling burned out. So in 2014, after they turned the corner and became profitable, they decided to close entirely on their slowest days, Tuesday and Wednesday nights. Revenues dropped 8 percent per year, but the lower gas and electricity bills more than offset the losses. Service also improved: full-time staff felt better rested, and turnover dropped. The inn also eliminated many part-time jobs, converted others into full-time positions, and started giving employees paid vacation, a novelty in the ryokan industry.

Two years later, in January 2016, Jinya started closing on Monday night. Working a more concentrated four-night schedule allowed them to further improve the balance sheet, services, and satisfaction among customers and staff. Closing to customers for several days gave staff the chance to train together, to do maintenance work, and to open the ryokan to film and TV crews without disturbing guests. The chefs had time to refine dishes and improve service. Tomoko developed a profitable wedding and reception business. Everyone had more opportunity to rest.

Tomio repackaged the IT platform as Jinya Connect, a commercial product, and started licensing it to other inns, charging a ¥100,000 installation fee and a monthly per-user fee of ¥3,500. The cloud-based system is now used in three hundred other inns, generates more than ¥200 million a year, and employs eighteen engineers. Voice recognition and speech-to-text was added in 2016 to make it easier for staff to record and share notes; the system can also keep track of social media posts by guests about their visits. It's also helped visitors: cross-country travelers can use the system to make reservations at several inns at once.

Those three hundred inns are also part of Jinya Expo, a social network and online marketplace. The Expo gives small, family-run inns—which have traditionally been geographically isolated and disconnected—a way to share advice, sell inventory, and post job announcements. It's also allowed for more complicated and interesting collaborations. Inns in the same region have banded together to buy supplies in bulk, allowing them to lower their expenses. Some seasonal facilities even share staff: summer resorts and ski lodges, for example, have made arrangements to use the same kitchen staff, allowing chefs and sous chefs to stay together for most of the year.

The experiments didn't stop with software and mobile devices. Underneath the carefully tended gardens and traditionally decorated rooms, Tomio started adding a layer of sensors that helps the staff manage the property and guests. An automated license plate reader identifies guests as they drive in and sends alerts to the doorman and receptionist, allowing customers to be greeted by name and automatically checked in. Sensors keep track of the number of people using the *onsen* (a public bath fed by a spring on the property) and alerts staff to replace towels or if there's a problem with water temperature or level in the bath. Sensors in the hallway alert staff when guests are leaving, so they can be greeted. Tomio has formed a partnership to develop commercial IT systems for hotels and other small businesses.

As a result, the inn's revenues have grown and diversified. The inn made ¥290 million in 2009, almost all from guests. In 2018, it made ¥613 million from guests, banquets, and special events. Even though they now charge more per night, the inn's average occupancy rate has risen to 76 percent, nearly twice the national average. Jinya Connect and Expo made another ¥200 million. And even though they increased the number of full-time staff—average salaries rose from ¥2.88 to ¥3.98 million (well above the industry average)—overall labor costs have dropped 25 percent and employee turnover has dropped below 4 percent.

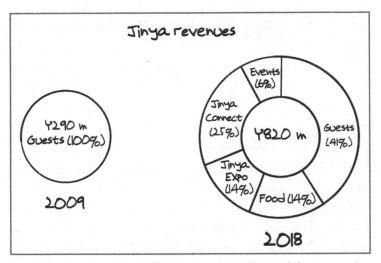

Jinya revenues, by category. The inn hasn't just survived despite moving to a four-day week; it's been able to diversify and prosper because it moved to a four-day week.

An inn whose roots date back to the European Middle Ages might not be an obvious place to prototype the future; it's like the Tower of London opening a tech incubator and maker space. But Jinya illustrates how companies that have moved to four-day workweeks are using their free time to improve service and staffing, create new products, and prototype a future for work that is happier, fairer, and built for the long term.

A decade after narrowly avoiding bankruptcy, the Miyazakis now see the inn as more than a test bed for new software. "I want to promote a way of working that can accommodate different stages of life, such as child-rearing and nursing care, for the entire industry," Tomoko told a reporter in 2018. "I'm aiming to make inns an industry in which people long to work."

BUILDING A NEW PARADIGM FOR WORK

Tomoko's evolution from struggling innkeeper to workplace evangelist is not unusual. During many of my interviews with company founders and leaders, our conversations start out grounded in the practical realities of strategy and operations, but move into more cultural or philosophical territory. Both Mark Merrywest and Emily West explain that flocc's six-hour day is but one expression of the company's quest for *lagom*, a Swedish word that roughly translates as "not too much, not too little." Henrik Stenmann says that IIH Nordic's four-day week was no longer "just about being closed on Fridays. It's more like a Nordic way of working. It's about the things that make four days working possible, and about working in better ways with better tools, not just working less." Pernille Garde Abildgaard, a Danish journalist who's written about the company, observes that their four-day week is shaped by, and in turn reinforces, "deep values in most Nordic workplaces: trust between boss and employees, a flat hierarchy, a huge focus on work-life balance, a desire for stable structures, and the pursuit of collective solutions. Almost nothing is to be forced, but we find the best solutions together."

Some talk about shorter hours as a way to moderate contemporary capitalism's winner-take-all ethos. Through most of our conversation, Tower Paddle Boards founder Stephan Aarstol sounds like an unsentimental, bottom-line kind of CEO—"I'm a capitalist, I'm looking at the five-hour day as a business owner who's trying to squeeze as much productivity out of my workforce as I can," he says at one point—but even he worries that too many companies are "trying to pay workers less and less, then automate what jobs they can and just squeeze more work out of them, while using the idea that the sixty-hour workweek makes you a true American." A shorter workday, he reflects, is the kind of "very tangible benefit" that workers need to see after decades of flat wages and growing inequality. (Indeed, even after Amazon entered the market and Tower's paddleboard sales plummeted from $7.5 million in 2016 to $1.5 million in 2019, Aarstol resisted giving up the five-hour day entirely. Instead, they switched to a "summer hours" model, working five-hour days from June through September, and diversified into other businesses. They converted part of their harbor-front office building into an event space, entered the electric bikes market, and launched a new business marketplace for other direct-to-consumer companies.)

Redesigning the workday often stimulates a bigger reconsideration within companies of how and why we work. A leader who wants to implement a four-day workweek must be willing to "rethink everything they think is an absolute truth, and then set out to test their assumptions, to challenge them, and to see if they're right," Marei Wollersberger says. "The five-day week is just one of them." Once they've opened the door to this kind of radical reimagining, she continues, "management must create the space and time and environment where people can experiment and find what works for them."

For many, what begins as a very practical exercise in solving specific, urgent problems in recruitment and retention, work-life balance, gender inequality, and sustainability leads to new ways of thinking about work, time, and leadership, and new ways of structuring the relationship between companies, workers, and technology. Framing the problem as a design challenge helps drive better schedules, more thoughtful management, more open communication, and smarter

tools. Implementing those changes, in turn, nudges companies to change how they think about attention, time, and
technology. In the course of shortening the workweek, companies lay the groundwork for a revolution in work.

That may sound overly dramatic, but history teaches us
that only in politics are revolutions sudden, noisy, violent affairs. In business, art, technology, and science, they're more
incremental. In most fields, revolutions start with solutions.

I was struck by this idea while standing in Liverpool
Street Station, a Victorian-era railway station a few blocks
from Normally. In the mid-nineteenth century, architects
lavished most of their attention on the classical or Gothic
passenger halls, and enclosed the trains and tracks with util-
itarian iron-and-glass vaults. They weren't trying to invent
a new visual language for an accelerating age, or create an
ironic juxtaposition of styles; they were satisfying the demands of public taste while solving a difficult engineering
problem in the most practical and economical means available to them. But for architects like Rennie Mackintosh and
Frank Lloyd Wright, who came of age at the end of the century, the sheds in back were the interesting part of the design: they demonstrated how iron and glass could be used to
create a new architectural style free from the burdens of the
past—a rational, scientific, and entirely modern architecture.
Mackintosh's and Wright's work, in turn, inspired the radical minimalism and functionalism of the Bauhaus and International Style in the 1920s and 1930s. The end result was a
revolution in architectural style, but one that unfolded incrementally, over decades.

The railway station was also the front end of a commercial and logistical system of unprecedented size and complexity that triggered revolutions in information management,

finance, and law. Coordinating millions of passengers, thousands of trains, daily deliveries of freight and fuel, capital, and workers created a demand for new managerial tools and information technologies. Railways were early adopters of novelties like the electrical telegraph, carbon paper, and filing systems, and they helped give birth to modern capital markets, regulatory agencies, and antitrust law—more revolutionary innovations that grew incrementally.

Finally, the railways changed how we think about time. In order to coordinate schedules and avoid collisions, railroads encouraged the adoption of standardized time services and time zones. Time ceased to be a local phenomenon. Seattle and San Diego, London and Lisbon, Munich and Milan now shared the same time. The problem of coordinating time across thousands of miles, of making all the clocks in a network strike the hour at exactly the same instant—and knowing that you had succeeded—turned out to be exceptionally hard, and building timekeeping systems for railroads occupied the efforts of many clockmakers, especially in Switzerland. These designs passed through the patent office in Bern, where they were read by a young examiner with a keen interest in time. Albert Einstein saw that clockmakers' efforts raised profound questions about how time and space are related. When he published his famous article on the theory of special relativity, Einstein used the problem of coordinating railroad network time as an illustration of the broader problem of measuring time and space.

Companies that redesign the workweek are moving from solving immediate problems with recruitment, work-life balance, and productivity to inventing new structures in time, writing new rules for how we work, and changing how we solve problems in the workplace and how we share the benefits of those solutions. They're building a new paradigm for business.

What are the features of this new paradigm?

1. **Leaders define problems; everyone solves them.** Companies can't shorten working hours without support from leaders, but leaders can't shorten working hours without engaging workers. No single person knows enough to successfully redesign a company's workday; you need to involve everyone. Conversely, no one but the CEO or owner can set a company on the path toward a shorter workday and make a final decision about whether to permanently adopt a shorter workday. This is a model for a more fluid, contingent style of strategy and decision-making in which commanders set goals, but teams figure out how to execute them.

2. **Focused hours beat long hours.** In today's business world we think of the best, most dedicated workers as the ones who put in long hours at their desks, and the best managers as the ones who are able to motivate their employees to stay late. This is backward. Anyone can sit in a chair for twelve hours, and workers who habitually put in long hours need coaching, not awards. Companies shortening their working hours prioritize focus over time: a few hours of intense concentration or highly effective teamwork is far more valuable than a long, less focused day. They also recognize the effectiveness of matching tasks and times to circadian rhythms, the natural rise and fall in our capacity for concentration and decision-making. Time is valuable, but not all hours are equally valuable.

3. **Boundaries are good.** Acknowledging the value of focus also means recognizing the importance of detachment and giving people time to recharge. During the day, having clearer divisions between focused time, time for less intensive activities, and social time raise the quality of all three. Likewise, days at work and days off are both improved if you're not always on and don't have to take work home. Finally, boundaries help temper passion, slow burnout, and encourage people to take a more sustainable approach to their careers.

4. **Attention is social.** We normally think of attention as something that happens between brains, eyes, and screens. But attention is actually social. It requires uninterrupted time—continuous, unbroken, and free from outside interruptions. My ability to focus depends on your willingness to not interrupt me and vice versa. Companies that fail to create preserves for attention, that break up the day with meetings and events, and that put workers in physical and online environments that amplify distractions undermine workers' efforts to concentrate on tasks that matter most. In workplaces that value attention, interruptions are the new smoking.

5. **Efficiency gains belong to workers.** Companies that move to four-day weeks have a social contract with workers: if you figure out how to redesign the workday and operate more efficiently, you get to keep the time savings. This provides an incentive for workers to sharpen their own skills, learn how to use existing technologies more effectively, and collaborate with coworkers to redesign processes, schedules, and

calendars. It provides a guarantee that workers won't be made redundant if they succeed in automating the easier parts of their jobs and allows them to become more valuable employees by deploying technologies to augment their more challenging tasks.

6. **Build superstructures, not just superpowers.** In today's workplace, we're taught to look for personal and bespoke solutions to problems with work-life balance, productivity, and burnout. The problem is, these solutions are unequally distributed (professionals and executives are more likely to get them), carry unintended consequences (ask any woman fighting flexibility stigma), and force us to take personal responsibility for failure while insulating the system from accountability. To make a success of the four-day week, we have to recognize that everyone is confronting the same challenges, and that we can solve them more efficiently—for everyone—by changing the system. Collective action is more important than personal improvement. Shorter hours require everyone to work more effectively, work together better, and reward everyone equally. Don't lean in, organize.

7. **Ask questions, then find answers.** Moving to a shorter workweek encourages you to challenge conventional wisdom, ask basic questions, and root out the obsolete logic behind everyday, taken-for-granted practices and products. But it also gives you the chance—even the obligation—to **answer** these questions too. You have to complain less and prototype more.

8. **Customers are your allies.** Customers naturally have lots of questions about your trial, but if you can explain

it well, they can be important allies in your quest for shorter working hours, supporting you during the trial, helping you stay on track, and providing feedback about your work. Everyone faces challenges today with work-life balance, talent development, and sustainability and worries about even bigger disruptions on the horizon. The fact that you're prototyping a way to solve these issues makes you more valuable than ever.

9. **Communicate openly and intelligently.** Redesigning the workweek is a group effort, and it requires a lot of communication about everything from logistics and best practices to social norms and company culture. At an everyday level, teams have to communicate well to coordinate their work more quickly and become more efficient. But they also have to be thoughtful: communication at the wrong times becomes a distraction.

10. **Never stop evolving.** Companies never stop changing: people come and go, new competitors appear, tastes change, and markets evolve. Smart leaders recognize this and always try to push their companies to avoid complacency and stay open to new things. One of the benefits of the design thinking process is that it helps people and companies become comfortable with continuous change.

This new paradigm not only offers leaders and companies a set of principles that can improve workplaces and working life today; they can help address some of the most pressing problems business, labor, and all of us will face in the future.

IMPROVING THE FUTURE OF WORK

The idea of using innovations in time and technology to improve work couldn't be more timely or necessary. There's a widespread unease with the way work has evolved over the last few decades, and what's going to happen to it. We deal every day with problems like overwork, work-life balance, the gig economy, matching the demands of work and family, and the mismatch between the passion we're expected to display at work and the loyalty companies feel themselves obliged to return.

These connect to bigger problems with globalization and inequality. Globalization has produced increases in the living standards of many. But it's also hollowed out older industries, decimated the economies and prospects of entire regions, and allowed elites to emerge, grow fabulously wealthy, and insulate themselves from the global economy's worst problems and predations.

We also have to deal with the backlash against globalization and neoliberalism taking the forms of populism, rising nationalism, and new forms of authoritarianism. Climate change and environmental destruction are problems we have to start dealing with now, and which we and our children will have to deal with for decades to come.

And, on the horizon and closing in fast, artificial intelligence and robotics are poised to further transform our daily lives and work, our workplaces and companies, and markets and economies.

This is a critical time to think about the future of work, about how individuals and society think about jobs, about the place work has in our lives, and about how we share the benefits of labor, productivity, and automation.

The four-day workweek can help us tackle all these issues. It addresses many of our everyday personal problems with work today. It can be part of our strategy for addressing the unequal distribution of wealth between elites and workers, the unequal spread of wealth between geographical regions, and the challenges industries and economies will face as workforces grow older. A shorter workweek can help alleviate work's impact on energy consumption and the environment. And it provides a model for how we can use AI and robotics to augment and increase productivity, improve workers' lives, and preserve jobs, not destroy them.

HEALTH AND HAPPINESS

Four-day workweeks could improve physical and mental health in developed economies. We no longer light up in the office like in the *Mad Men* days, but today's smoke-free offices expose workers to other risks: bad management, economic insecurity, overwork, work-family conflict, and burnout contribute to high levels of hypertension, chronic stress, anxiety, alcohol and drug abuse, and heart disease.

Four-day workweeks improve physical health by giving people more time for recovery, exercise, and self-care. They increase happiness by reducing work-home conflict and giving people more time for friends and social activities.

Redesigning work also results in better-run, better-led, healthier workplaces. By giving people more control over how they work, four-day workplaces also increase happiness and job satisfaction. Studies of high-pressure occupations have long found that people who have higher levels of control over their work are happier and less stressed than those who have less control. (This is even true in dangerous professions: during World War II, even though they had far higher mortality rates, fighter pilots had higher morale than bomber pilots. Why? Fighter pilots had more control over how and where they flew than bomber pilots.)

Redesigning the workday to set aside regular time for focused work may also have an indirect effect on employee happiness. A series of studies by York University business professor Ronald Burke and his students helps explain why. In studies of Egyptian and Turkish workers, they find that work **intensity**—for example, how hard you work, rather than how many hours you're on the job—can have a positive effect on employee well-being. Another study, this time of hotel managers in China, found that people who put in seventy or more hours per week score higher on measures for work-related "Passion" and "Addiction" than people who work normal hours. However, those who score higher on Passion are less obsessive, more satisfied with their jobs, and have happier home and personal lives than those who score higher on Addiction. By designing work that explicitly prioritizes intensity instead of overwork, and encourages people to find ways of working that bank rather than burn through their passion, companies on four-day schedules end up producing happier employees.

A survey of New Zealand trusts company Perpetual Guardian also provides some measure of how moving to a four-day workweek influences social and psychological factors related to work, performance, and well-being. University of Auckland professor Jarrod Haar surveyed executives and employees before and after the trial. He found that team psychosocial capital and cohesion—both of which predict the ability of groups to work together productively, as well as job satisfaction and well-being—were higher after the four-day-week trial than before, as well as team creativity. Employees reported higher readiness to change, job satisfaction, and engagement, and improved capacity to achieve work-life balance—all of which further boosted workplace happiness.

Shortening the workweek can also improve the lives and well-being of entrepreneurs. Entrepreneurship can present substantial mental health challenges. A team led by University of California San Francisco professor Michael Freeman has found that half of entrepreneurs have at least one mental health condition and have significantly higher than normal rates of depression and other issues. Founder burnout is a major factor in 65 percent of new company failures.

Clinical psychotherapist Paul Hokemeyer estimates that up to 80 percent of entrepreneurs "struggle with a host of personality disorders such as narcissism, sudden wealth syndrome and the impostor syndrome," as he wrote in 2019.

Founders are more likely to deal with serious mental health issues:

Depression	30%	2x*
ADHD	30%	2x
Anxiety	27%	same
Substance abuse	12%	3x
Bipolar disorder	11%	10x

*compared to the general population

Founders of companies may deal with substantial mental health issues and are far more prone to some problems than the general population.

pparently, demanding long hours and huge sacrifices from employees, dealing with enormous pressure from investors to deliver gigantic returns, living with intense uncertainty and social isolation, treating burnout as an occupational hazard and self-care as contemptible weakness, and then suddenly being showered with rock-star levels of praise and wealth doesn't encourage great mental health.

How can shorter hours help improve the mental health of entrepreneurs? Founders often report spending more time with family when they shift to four-day weeks and exercising more regularly. A study of Swedish entrepreneurs explains why this is a sensible strategy. Kristina Gunnarsson and Malin Josephson tracked the happiness and well-being of a group of 246 Swedish entrepreneurs for five years, measuring their physical health, mental health, job satisfaction, working hours, and how they spent their time outside work. They found that the most important factor influencing happiness was social life: a wide circle of friends and active social lives translated into higher levels of social support—especially important for company heads who have few peers at work—and greater ability to mentally detach from work. The second most important was exercise.

AGING SOCIETIES AND WORKFORCES

The four-day workweek could be good for aging workforces and countries. In developed countries, the average age of workers is rising as birth rates decline, life spans increase, and retirement becomes less predictable. Globally, the percentage of people sixty-five or older in the workforce grew dramatically between 1990 and 2015, and the growth of older workforces is especially pronounced in countries like China, the United States, and the United Kingdom.

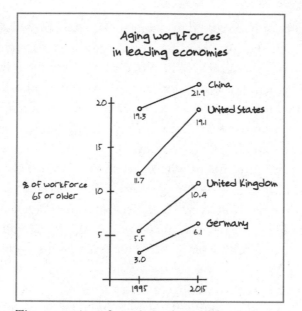

The proportion of people in the workforce who are sixty-five and older is growing in most developed countries. Partly, this reflects nationwide demographic changes: there are fewer young workers and more older people healthy enough to work. But it can also be driven by inadequate retirement savings, labor policies that encourage older workers to stay employed, and other factors.

As more older workers stay employed, national workforces are getting older. In the United States, according to the Bureau of Labor Statistics, the proportion of the American workforce that's under fifty-five has been dropping since the mid-1990s (and the percentage of workers under twenty-five peaked in the 1970s). In 2024, 8 percent of the American workforce will be sixty-five or older, and 18 percent of the workforce will be fifty-five or older. Older workers stay at work longer and are less likely to retire at sixty-five, either because they can't afford to or they don't want to. Japan's

Ministry of Internal Affairs estimated in 2018 that 12.4 percent of the Japanese workforce is already sixty-five or older, and 20 percent of the nation's population is seventy or older.

These trends will continue. According to the World Health Organization, global average life expectancy increased from sixty-six and a half years in 2000 to seventy-two years in 2016. Children born in Japan and Singapore in 2019 have an estimated life expectancy of over eighty-five years; in most European countries, life expectancy is over eighty; in the United States, it's seventy-nine. Not only are people living longer, they're enjoying a higher quality of life and greater health later in life. Our assumptions about how careers, lives, and livelihoods unfold—with people completing their formal education in their teens or twenties, working full-time jobs until their sixties, and then living off their pensions—don't work very well now, and will completely break down in a world in which people are physically and mentally capable into their eighties or nineties, and can reasonably live to be one hundred. The model where you work enormously long hours in your twenties in an effort to become rich enough in your thirties to retire before you burn out in your forties won't make any sense at all.

Economists worry that aging countries have to deal with ever-rising social welfare costs and lower levels of national productivity. By delaying retirement and keeping people healthier, the four-day workweek would help ease pressure on pensions and lower health-care spending. By allowing people to stay employed longer, national productivity levels would rise.

Further, making it possible for people to stay in jobs and professions that they enjoy will increase happiness more than forcing people into retirement. Good work can be a huge source of meaning and satisfaction in people's lives. As the cellist Pablo Casals wrote in his autobiography, "Work helps prevent one from getting old." Even at ninety-three, he argued, "The man who works and is never bored is never old. Work and interest in worthwhile things are the best remedy for age."

Cognitive scientists talk about the "use it or lose it" hypothesis, which argues that cognitive ability is like a muscle: if you don't exercise it continuously it will atrophy, but if you push it too hard you risk injury. A number of studies have found that older people who are still working or otherwise active are physically and mentally healthier than those who are not active. An Australian study suggests that working reduced hours not only helps older workers stay employed and productive, but working a few hours a day can also have a positive effect on cognitive aging—that is, the rate of mental decline. A 2016 Australian study found that people over forty who work up to twenty-five hours a week perform better on cognitive function tests than those who work full-time or don't work at all.

Stanford Center on Longevity director Laura Carstensen argues that we should see careers as marathons rather than sprints, and that such careers would make it easier to move in and out of work when children are young or as parents get old and to stay engaged in the workplace longer. The four-day workweek would make that possible by allowing us to work more sustainably, for more of our lives. By making long hours and overwork less valuable or desirable, it would also create greater equality between younger and older workers. Finally, the challenge of continually figuring out how to further shorten working hours—by learning new tools, automating routine processes, and being more discerning in how you manage your work—can be of particular benefit to older workers. Sociologists argue that "job crafting," the ability to change how you work and the scope of your work, can help older workers adjust their jobs so they can remain engaged and productive.

TRAFFIC AND COMMUTING

Moving to a shorter workweek could have a significant effect on commuting times and traffic.

For individuals, a four-day workweek can mean a significant reduction in traffic time. When Toyota Center Gothenburg introduced a six-hour day, they found that commuting during off-peak periods cut mechanics' daily commute times in half. In large cities like New York, Mexico City, Rio de Janeiro, and Los Angeles, people who take public transit to work spend two hours or more per day commuting, and those working in large buildings can spend additional minutes waiting for elevators. American workers with an average one-way commute of twenty-seven minutes would save nearly two full days per year in commuting time if they moved from a five-day to a four-day workweek. They would also generate less air pollution (driving generates about 25 percent of all air pollution) and be healthier because they were exposed to less of it.

Regional or national adoption of shorter working hours would give policy makers a tool for reducing congestion and pollution. Staggering government and business working hours to ease congestion has been tried in a number of cities, generally with mixed success, but it has yet to be tried in combination with reduced working hours, which would give companies more flexibility in scheduling when the workday begins and ends. In the Philippines, the government has debated a bill to allow employees to work a four-day week to help workers deal with long commutes and eternal traffic jams in Manila. In Mumbai, India, where three thousand people are injured on overcrowded commuter trains every year, the railway ministry suggested moving to a four-day workweek and staggering working hours to alleviate congestion and make commutes safer.

ENVIRONMENTAL IMPACTS

Reducing working hours could also lead to substantial reductions in carbon emissions and energy consumption. As one study of working hours and energy use in OECD countries put it, "working hours are significantly associated with greater environmental pressures." As countries lengthen their workweeks and people work more hours, they consume more energy and expand their carbon footprints: one study found that a 1 percent increase in working hours raises energy use by up to 1.3 percent, carbon footprint by 1.3 percent, and overall environmental footprint by 1.2 percent. Researchers estimate that by reducing commuting, lowering workplace energy use, and other effects, adopting a four-day workweek would cut a nation's carbon emissions by between 16 and 30 percent (though the higher range assumes that wages would also fall). One Swedish study concluded that reducing working hours to an average of thirty hours per week by 2040 "would result in a significantly slower growth of energy demand, which would also make it easier to reach climate targets." An American study that looked at the impact of reduced working hours on global temperatures to 2100 estimates that reducing average annual hours by 0.5 percent per year "would very likely mitigate one-quarter to one-half, if not more, of any [global] warming which is not yet locked-in" (that is, already bound to happen in the coming decades given the amount of carbon currently in the atmosphere) and reduce global temperatures by 0.2 to 1.2 degrees centigrade.

But doesn't having more free time also mean having more free time for energy- and carbon-intensive activities— driving to the mountains to ski, or jetting to the city for a long weekend, or flying home to visit family? The risks are lower than you'd think, for a couple reasons. First, people spend their newly won free time locally, on things like life admin, exercise, and time with family. Second, studies indicate that as a general rule, people are actually less likely to engage in energy-intensive activities and consumption when they have more free time. A 2013 study of working hours and consumption found that long working hours lead households to consume more energy-intensive goods: they eat more frozen and packaged foods, order out more often, and are more likely to use cars or taxis. When people have more free time, they're more likely to cook for themselves, walk or bicycle, and have more time to plan more energy-efficient activities. Greater time stress also correlates to more energy- and materially intensive leisure activities, not less: people who work long hours are more likely to vacation abroad rather than close to home and go on all-terrain vehicle adventures rather than hikes. (Such choices are reinforced by social norms within hard-charging companies, in energy consulting firms, it's more acceptable to take a three-week vacation in the South Pacific than to take an afternoon off with one's young children.)

REGIONAL DEVELOPMENT

Henrik Stenmann argues that IIH Nordic's four-day work-week represents a "Nordic style" of working, one that uses technology and intelligent management to achieve a more balanced life. For companies in locations like Tasmania and central England, a shorter workweek can draw workers from metropolitan centers. This points to a potential role that four-day weeks could play in the future as a tool for regional differentiation, or for attracting workers back to economically struggling regions.

In Korea, a group of companies in an industrial hub in the southeastern province of Gyeongbuk has announced a plan to move to four-day weeks to attract workers from Seoul. The provincial governor described it as an effort "to create advanced labor culture and create jobs."

One Japanese company sees the four-day workweek as a tool for attracting people back to rural areas that have struggled to retain companies and workers. Kunisaki Time—a fifteen-person company that makes 3-D mannequins, animals, and other objects from cardboard—has operated on a 4/8 schedule since 2013. Yuki Matsuoka first developed the method of applying CAD to designing patterns that could be laser cut on cardboard in 1995; after three years of trying to license the patent, he founded his own company in 1998. Since then, his designs have been featured in commercial and art exhibitions, museums, and department stores in Tokyo, Berlin, and New York.

For Yuki, the decision to move Kunisaki Time to a four-day week was driven by equal parts philosophy, geography, and economics. The remote, rural province of Oita, where Yuki was born and where Kunisaki Time is based, has become more connected to the rest of Japan in recently decades (Sony, Sharp, and other electronics companies started making semiconductors, chips, and sensors there in the 1970s), yet its population is aging and shrinking; in fact, the company is located in an elementary school that closed for lack of students. Yuki sees the four-day week as a way to attract talent that otherwise would stay in Tokyo, Kobe, or Nagoya. More profoundly, it's a way to "create a 'new life' for [the next] generation" that builds on "the culture and unique times of this land," drawing in new talent without disrupting the region's slower, more natural rhythm, Yuki told a Japanese retailer. A four-day week also suits creative industries that locate to the country: it gives people more time to "go hiking, fishing, read, or do whatever we want," while it also "leads to individual skill development and improves business efficiency." For Yuki, it's a way to renew people, to renew work, and to renew the region.

TECHNOLOGICAL INNOVATION

Like all businesses, companies that have moved to four-day workweeks rely on technology to help workers be more productive and efficient, to improve communication and collaboration between workers, to give leaders the data they need to manage effectively, and to coordinate with clients. But their adoption and use of technology has distinctive features that are worth noting, because they offer clues about how we can more effectively and humanely bring new technologies into the workplace of the future.

First, they use technologies to augment workers' cognitive and physical abilities, not to replace workers. New technologies can be deployed to augment and extend the senses, strengths, and skills of humans, and thus to help preserve human jobs and work, or they can be designed to replicate human abilities, pit machines against people, reduce capital's need for labor, and ultimately destroy human jobs and work. When Blue Street adopts DocuSign, Farnell Clarke moves to cloud-based accounting systems, and Normally uses collaborative software, they do so with the aim of helping individuals and teams work faster.

Second, because companies moving to four-day work-weeks give workers the power to adopt and experiment with new tools, they are letting workers own the means of production (and algorithms and data). IIH Nordic's bottom-up approach to technological innovation, which gives programmers the freedom to try out new methods and practices, gives workers a lot of power in the workplace. When workers own their own technologies, they're more likely to prosper, to become more skilled over time, and to seek out opportunities for higher-value work. Further, mastering and using well-designed technologies is itself a source of satisfaction. Not only does designing for augmentation reduce technology-driven unemployment, it makes for better, happier workers.

Techniques that emphasize augmentation and worker ownership are worth paying attention to because they offer a design template for creating the next generation of AI and robots. For the last several years, a vigorous debate over the future of work has centered around whether these technologies will eliminate jobs or will ultimately create new and better kinds of work. So far, the record has been mixed. Consider two very different impacts of new technology on two medical specialties, radiology and surgery. Traditionally, radiologists were some of the most highly skilled doctors on hospital staffs, and radiology fellowships were long and highly coveted. But online systems that allowed overseas doctors to read X-rays at a fraction of the cost of American doctors, and more recently by machine vision systems that are proving more accurate than professionals, have made radiology less attractive to young physicians choosing their specialties.

At the same time, robotic surgical systems have allowed specialists to operate on patients thousands of miles away, or to handle emergency surgery in field hospitals. But they haven't replaced surgeons; instead, the technologies have been incorporated into surgical practice, and new specialties in laparoscopic and robotic surgery have flourished in the last decade. Surgery is a physically and socially complex enterprise; even a routine surgical procedure requires teams of doctors, nurses, and other specialists (even the people who clean operating rooms can be specially trained) working together.

Cooking or working on a new ad campaign is like surgery: both require a mix of technical skill, collaboration, and cooperation. Indeed, lots of apparently "simple" work turns out to be fiendishly complex once you look at it closely. For these kinds of jobs, the best routes to technologically enhanced increases in productivity will come in designing and applying tools that help already-skilled workers do their jobs better, rather than trying to create systems to replace workers. Companies that have moved to four-day workweeks show that by giving workers the freedom to innovate and more control over how new technologies are chosen and adopted, we can avoid a dystopian scenario in which new technologies hollow out tens of millions of jobs, and instead create a future workplace that preserves jobs, improves work, and makes companies more productive.

THE SPREAD OF THE MOVEMENT

In the last year, interest in the four-day workweek has grown considerably. Some of the interest comes from well-publicized examples like New Zealand–based Perpetual Guardian, whose founder, Andrew Barnes, has become a public advocate of shorter hours. Perpetual Guardian first trialed a four-day week in March 2018 and adopted it permanently in July. Nine months later, another eighteen companies in New Zealand in a variety of industries had adopted four-day weeks. Dozens of companies contacted Tash Walker after The Mix published a report on their experiences with the four-day week, and of those "perhaps twenty or thirty," she says, had tried it themselves by July 2019. Urban clusters of companies switching to shorter hours are also popping up. In Edinburgh, two restaurants followed Aizle in adopting four-day weeks in 2019: the Michelin-starred 21212 and the new restaurant Fhior. The town of Norwich, England, has three companies—Farnell Clarke, flocc, and Curveball—that have adopted a six-hour day, and they've shared notes about their respective experiences. Gothenburg, Sweden, has seen experiments with six-hour days in local government, an academic hospital, a nursing home, and in the Toyota repair center.

Four-day workweeks are also spreading organically within industries. In the restaurant industry, chefs who discover the four-day week while working at places like Noma and L'Astrance are starting their own restaurants and bringing the four-day week to the restaurant scene in new cities. The movement to experiment with shorter hours is spreading to more casual restaurants now too. Baumhower's Victory Grille is an Alabama chain of sports-themed restaurants owned by former pro football player Bob Baumhower. In late 2018, facing industry-wide challenges in keeping good staff in the kitchen and front office, the chain started offering four-day weeks to its managers and cooks. As Baumhower said in a 2018 article, "Allowing our managers to have the life-work balance they desire while being able to better serve our guests" is "a no-brainer. It's funny how ideas come to you, and you wonder to yourself—'Why didn't we do this years ago?'" Fast-food chain Shake Shack announced that it was trialing a four-day week for managers at its Las Vegas location in March 2019 and extended the program to other stores on the West Coast later that spring.

The companies I've described have adopted the four-day workweek for their own reasons: to increase recruitment, decrease turnover, support work-life balance and sustainability, boost creativity, and so on. Government regulation hasn't played a role in their decisions, but in the future states could play a bigger role in promoting the four-day workweek.

In Europe, unions and political parties in Belgium, Denmark, and Sweden have proposed transitioning to a four-day or thirty-hour week as a response to automation or to help working parents with young children. The UK Trades Union Congress made the case for a four-day workweek in late 2018; the next year, groups within the UK Labour Party proposed that the party embrace a four-day workweek. In some countries, union agreements now mandate that workers over fifty-five have the option to work flexible hours.

These efforts could make the four-day workweek more widespread in Western countries. An even bigger wild card is China. In early 2019, the northern province of Hebei floated a proposal for businesses and local governments to close on Friday afternoons, in an effort to stimulate domestic consumption and leisure spending. This followed a 2018 Chinese Academy of Social Sciences proposal to shift the entire country to a four-day workweek by 2030. It outlined a ten-year ramp-up period, with state-owned enterprises in cities like Shanghai, Chongqing, and Beijing moving to a four-day week from 2020, and other regions and industries moving to four-day weeks from 2025. The four-day week, the report argued, would help maintain productivity of an aging workforce; nudge the country toward more spending on services, leisure, and tourism; and make it easier for parents to stay in the workforce.

By then, economists predict, China will have a population of 1.45 billion people. It will be the world's largest economy, and Asia will be the engine of the global economy. (Of the world's five largest national economies in 2030, four—China, India, Japan, and Indonesia—could be in Asia.) China will set the example for economic growth and corporate behavior in the twenty-first century, and if it shifts to a four-day week, it may be difficult for the rest of the world not to follow. Foreign companies working with Chinese businesses will fall into synchrony with them, while competing businesses will be pressed to imitate them. (In the nation's early years, Israel's workweek started on Sunday and finished on Friday afternoon, before the Sabbath. Now, though, most Israeli software companies work Monday through Friday, in order to coordinate with American and European clients.)

If moving a giant economy to a new workweek sounds impossible, remember this: China has done it before, and not that long ago. On May 1, 1995, after eight years of studies and a year of trials, the nation's workweek shifted from six days to five—and the economy continued to grow by double digits. China is not the only country in living memory to have shifted to a five-day week. Countries in Scandinavia, famous now for their relaxed working hours and work-life balance, officially adopted five-day weeks in the 1960s. Korea moved to a five-day week in the 1970s, and in 2018 passed legislation capping most workweeks at fifty-two hours. Just as the five-day week and eight-hour day became the global standard in the twentieth century, China's adoption of the four-day week in 2030 would make it the standard in the twenty-first.

CONCLUSION

In an interview with Australian author Kura Antonello, Kester Black founder Anna Ross said, "We work four days a week because, after a three-day weekend, anything is possible." For a long time, a four-day week has seemed impossible. The pervasiveness and sheer familiarity of overwork; the diversity of cultural, psychological, organizational, and economic forces that drive or defend it; and the absence of notable exceptions to the cult of busyness all combine to make overwork seem natural and inevitable.

But companies are discovering that it **is** possible to create new and more balanced ways of working. By redesigning their days and eliminating distractions and busywork, providing more uninterrupted time for intensive focused work, planning and managing projects and work processes to avoid surprises and the need for overtime, respecting the need to detach from work, and trusting that downtime will make workers more productive and effective on the job, companies like IIH Nordic, Zozo, Woowa Brothers, Noma, Normally, and Cockroach Labs illustrate that it's possible to shorten the workday or workweek without losing productivity, sacrificing revenues or profitability, or ceding ground to the competition.

The four-day workweek also offers internal, cultural benefits. It provides an unusually clear incentive for experimenting with new ways of working, adopting new technologies, finding ways of automating routine tasks, and building a more productive culture. It reveals that attention and job satisfaction have an important and usually overlooked social dimension. It encourages people to see the challenges of juggling parenting and career, and of finding work-life balance, as structural issues rather than merely personal quests. It reorients leaders' attitudes toward time and encourages them to treat overwork not as a sign of dedication but as an indication of inefficiency or a symptom of organizational sickness. The four-day workweek provides a way to share productivity gains between companies and workers, in a manner that makes the connection between better work and more time crystal-clear. In an era when critics of neoliberalism and globalization point out that working-class wages have remained flat for decades, and even professional work suffers from increasing uncertainty, programs to reduce working hours offer workers the one truly irreplaceable resource: more time.

The diversity of companies that have already made the leap to four-day weeks, the variety of industries they're in, and the range of countries in which they're located shows that while it's still small, this is a global movement, and it's growing. (In the day before I wrote this conclusion, two more companies announced that they were starting four-day-week trials!) It's time that we treat them as early adopters, study their examples, and learn from their experience. It's time to work a four-day week, because when you do, anything is possible.

Acknowledgments

A book like this is only possible if people are willing to tell their stories, answer your questions, share documents, and show you around their offices and restaurants. I'm grateful for the generosity of the people who are making shorter workdays a reality: Stephan Aarstol, Rafat Ali, Jen Anderson, Helen Andrews, Iain Brown, Patrick Byrne, Lee Carnihan, Bruno and Christie Chemel, Jonathan Cook, Paul Corcoran, Ffyona Dawber, Gretchen DeVault, Chris Downs, Atemad El-Berjiji, Jonathan Elliot, Linus Feldt, Joi Foley, Alex Gafford, Eileen Gallagher, Steve Goodall, Lorraine Gray, Jessica Gregory, Jhanvi Gudka, Michael Honey, Warren Hutchinson, Jade Johnston, Vicki Kavanaugh, Frances and James Kay, Kenn Kelly, Bong-Jin Kim, Spencer Kimball, Marek Kříž, Grace Lau, Lokman Lau, Oliver Lawer, Rich Leigh, Gemma Mitchell, Mark Merrywest, Natalie Nagele, Yumika Nakane, Ho Nam, Ikuo Nishina, Chad Pytel, John Peebles, Kay Pollingsworth, Stuart Ralston, Lasse Rheingans, David Rhoads, Georgina Robilliard, Anna Ross, Jin Ryu, Jan Schulz-Hofen, David Scott, John Sloyan, Daniel Spencer, Henrik Stenmann, Jason Stockwood, Ross Tavendale, Annie Tevelin, Chris Torres, Amritan Walia, Tash Walker, Rosie

Warin, Sam Werngren, Emily West, Marei Wollersberger, and Robert Yuen.

I'm also grateful to Pernille Garde Abildgaard, Lawrence Ampofo, Hope Bastine, Isabel Behncke, Katie Bell, James Berman, Monika Cheney, Heejung Chung, Michael Aaron Dennis, Paul Dickinson, Maaike Dijkstra, Paula Ganhão, Nils Gilman, Alexandra Goldstein, Lynda Gratton, Adrian Harper, Lyn Jeffery, Paul Kim, Nataly Kogan, Christopher Lindholst, Hamish Macaskill, Gloria Mark, Jack Muirhead, Roy Pak, Mark Rice-Oxley, Lena Rübelmann, Bansri Shah, Daljit Singh, Thomas Söderqvist, Lord Dennis Stevenson, Will Stronge, Clive Thompson, Greg Vlahos, James Wallman, Ed Whiting, and Juliana Wölfsberger for their advice, feedback, and encouragement. In Japan, Akira Takauchi and Momoku Tokushige helped greatly with logistics and local arrangements. In Korea, Hyungsub Choi acted as interpreter and local guide, while Angela Kim translated a number of articles.

My thanks as always to Zoë Pagnamenta, Alison Lewis, and Jess Hoare at the Zoë Pagnamenta Agency. Colleen Lawrie at PublicAffairs and Martina O'Sullivan at Penguin Business offered critical editorial advice from the first word to the last.

Finally, my eternal gratitude to my wife, Heather, and to my children, Elizabeth and Daniel, who I hope will work in a world where the four-day week is business as usual.

Appendix

Companies Studied for This Book

This list includes the companies researched and described in this book.

Companies with an asterisk (*) beside their name experimented with shorter hours but have returned to normal working hours.

Companies working four-day weeks operate eight-hour days (for a total of thirty-two hours per week) unless noted. I've also noted the companies that combine shorter hours and flexible schedules, or combine four-day weeks with Free Fridays, days when the office is open and people are free to work on personal projects or professional development.

While restaurants included in this list work four-day weeks, their days often last far longer than eight hours—but working four twelve-hour days is still a big improvement over working five or six.

Name	Country	Industry	Schedule
21212	UK	Restaurant	Four-day week
10 Minds Breo	Korea	O2O	Thirty-five-hour week
Administrate	UK	Software	Four-day week
Advice Direct Scotland	UK	Call center	Four-day week
AE Harris	UK	Manufacturing	Four-day week (thirty-six hours)
Agent Marketing*	UK	Marketing	Four-day week
Aizle	UK	Restaurant	Four-day week
Aloha Hospitality	US	Restaurant	Four-day week
Aniar	Ireland	Restaurant	Four-day week
AO Pasta	Canada	Restaurant	Four-day week
APV*	Hong Kong	Video	Four-day week
atrain	Hong Kong	Consulting	Four-day week
Attica	Australia	Restaurant	Four-day week
Background	Sweden	Software	Thirty-hour week
Barley Publishing House (보리출판사가)	Korea	Publishing	Four-day week
Bauman Lyons*	UK	Architecture	Four-day week
Baumé	US	Restaurant	Four-day week
Bell Curve	US	Software	Four-day week
Big Potato Games	UK	Board games	Four-day week
Bike Citizens	Austria	Magazine	Four-day week
Blue Street Capital	US	Finance	Twenty-five-hour week
Bråth AB	Sweden	Software	Thirty-hour week
Century Office	UK	Furniture	Thirty-two-and-a-half-hour week
CLiCKLAB	Denmark	Digital marketing	Four-day week

Name	Country	Industry	Schedule
Cockroach Labs	US	Software	Four-day week + Free Fridays
Collective Campus	Australia	Incubator	Thirty-hour week
Collins SBA	Australia	Accounting	Twenty-five-hour week
Creative Mas	Korea	Advertising	Four-day week
Curveball Media	UK	Animation and film	Thirty-hour week
Cybozu	Japan	Software	Four-day week + flex
Devonshire Arms	UK	Restaurant	Four-day week
Devx	Czech Republic	Software	Four-day week
Doctor Travel (여행박사)	Korea	O2O	Four-day week
DVQ Studio*	US	Marketing	Four-day week
Elektra Lighting	UK	Design	Four-day week
Elisa	Estonia	Telecom	Thirty-hour week
ELSE	UK	Design	Four-day week + Free Fridays
eMagnetix	Austria	O2O	Thirty-hour week
Enesti (에네스티)	Korea	Cosmetics	Four-day week
Enoteca Sociale	Canada	Restaurant	Four-day week
eSmiley	Denmark	Food safety	Four-day week
Farnell Clarke	UK	Accounting	Thirty-hour week + flex
Fhior	UK	Restaurant	Four-day week
Filimundus*	Sweden	Software	Thirty-hour week
flocc	UK	Marketing	Thirty-hour week

Name	Country	Industry	Schedule
Geranium	Denmark	Restaurant	Four-day week
Gimm-Young Publishers (김영사)	Korea	Publishing	Thirty-five-hour week
Goodall Group	UK	Marketing	Four-day week
Graf Miville	Switzerland	Marketing	Four-day week
Hugsmidjan	Iceland	Marketing	Thirty-hour week
Icelab	Australia	Software	Four-day week + flex
IIH Nordic	Denmark	Software	Four-day week
Indycube	UK	Coworking	Four-day week
Ingrid & Isabel*	US	Fashion	Four-day week
Insured by Us	Australia	Insurtech	Four-day week + flex
Intrepid Camera	UK	Manufacturing	Four-day week
J & CoCeu	Korea	Cosmetics	Four-day week
Jinya	Japan	Hotel	Four-day week
Kai Cafe	Ireland	Restaurant	Four-day week
Kester Black	Australia	Cosmetics	Four-day week
Kin&Co	UK	Advertising	Thirty-five-hour week
Kunisaki Time	Japan	Manufacturing	Four-day week
Lara Intimates	UK	Fashion	Four-day week
Maaemo	Norway	Restaurant	Four-day week
Mahabis*	UK	Fashion	Four-day week
Marquette	US	Nursing home	Four-day week
Model Milk	Canada	Restaurant	Four-day week
Monograph	US	Software	Four-day week
MRL Consulting	UK	Consulting	Four-day week
n/naka	US	Restaurant	Four-day week
Noma	Denmark	Restaurant	Four-day week

Name	Country	Industry	Schedule
Normally	UK	Creative agency	Four-day week
ntegrity	Australia	Marketing	Four-day week
Ogada	Korea	Restaurant	Thirty-five-hour week
OX Restaurant	Northern Ireland	Restaurant	Four-day week
Perpetual Guardian	NZ	Financial/legal services	Four-day week
Pigeonhole	Canada	Restaurant	Four-day week
Planio	Germany	Software	Four-day week
Pursuit Marketing	UK	Call center	Four-day week
Raby Hunt	UK	Restaurant	Four-day week
Radioactive PR	UK	Marketing	Four-day week
Reflect Digital	UK	Marketing	Four-day week
Relae	Denmark	Restaurant	Four-day week
Rheingans Digital Enabler	Germany	Software	Twenty-five-hour week
Riordan ((주)리오단은)	Korea	Vitamins	Four-day week
Rockwood Leadership Institute	US	Nonprofit	Four-day week
Sat Bains	UK	Restaurant	Four-day week
Satake Corporation	Japan	Manufacturing	Four-day week
Shake Shack	US	Restaurant	Four-day week
Simply Business	UK	Insurance	Four-day week
SkinOwl	US	Skin care	Twenty-four-hour week
Sugar Helsinki	Finland	Marketing	Four-day week + Free Fridays
Suprema (슈프리마에이치큐)	Korea	Electronics	Thirty-five-hour week

Name	Country	Industry	Schedule
Svartedalens Nursing Home	Sweden	Nursing home	Four-day week
Synergy Vision	UK	Health care	Four-day week
Team Elysium	Korea	Med tech	Four-day week
The Glebe	US	Nursing home	Thirty-hour week
The Mix	UK	Creative agency	Four-day week
thoughtbot	US	Software	Four-day week + Free Fridays
Tourism Marketing Agency*	UK	Marketing	Thirty-hour week
Tower Paddle Boards	US	O2O	Twenty-five-hour week
Toyota Center Gothenburg	Sweden	Automotive	Thirty-hour week
Treehouse*	US	Software	Four-day week
Type A Media	UK	Marketing	Four-day week
Unterweger	Austria	Cosmetics	Four-day week
Utah state government*	US	Government	Four-day week (forty hours)
VERSA	Australia	Marketing	Four-day week
Wildbit	US	Software	Four-day week + flex
With Innovation (위드이노베이션)	Korea	O2O	Thirty-five-hour week
Woowa Brothers (우아한형제들)	Korea	O2O	Thirty-five-hour week
Work It Daily	US	HR	Thirty-five-hour week
Zipdoc (집닥)	Korea	O2O	Thirty-five-hour week
Zozo	Japan	O2O	Thirty-hour week

Bibliography

Except where noted, quotes from founders and employees come from interviews I conducted with them in 2018 and 2019. Other sources for quotes, statistics, and background material are below.

INTRODUCTION

Stephan Aarstol discusses Tower Paddle Board's transition to a five-hour day in his book, *The Five-Hour Workday: Live Differently, Unlock Productivity, and Find Happiness* (Lioncrest, 2016).
What's Wrong with Work. Bertrand Russell writes about the future of work in "In Praise of Idleness," *Harper's*, October 1932, https://harpers.org/archive/1932/10/in-praise-of-idleness. Working hours from 1870 to 1950 were estimated by Michael Huberman and Chris Minns, "The Times They Are Not Changin': Days and Hours of Work in Old and New Worlds, 1870–2000," *Explorations in Economic History* 44, no. 4 (October 2007): 538–567, https://personal.lse.ac.uk/minns/Huberman _Minns_EEH_2007.pdf. Statistics on temporary, gig, or zero-hour jobs are from the Bureau of Labor Statistics (United States), Trade Union Council (United Kingdom), Lancers (Japan), Korea Labor and Society Institute (Korea). On the costs of overwork for individuals and companies, see John Pencavel, "The Productivity of Working Hours," *Economic Journal* 125, no. 589 (December 2015): 2052–2076, https://doi .org/10.1111/ecoj.12166; Jeffrey Pfeffer, *Dying for a Paycheck:*

How Modern Management Harms Employee Health and Company Performance—and What We Can Do About It (New York: Harper Business, 2018). Statistics on overwork are from the OECD Better Life Index, 2019, http://www.oecdbetterlifeindex.org /topics/work-life-balance/. On women and stress in part-time work, see Tarani Chandola et al., "Are Flexible Work Arrangements Associated with Lower Levels of Chronic Stress–Related Biomarkers? A Study of 6025 Employees in the UK Household Longitudinal Study," *Sociology* 53, no. 4 (August 2019): 779–799, https://doi.org/10.1177/0038038519826014. On labor force participation rates of mothers, see "Labor Force Participation: What Has Happened Since the Peak?" *Monthly Labor Review* (September 2016), figure 8, www.bls.gov/opub/mlr/2016 /article/pdf/labor-force-participation-what-has-happened -since-the-peak.pdf.

CHAPTER 1

Sowol-Ro, Seoul, South Korea. Bong-Jin Kim talks with Sam Kim in "Coming Soon to Seoul: Robot-Delivered Jajangmyeon Noodles," *Bloomberg*, February 27, 2019, www.bloomberg .com/news/articles/2019-02-27/coming-soon-to-seoul-robot -delivered-jajangmyeon-noodles; he talks about being a designer-CEO in *Digital Insight Today*, www.ditoday.com/articles /articles_view.html?idno=14603, translated by Angela Kim.

Design Thinking. Good introductions to design thinking are Tim Brown, *Change by Design: How Design Thinking Transforms Organizations and Inspires Innovation* (New York: Harper Business, 2009), and Michael Lewrick, Patrick Link, and Larry Leifer, *The Design Thinking Playbook: Mindful Digital Transformation of Teams, Products, Services, Businesses and Ecosystems* (New York: Wiley, 2018). The case for shortening working hours has been made recently in Rutger Bregman, *Utopia for Realists: How We Can Build the Ideal World* (New York: Little, Brown, 2017); Stan De Spiegelaere and Agnieszka Piasna, *The Why and How of Working Time Reduction* (European Trade Union Institute, 2017); and Will Stronge and Aidan Harper, eds., *The Shorter Working Week: A Radical and Pragmatic Proposal* (Autonomy,

2019), http://autonomy.work/wp-content/uploads/2019/01
/Shorter-working-week-final.pdf.

CHAPTER 2

The Companies. The restaurant industry's struggles are frequently discussed in industry magazines; a good entry point is Kat Kinsman's website Chefs with Issues (http://chefswithissues.com). On the survey of the restaurant industry, see Katherine Miller, "It's Time to Speak Out on the Kitchen's Toll: Addressing Mental Health in the Restaurant Industry," James Beard Foundation website, June 20, 2018, www.jamesbeard.org/blog/its-time-to -speak-out-on-the-kitchens-toll. On stress in advertising, see Shareen Pathak, "No Slack on Weekends: Agencies Look for Ways to Tackle Employee Burnout," *Digiday*, March 13, 2019, https://digiday.com/marketing/agencies-employee-burnout; Pippa Chambers and Mariam Cheik-Hussein, "Reduce Stigma and Provide Support; Adland's Mental Health Task," *AdNews*, April 9, 2019, www.adnews.com.au/news/reduce-stigma-and -provide-support-adland-s-mental-health-task; Rebecca Stewart, "Two-Thirds of Marketers Have Considered Leaving Industry Because of Poor Workplace Wellbeing," *Drum*, February 20, 2018, www.thedrum.com/news/2018/02/20/two-thirds -marketers-have-considered-leaving-industry-because-poor -workplace. For the tech industry, see Nate Swanner, "Depression Far Too Common Among Tech Pros: Survey," *Dice*, December 5, 2018, https://insights.dice.com/2018/12/05/depression -tech-pros-common-study, and Stack Overflow Developer Survey Results 2019, https://insights.stackoverflow.com /survey/2019/.

The Leaders. Anna Ross's 2016 quote comes from Kate Stanton, "From Unhappy Employee to Successful Entrepreneur," *BBC News*, March 6, 2016. On Ryan Carson, see Richard Feloni, "This Tech CEO and His Employees Only Work 4 Days a Week," *Business Insider*, June 23, 2015; Ryan Carson, "Begin With the End in Mind," talk given at Adobe's 99U conference, May 5–6, 2016, https://99u.adobe.com/videos/53977 /ryan-carson-begin-with-the-end-in-mind. Cybozu CEO

Yoshihisa Aono describes his ambitions in Nicole Jones, "What a Radical Japanese Tech Company Can Teach Us About Retaining Happy Employees," blog post on *Kintone* website, July 25, 2016, https://blog.kintone.com/business-with-heart/what-a-radical-japanese-tech-company-can-teach-us-about-keeping-employees-happy. Japanese Ministry of Labor statistics on four-day weeks are cited in Masumi Koizumi, "Japanese Companies Warming Up—Slowly—to Four-Day Workweek," *Japan Times*, February 12, 2019, www.japantimes.co.jp/news/2019/02/12/reference/japanese-companies-warming-slowly-four-day-workweek/#.XXaVOZNKhEI. Gallup's 2017 survey of email use is summarized in Frank Newport, "Email Outside of Working Hours Not a Burden to U.S. Workers," *Gallup*, May 10, 2017, https://news.gallup.com/poll/210074/email-outside-working-hours-not-burden-workers.aspx. Esben Holmboe Bang discusses sustainability at his Food on the Edge 2017 talk, at https://youtu.be/m3jasqTAZcQ. William Becker is quoted in "Mere Expectation of Checking Work Email After Hours Harms Health of Workers and Families," *EurekAlert!/American Association for the Advancement of Science*, August 10, 2018, www.eurekalert.org/pub_releases/2018-08/vt-meo080618.php.

CHAPTER 3

Tanner Street, London, England. While my account of The Mix's experience draws on interviews and site visits, Tash Walker and The Mix have also written about their experience with four-day weeks: see Walker, "4 Days a Week," LinkedIn, July 26, 2018, www.linkedin.com/pulse/4-days-week-tash-walker/, and their 2019 report, *Four: What Is It Good For?*, http://themixlondon.com/fourdayweek.

First Impressions. On Cambridge University project on "The Employment Dosage" and working hours and well-being, see Daiga Kamerāde et al., "A Shorter Working Week for Everyone: How Much Paid Work Is Needed for Mental Health and Well-Being?" *Social Science & Medicine*, June 18, 2019, https://doi.org/10.1016/j.socscimed.2019.06.006. Ben Shewry describes the shift at Attica in his talk, "No More Cock-Rock," at the

2018 MAD Symposium: Food on the Edge, www.madfeed. co/video/no-more-cock-rock-ben-shewry. Natasha Gillezeau writes about "The Burnout Generation" in the *Australian Financial Review*, July 12, 2019, www.afr.com/work-and-careers /careers/the-price-of-burnout-culture-20190531-p51t68. The Kin&Co survey of companies and Warin's comment are from Phillip Inman and Jasper Jolly, "Productivity Woes? Why Giving Staff an Extra Day Off Can Be the Answer," *Guardian*, November 17, 2018, www.theguardian.com/business/2018/nov/17 /four-day-week-productivity-mcdonnell-labour-tuc, and https:// wednesdayoff-ternoon.com/the-research/.

Choosing Which Day to Eliminate from the Workweek. There is a large literature on the impact of sleep deprivation on judgment and decision-making, which I summarize in my book *Rest: Why You Get More Done When You Work Less* (Basic, 2016), 280–282. William Dement's comment on law enforcement is from Bryan Vila, *Tired Cops: The Importance of Managing Police Fatigue* (Washington, DC: Police Executive Research Forum, 2000), xiv. On Utah state government energy and carbon savings during its four-day week, see Jenny Brundin, "Utah Finds Surprising Benefits in Four-Day Workweek," *NPR Morning Edition*, April 10, 2009, www.npr.org /templates/story/story.php?storyId=102938615, and Alex Williams, "To Fight Climate Change, Institute Three-Day Weekends," *Quartz*, October 10, 2016, https://qz.com/770758/how -three-day-weekends-can-help-save-the-world-and-us-too.

Company Profile: AE Harris. Russell Luckock writes about AE Harris in Graeme Brown, "Post Columnist Russell Luckock Looks Back on 60 Years of the Newspaper," *Birmingham Post*, September 17, 2014, www.business-live.co.uk/news /local-news/post-columnist-russell-luckock-looks-7839675, and Luckock, "Four-Day Week Has Triumphed," *Birmingham Post*, December 10, 2010, www.business-live.co.uk/business /russell-luckock-four-day-week-triumphed-3925111.

Free Fridays. On the worldview of software developers, see Clive Thompson's *Coders: The Making of a New Tribe and the Remaking of the World* (New York: Penguin, 2019), and Ellen Ullman,

Close to the Machine: Technophilia and Its Discontents (New York: Picador, 2012).

Shorter Hours Versus Flexible Time. My thinking about flexible work and its challenges draws on the work of sociologist Heejung Chung, in particular her "'Women's Work Penalty' in Access to Flexible Working Arrangements Across Europe," *European Journal of Industrial Relations* 25, no. 1 (March 2019): 23–40, https://doi.org/10.1177/0959680117752829; "Gender, Flexibility Stigma, and the Perceived Negative Consequences of Flexible Working in the UK," *Social Indicators Research* (November 2018): 1–25, https://doi.org/10.1007/s11205-018-2036-7; Chung and Yvonne Lott, "Gender Discrepancies in the Outcomes of Schedule Control on Overtime Hours and Income in Germany," *European Sociological Review* 32, no. 6 (December 2016): 752–765, https://doi.org/10.1093/esr/jcw032; Chung and Mariska van der Horst, "Women's Employment Patterns After Childbirth and the Perceived Access to and Use of Flexitime and Teleworking," *Human Relations* 71, no. 1 (January 2018): 47–72, https://doi.org/10.1177/0018726717713828.

Metrics and Key Performance Indicators. Martin Banck describes Toyota Center Gothenburg's thirty-hour week in his 2015 talk at Woohoo's International Conference on Happiness at Work, "Introducing a 30-Hour Work Week at Toyota Gothenburg," available online at https://youtu.be/aJUEXPP0Hao; see also Liz Alderman, "In Sweden, an Experiment Turns Shorter Workdays into Bigger Gains," *New York Times*, May 20, 2016, www.nytimes.com/2016/05/21/business/international/in-sweden-an-experiment-turns-shorter-workdays-into-bigger-gains.html.

FAQs, Scenarios, and Contingency Plans. On SK Group's experiments with the four-day week, see Young-jin Oh, "4-Day Work Week in Korea: SK Starts with Hope, Doubt," *Korea Times*, May 21, 2019, www.koreatimes.co.kr/www/nation/2019/05/356_269248.html, and Jung Min-hee, "SK Group Introduces 4-day Workweek System," *Business Korea*, May 22, 2019, www.businesskorea.co.kr/news/articleView.html?idxno=32088. The Wellcome's flirtation with four-day weeks is recounted in Ed Whiting, "Investigating a Four Day Week—3 Things We Did, 3 Things We Learned," LinkedIn, April 25, 2019, www.linkedin.com/pulse/investigating-four-day-week-3 -things-we-did-learned-ed-whiting.

CHAPTER 4

Redesign the Workday. On efforts to shorten the workweek in the 1960s, see "Four-Day Week," *CQ Researcher*, August 11, 1971, https://library.cqpress.com/cqresearcher/document.php?id =cqresrre1971081100; Janice Neipert Hedges, "A Look at the Four-Day Workweek," *Monthly Labor Review* 94, no. 10 (October 1971): 33–37. For more on walking meetings, see Pang, *Rest*, 94–97, 275–276. On meetings at Zozo, see "Doubt the Obvious: Aiming to Introduce the Six-Hour Workday," Toyo Keizai, n.d., https://toyokeizai.net/articles/-/18028 (translated for the author by Alexander Steullet). On Roombot, see the video "O3 Roombot: Keeping Meetings on Schedule" at https://youtu.be /CdgjBYYKHRI.

Defragment the Workday. For more on flocc, see Emily West's talk at SyncNorwich, "Lagom—Just the Right Amount (Of Work!)," at https://youtu.be/HY7gLFCzK3o. The relationship between circadian rhythms and focus, and the ways creative people have adapted working schedules to them, is described in Pang, *Rest*, especially 53–92. Yeon-ju Ahn is quoted in "Woowa Brothers: Elegant Goddesses," *Women Economy*, December 31, 2017, www.womaneconomy.kr/news/articleView.html ?idxno=56240 (translated for the author by Angela Kim). On judgment in open offices, see Art Markman, "Your Open Office Is Causing Your Coworkers to Judge You More Harshly," *Fast Company*, January 24, 2019, www.fastcompany.com/90295000 /your-open-office-is-causing-your-coworkers-to-judge-you -more-harshly. Big Potato's schedule is described in Hazel Sheffield, "Why Four-Day Working Weeks May Not Be the Utopia They Seem," *Wired*, September 16, 2019, www.wired.co.uk /article/four-day-work-week-analysis.

Redesign Technology. On email and distraction, see Gloria J. Mark et al., "'A Pace Not Dictated by Electrons': An Empirical

Study of Work Without Email" in *Proceedings of the SIGCHI Conference on Human Factors in Computing Systems* (New York: ACM, 2012).

Company Profile: Farnell Clarke and Cloud-Based Accounting. Will Farnell discusses Farnell Clarke's work in a May 27, 2017, interview, "Will Farnell from Farnell Clarke Accountants Talks About Company Culture," at https://youtu.be/m72uVR4ZDqc. Gallup's 2018 survey on friendships at work is described in Annamarie Mann, "Why We Need Best Friends at Work," Gallup, January 15, 2018, www.gallup.com/workplace/236213/why -need-best-friends-work.aspx.

Redesign Sociability. René Redzepi talks about restaurant staff eating together in "Culture of the Kitchen," MADfeed, August 19, 2015, www.madfeed.co/2015/culture-of-the-kitchen-rene -redzepi/. The survey on workplace attitudes toward lunch is summarized in Joanna Hein and Weber Shandwick, "Tork Survey Reveals Lunch Break Impact on Workplace Engagement," Tork, May 16, 2018, www.torkusa.com/about/pressroom/tbtlb. On shared meals and fire station morale, see Kevin M. Kniffin et al., "Eating Together at the Firehouse: How Workplace Commensality Relates to the Performance of Firefighters," *Human Performance* 28, no. 4 (2015): 281–306, https://doi.org/10.1080 /08959285.2015.1021049.

Give Employees Control. On the IKEA effect and examples of control improving satisfaction, see Michael I. Norton et al., "The IKEA Effect: When Labor Leads to Love," *Journal of Consumer Psychology* 22, no. 3 (July 2012): 453–460, https:// doi.org/10.1016/j.jcps.2011.08.002; Farah Mohammed, "Why We Pay to Do Stuff Ourselves," *JSTOR Daily*, August 16, 2019, https://daily.jstor.org/why-we-pay-to-do-stuff-ourselves; Craig Knight and S. Alexander Haslam, "The Relative Merits of Lean, Enriched, and Empowered Offices: An Experimental Examination of the Impact of Workspace Management Strategies on Well-Being and Productivity," *Journal of Experimental Psychology: Applied* 16, no. 2 (June 2010): 158–172, http://dx.doi .org/10.1037/a0019292; John J. Zentner, *The Art of Wing Leadership and Aircrew Morale in Combat*, CADRE Paper 11 (Maxwell

Air Force Base, AL: Air University Press, 2001), https://media
.defense.gov/2017/Nov/21/2001847044/-1/-1/0/CP_0011
_ZENTNER_ART_OF_WING_LEADERSHIP.PDF.

CHAPTER 5

How Clients React. Bauman Lyons architects documented their
experience with the four-day week at https://baumanlyons
architects.wordpress.com.

Four-Day Weeks Improve Performance. Esben Holmboe Bang's
Food on the Edge 2017 talk is at https://youtu.be/m3jasq
TAZcQ.

**Company Profile: The Glebe: Using Thirty-Hour Weeks to
Lower Nursing Turnover and Improve Care.** Ellen D'Ardenne is quoted in Tim Regan, "CCRC to Pay Full-Time for
30 Hours of Work for CNAs," *Senior Housing News*, March 30,
2018, https://seniorhousingnews.com/2018/03/30/ccrc-pay
-full-time-30-hours-work-cnas; see also James M. Berklan,
"Aid for Aides: 40 Hours' Pay for 30 Hours' Work," *McKnight's
Long-Term Care News*, April 5, 2018, www.mcknights.com/daily
-editors-notes/aid-for-aides-40-hours-pay-for-30-hours-work;
Lois A. Bowers, "CCRC Tests 8-Hour Pay for 6-Hour Day,"
McKnight's Senior Living, April 3, 2018, www.mcknights
seniorliving.com/home/news/ccrc-tests-8-hour-pay-for-6-hour
-day. Emilie Telander is quoted in Maddy Savage, "What Really
Happened When Swedes Tried Six-Hour Days?" BBC News,
February 8, 2017, www.bbc.com/news/business-38843341. On
law firms, flexible work, and retention, see Cynthia Thomas
Calvert et al., *Reduced Hours, Full Success: Part-Time Partners
in U.S. Law Firms* (The Project for Attorney Retention, 2009);
Ivana Djak, "The Case for Not 'Accommodating' Women at
Large Law Firms: De-Stigmatizing Flexible Work Programs,"
Georgetown Journal of Legal Ethics 28 (2015): 521–546.

Women and Flexible Careers. On the challenges and financial
penalties of flexible work and career breaks, the Timewise study
is cited in "Two Thirds of Female Professionals Are Estimated to
be Working Below Their Potential When They Return to Work
from Career Breaks," PwC press release, November 14, 2016,

pwc.blogs.com/press_room/2016/11/two-thirds-of-female
-professionals-are-estimated-to-be-working-below-their
-potential-when-they-retur.html; the 2017 KPMG study is
summarized in "I Felt Like My Career Break Wiped Clean All
of My Previous Achievements," Vodafone, March 8, 2018, www
.vodafone.com/content/index/what/connected-she-can/i
-felt-like-my-career-break-wiped-clean-all-of-my-previous
-achievements.html. On UK working women, see Yong Jing
Teow and Priya Ravidran, *Women Returners: The £1 Billion
Career Break Penalty for Professional Women* (PwC, November
2016), www.pwc.co.uk/economic-services/women-returners
/pwc-research-women-returners-nov-2016.pdf. On wage
differences over time, see Marianne Bertrand et al., "Dy-
namics of the Gender Gap for Young Professionals in the Financial and Corporate Sectors," *American Economic Journal:
Applied Economics* 2, no. 3 (July 2010): 228–255, www.aea-
web.org/articles?id=10.1257/app.2.3.228; Henrik Kleven et
al., "Children and Gender Inequality: Evidence from Denmark," *NBER Working Paper Series* 24219 (National Bureau of Economics, January 2018), www.nber.org/papers
/w24219. Arturo Perez is quoted in Valérie Gauriat, "Sweden: Shorter Workdays, Happier and More Productive Staff?"
Euronews, June 10, 2016, www.euronews.com/2016/10/06
/sweden-shorter-workdays-happier-and-more-productive-staff.
Four-Day Weeks Boost Creativity. On Reusser Design's four-
day week, see Andy Welfle, "Why We Switched to a Four-Day
Work Week," Reusser Design, February 25, 2013, https://
reusserdesign.com/resources/articles/why-we-switched-to-a-4
-day-work-week; Jeanne Sahadi, "The Four-Day Workweek Is
Real . . . for Employees at These Companies," CNN Money,
April 27, 2015, https://money.cnn.com/2015/04/27/pf/4
-day-work-week/. Cristian Rennella describes his experience in
Rennella, "Why Our Startup Has No Bosses, No Office, and
a Four-Day Work Week," *Quartz*, September 6, 2014, https://
qz.com/260846/why-our-startup-has-no-bosses-no-office
-and-a-four-day-work-week. Maria Bråth is quoted in David
Crouch, "Efficiency Up, Turnover Down: Sweden Experiments

with Six-Hour Working Day," *Guardian*, September 17, 2015, www.theguardian.com/world/2015/sep/17/efficiency-up -turnover-down-sweden-experiments-with-six-hour-working -day. Iain Tate is quoted in Patrick Coffee, "W+K London Experiments with Forcing Employees Not to Overexert Themselves," *Adweek*, March 25, 2016, www.adweek.com/agencyspy /wk-london-experiments-with-forcing-employees-not-to -overexert-themselves/104813, and Tate, "Working Differently at W+K London," *Medium*, March 15, 2016, https://medium .com/@iaintait/thoughts-about-working-differently-at-w-k -london-802b09763ec5. On relaxation, the default mode network, and creativity, see Pang, *Rest*, 33–50.

Four-Day Weeks Boost Long-Term Happiness and Job Satisfaction. The classic study of the Hawthorne Effect is Richard Gillespie, *Manufacturing Knowledge: A History of the Hawthorne Experiments* (Cambridge, UK: Cambridge University Press, 1991). The Swedish study of reduced working hours and happiness is in Helena Schiller et al., "Total Workload and Recovery in Relation to Worktime Reduction: A Randomised Controlled Intervention Study with Time-Use Data," *Occupational and Environmental Medicine* 75 (2018): 218–226, https://oem.bmj.com /content/75/3/218.

Four-Day Weeks Make Better Leaders. On Henrik Stenmann, coaching, and evolution, see Mathilde Fischer Thomsen, "Virksomhed har 4-dages Arbejdsuge: 'Vi Passer på Vores Medarbejdere,'" TV 2 Lorry, February 10, 2017, www.tv2lorry.dk /artikel/virksomhed-har-firdages-arbejdsuge-vi-passer-paa -vores-medarbejdere; "Her er Hemmeligheden Bag en 4-dages Arbejdsuge," StepStone, February 21, 2017, www.step stone.dk/virksomhed/videncenter/hr-og-rekruttering/her-er -hemmeligheden-bag-en-4-dages-arbejdsuge?lang=en. On tech workers' complaints about leadership, see "Tech Workers Say Poor Leadership Is Number One Cause for Burnout," Ladders, October 30, 2018, www.theladders.com/career-advice/tech -workers-say-poor-leadership-is-number-one-cause-for-burn out; on entrepreneurs and coping, see M. A. Uy et al., "Joint Effects of Prior Start-Up Experience and Coping Strategies on

Entrepreneurs' Psychological Well-Being," *Journal of Business Venturing* 28 (2013): 583–597, www.mawder.com/wp-content /uploads/2017/08/2013JBV.pdf.

CHAPTER 6

Tsurumakikita, Hadano, Japan. Tomoko Miyazaki is quoted in Kazuyo Nakamura, "The Kindest Cut: Inn Reduces Work Hours—Yet Staff Pay Rises 40%," *Straits Times*, June 16, 2018, www.straitstimes.com/asia/east-asia/the-kindest-cut-inn -reduces-work-hours-yet-staff-pay-rises-40. Other articles on Jinya in the English-language press include Daisuke Yamazaki, "Engineer Saves Ryokan and Totoro Tree," *Tokyo Business Daily*, February 3, 2015, https://toyokeizai.net/articles/-/58648; Michio Watanabe, "Time-Honored Japanese Inn Rebuilds Business Using Modern Technology," *Kyodo News*, December 9, 2017, https://english.kyodonews.net/news/2017/12/54607a19c365 -feature-time-honored-japanese-inn-rebuilds-business-using -modern-technology.html; Kazuyo Nakamura, "IT, Four-Day Work Week Help Inn Cut Waste and Double Sales," *Asahi Shimbun*, February 2, 2018, www.asahi.com/ajw/articles /AJ201802020011.html.

Building a New Paradigm for Work. On Victorian railways and modern architecture, see Wolfgang Schivelbusch, *The Railway Journey: The Industrialization of Time and Space in the Nineteenth Century* (Oakland: University of California Press, 1986); Michael Freeman, *Railways and the Victorian Imagination* (New Haven, CT: Yale University Press, 1999); Reyner Banham, *Theory and Design in the First Machine Age* (Cambridge, MA: MIT Press, 1980); William Curtis, *Modern Architecture Since 1900* (London: Phaidon, 1982). The influence of railroad clock systems on Einstein's thinking is described by Peter Galison in "Einstein's Clocks: The Place of Time," *Critical Inquiry* 26, no. 2 (Winter 2000): 355–389, www.jstor.org/stable/1344127; and Galison, *Einstein's Clocks and Poincaré's Maps: Empires of Time* (New York: Norton, 2004).

Health and Happiness. On focus and employee happiness, see Ronald J. Burke et al., "Work Hours, Work Intensity,

Satisfactions and Psychological Well-Being Among Turkish Manufacturing Managers," *Europe's Journal of Psychology* 5, no. 2 (2009): 12–30, https://ejop.psychopen.eu/index.php/ejop /article/view/264; Burke et al., "Work Motivations, Satisfaction and Well-Being Among Hotel Managers in China: Passion Versus Addiction," *Interdisciplinary Journal of Research in Business* 1, no. 1 (January 2011): 21–34, http://citeseerx.ist.psu.edu /viewdoc/download?doi=10.1.1.472.6646&rep=rep1&type =pdf; and Parbudyal Sin et al., "Recovery After Work Experiences, Employee Well-Being and Intent to Quit," *Personnel Review* 45, no. 2 (March 2016): 232–254, https://doi .org/10.1108/PR-07-2014-0154. Perpetual Guardian's four-day week experiment was studied by Jarrod Haar, *Overview of the Perpetual Guardian 4-day (Paid 5) Work Trial* (unpublished ms., June 6, 2018), https://static1.squarespace.com /static/5a93121d3917ee828d5f282b/t/5b4e4237352f53b0c c369c8b/1531855416866/Final+Perpetual+Guardian+report _Professor+Jarrod+Haar_July+2018.pdf. On founders and mental health, see Michael Freeman et al., "The Prevalence and Co-occurrence of Psychiatric Conditions Among Entrepreneurs and Their Families," *Small Business Economics* (May 2018): 1–20, www.researchgate.net/publication/325089478_The _prevalence_and_co-occurrence_of_psychiatric_conditions _among_entrepreneurs_and_their_families; Paul Hokemeyer quoted in Marcel Muenster and Hokemeyer, "There Is a Mental Health Crisis in Entrepreneurship. Here's How to Tackle It," World Economic Forum, March 22, 2019, www.weforum.org /agenda/2019/03/how-to-tackle-the-mental-health-crisis-in-entrepreneurship; Kristina Gunnarsson and Malin Josephson, "Entrepreneurs' Self-Reported Health, Social Life, and Strategies for Maintaining Good Health," *Journal of Occupational Health* 53, no. 3 (March 2011): 205–213, www.researchgate.net /publication/50596291_Entrepreneurs'_Self-reported_Health _Social_Life_and_Strategies_for_Maintaining_Good_Health.

Aging Societies and Workforces. I draw on Theodore Roszak, *Longevity Revolution: As Boomers Become Elders* (Berkeley Hills Books, 2001); Lynda Gratton and Andrew Scott, *The 100-Year*

Life: Living and Working in an Age of Longevity (London: Blooms-bury Business, 2017). Pablo Casals discusses aging and work in Casals and Alfred E. Kahn, *Joys and Sorrows: Reflections* (New York: Simon and Schuster, 1970). On aging, cognition, and work, see Shinya Kajitani et al., "Use It Too Much and Lose It? The Effect of Working Hours on Cognitive Ability," Melbourne Institute Working Paper No. 7/16 (2016), https://melbourne institute.unimelb.edu.au/publications/working-papers/search /result?paper=2156560; Corinne Purtill, "A Stanford Researcher Says We Shouldn't Start Working Full Time Until Age 40," *Quartz at Work*, June 27, 2018, https://qz.com/work/1314988 /stanford-psychologist-laura-carstensen-says-careers-should-be -mapped-for-longer-lifespans/. On job crafting, see Dorien Kooij et al., "Successful Aging at Work: The Role of Job Craft-ing," in *Aging Workers and the Employee-Employer Relationship* (New York: Springer, 2015), 145–161, www.researchgate.net /publication/283807994_Successful_Aging_at_Work_The _Role_of_Job_Crafting; K. A. S. Wickrama et al., "Is Working Later in Life Good or Bad for Health? An Investigation of Mul-tiple Health Outcomes," *Journals of Gerontology, Series B: Psy-chological Sciences and Social Sciences* 68, no. 5 (September 2013): 807–815, https://doi.org/10.1093/geronb/gbt069.

Traffic and Commuting. See Gabriela Saldivia, "Stuck in Traffic? You're Not Alone. New Data Show American Commute Times Are Longer," *Here and Now*, September 20, 2018, www.npr .org/2018/09/20/650061560/stuck-in-traffic-youre-not-alone -new-data-show-american-commute-times-are-longer; Helen Flores, "Government Urged to Try 4-Day Work Week Amid Traffic," *Philippine Star*, August 20, 2018, www.philstar.com /headlines/2018/08/20/1844163/government-urged-try-4-day -work-week-amid-traffic; "4-Day Workweek Possible in BPO, Say Stakeholders," *Business Mirror*, September 25, 2018, https:// businessmirror.com.ph/2018/09/25/4-day-workweek-possible -in-bpo-say-stakeholders/.

Environmental Impacts. See Juliet Schor, "Sustainable Con-sumption and Worktime Reduction," Working Paper No. 0406, Johannes Kepler University of Linz, Department of Economics

(2004), www.econstor.eu/bitstream/10419/73279/1/wp0406
.pdf; Anders Hayden and John M. Shandra, "Hours of Work
and the Ecological Footprint of Nations: An Exploratory Analysis," *Local Environment* 14, no. 6 (2009): 575–600, https://doi
.org/10.1080/13549830902904185; François-Xavier Devet-
ter and Sandrine Rousseau, "Working Hours and Sustainable
Development," *Review of Social Economy* 69, no. 3 (2011): 333–
355, https://doi.org/10.1080/00346764.2011.563507; Carlo
Aall et al., "Leisure and Sustainable Development in Norway:
Part of the Solution and the Problem," *Leisure Studies* 30, no. 4
(2011): 453–476, https://doi.org/10.1080/02614367.2011.5898
63; Kyle W. Knight et al., "Could Working Less Reduce Pressures on the Environment? A Cross-National Panel Analysis of
OECD Countries, 1970–2007," *Global Environmental Change*
23, no. 4 (August 2013): 691–700, https://doi.org/10.1016/j
.gloenvcha.2013.02.017; Martin Pullinger, "Working Time
Reduction Policy in a Sustainable Economy: Criteria and Options for Its Design," *Ecological Economics* 103 (July 2014):
11–19, https://doi.org/10.1016/j.ecolecon.2014.04.009; David
Frayne, "Stepping Outside the Circle: The Ecological Promise
of Shorter Working Hours," *Green Letters: Studies in Ecocriti-
cism* 20, no. 2 (2016): 197–212, https://doi.org/10.1080/146884
17.2016.1160793; Giorgos Kallis et al., "'Friday Off': Reducing
Working Hours in Europe," *Sustainability* 5, no. 4 (April 2013):
1545–1567, www.researchgate.net/publication/273220828
_Friday_off_Reducing_Working_Hours_in_Europe; Qinglong
Shao, "Effect of Working Time on Environmental Pressures:
Empirical Evidence from EU-15, 1970–2010," *Chinese Journal
of Population Resources and Environment* 13, no. 3 (2015): 231–
239, https://doi.org/10.1080/10042857.2015.1033803; Lewis C.
King and Jeroen C. J. M. van den Bergh, "Worktime Reduction
as a Solution to Climate Change: Five Scenarios Compared for
the UK," *Ecological Economics* 132 (February 2017): 124–134,
https://doi.org/10.1016/j.ecolecon.2016.10.011.
Regional Development. Yuki Matsuoka is quoted in "FLATS
by Kunisakitime," Alexicious, www.alexcious.com/brands
/detail101.html; see also "Flexible Work Hours Can Be an

Aid to Motivation," *Gulf News*, January 23, 2015, https://
gulfnews.com/how-to/employment/flexible-work-hours-can
-be-an-aid-to-motivation-1.1445238.

Technological Innovation. Automation in radiology and surgery are the subjects of enormous literatures; for recent reviews,
see Ahmed Hosny et al., "Artificial Intelligence in Radiology,"
Nature Reviews Cancer 18 (August 2018): 500–510, www.ncbi
.nlm.nih.gov/pmc/articles/PMC6268174; Brian S. Peters et al.,
"Review of Emerging Surgical Robotic Technology," *Surgical
Endoscopy* 32, no. 4 (2018): 1636–1655, https://doi.org/10.1007
/s00464-018-6079-2. Likewise, the literature on automation,
robotics, and the future of work is vast; Erik Brynjolfsson and
Andrew McAfee, *The Second Machine Age: Work, Progress, and
Prosperity in a Time of Brilliant Technologies* (New York: Norton,
2014) and Martin Ford, *Rise of the Robots: Technology and the
Threat of a Jobless Future* (New York: Basic Books, 2015) provide
accessible introductions to the subject.

The Spread of the Movement. Bob Baumhower is quoted in
"Alabama's Aloha Hospitality Launches 4-Day Workweek,"
AL.com, March 28, 2019, www.al.com/press-releases/2018/10
/alabamas_aloha_hospitality_lau.html. On unions and advocacy
of a four-day week, see Guy Chazan, "Germany's Union Wins
Right to 28-Hour Working Week and 4.3% Pay Rise," *Financial
Times*, February 6, 2018, www.ft.com/content/e7f0490e-0b1c
-11e8-8eb7-42f857ea9f09; Benjamin Kentish, "Give Workers
Four-Day Week and More Pay, Unions Urge Businesses," *Independent,* September 9, 2018, www.independent.co.uk/news
/uk/politics/four-day-week-uk-technology-tuc-frances-ogrady
-amazon-a8530386.html; Rebecca Wearn, "Unions Call for
Four-Day Working Week," BBC News, September 10, 2018,
www.bbc.com/news/business-45463868; Sonia Sodha, "How
to Make a Four-Day Week Reality," *Guardian*, October 26,
2018, www.theguardian.com/commentisfree/2018/oct/16/four
-day-week-parents. On calls for a four-day week in China, see
Weida Li, "Four-Day Week Proposed in China as Free Time
Decreases," *GB Times*, July 16, 2018, https://gbtimes.com
/average-leisure-time-for-chinese-people-decreased-in-2017;

Cheng Si, "Study: Leisure Life Adds to Happiness," *China Daily*, July 16, 2018, www.chinadaily.com.cn/a/201807/16/WS5b4bf247a310796df4df68f7.html; Cao Zinan, "Four-Day Workweek by 2030 Called for in China," *China Daily*, July 16, 2018, www.chinadaily.com.cn/a/201807/16/WS5b4c7373a310796df4df6b95.html; Richard Macauley, "China Wants a 4.5-Day Work Week—To Boost Its Economy," *Quartz*, December 8, 2015, https://qz.com/568349/china-wants-a-4-5-day-work-week-to-boost-its-economy; "Is the Four-Day Workweek Proposal Feasible? The Proposal of a Four-Day Weekday Stirs Up a Lot of Debate," *Beijing Review*, August 2, 2018, www.bjreview.com/Lifestyle/201807/t20180730_800136855.html; Alex Soojung-Kim Pang, "Why Companies Should Say Goodbye to the 996 Work Culture, and Hello to 4-Day Weeks," *South China Morning Post*, April 20, 2019, www.scmp.com/comment/insight-opinion/article/3006873/why-companies-should-say-goodbye-996-work-culture-and-hello. Anna Ross is quoted in Kura Antonello, "Anna Ross: Founder & Director, Kester Black," The Cool Career, at www.thecoolcareer.com/anna-ross.

Index

Credit: Kristian Kettner

Alex Soojung-Kim Pang is the founder of Strategy+Rest, a Silicon Valley consulting company, and a visiting scholar at Stanford University. His previous books include *Rest: Why You Get More Done When You Work Less* and *The Distraction Addiction: Getting the Information You Need and the Communication You Want, Without Enraging Your Family, Annoying Your Colleagues, and Destroying Your Soul.*

PublicAffairs is a publishing house founded in 1997. It is a tribute to the standards, values, and flair of three persons who have served as mentors to countless reporters, writers, editors, and book people of all kinds, including me.

I. F. STONE, proprietor of *I. F. Stone's Weekly*, combined a commitment to the First Amendment with entrepreneurial zeal and reporting skill and became one of the great independent journalists in American history. At the age of eighty, Izzy published *The Trial of Socrates*, which was a national bestseller. He wrote the book after he taught himself ancient Greek.

BENJAMIN C. BRADLEE was for nearly thirty years the charismatic editorial leader of *The Washington Post*. It was Ben who gave the *Post* the range and courage to pursue such historic issues as Watergate. He supported his reporters with a tenacity that made them fearless and it is no accident that so many became authors of influential, best-selling books.

ROBERT L. BERNSTEIN, the chief executive of Random House for more than a quarter century, guided one of the nation's premier publishing houses. Bob was personally responsible for many books of political dissent and argument that challenged tyranny around the globe. He is also the founder and longtime chair of Human Rights Watch, one of the most respected human rights organizations in the world.

•   •   •

For fifty years, the banner of Public Affairs Press was carried by its owner Morris B. Schnapper, who published Gandhi, Nasser, Toynbee, Truman, and about 1,500 other authors. In 1983, Schnapper was described by *The Washington Post* as "a redoubtable gadfly." His legacy will endure in the books to come.

Peter Osnos, *Founder*